CONTEMPORARY ASCETICS OF MOUNT ATHOS

Volume II

ICON OF ALL THE SAINTS OF MOUNT ATHOS

CONTEMPORARY ASCETICS OF MOUNT ATHOS

Volume II

By
ARCHIMANDRITE CHERUBIM
(KARAMBELAS)

ST. HERMAN OF ALASKA BROTHERHOOD
2000

Copyright 1992 by the
St. Herman of Alaska Brotherhood

Address all correspondence to:
St. Herman of Alaska Brotherhood
P. O. Box 70
Platina, California 96076

First Printing: 1992
Second Printing: 2000

Front cover: Grigoriou Monastery, Mount Athos, Greece.

Karambelas, Archimandrite Cherubim.
　　Contemporary Ascetics of Mount Athos, Volume Two.
　　Translated from the Greek.

Library of Congress Catalogue Card Number 91-68395
ISBN 0-938635-56-5 (paper)
　　　0-938635-57-3 (cloth)

Contents

INTRODUCTION TO VOLUME II	365
1. ELDER SABBAS THE FATHER CONFESSOR	371
Author's Prologue to the Greek Edition	373
I. The Children of the Desert	375
II. The Ascent	393
III. The Renowned Father Confessor	406
IV. The Pilgrim	420
V. War with the Demons	431
VI. "Make Known to Me the Ways of Life"	442
2. ELDER IGNATIUS THE FATHER CONFESSOR	457
I. His Spiritual Formation	459
II. Fathers and Sons	477
III. The Harbor of Salvation	494
IV. The Light of Grace	517
3. ELDER CODRATUS OF KARAKALLOU	533
Author's Prologue to the Greek Edition	535
I. At the Place of Sanctification and Asceticism	537
II. A Model Abbot	550
III. An Exemplary Confessor	566
IV. "Well Done, Good and Faithful Servant"	579
4. ELDER PHILARET OF CONSTAMONITOU	587
Author's Prologue to the Greek Edition	589
I. "O Lord, I Have Loved Thy Tabernacles"	591
II. "O How I Have Loved Thy Law, O Lord"	605
III. "For I Am Thy Slave"	613
IV. "The Exposition of Thy Words Enlightens and Instructs Infants"	626
V. "Thy Judgments Have I Not Forgotten"	635

5. ELDER GERASIM MENAGIAS 643
   I. From Birth to Rebirth 645
   II. "Life is Blessed for Those Who Dwell in the Wilderness,
      For They Fly Upon the Wings of Divine Love" 657
   III. "On the Lampstand" 671
   IV. "The Righteous Live Forever" 685

APPENDICES

Appendix 1: An Event That Occurred During the Sebastopol
Campaign 697
Appendix 2: The Blind Confessor Ignatius: A Clairvoyant
Elder 704
INDEX 709

Introduction to Volume II of
Contemporary Ascetics of Mount Athos

The second half of Archimandrite Cherubim's book of brief monographs of Athonite personalities comprise only three Lives by his own pen. The other two were added in the same spirit by the original Greek publisher. The St. Herman Brotherhood has added photographs, appendices, and an index for both volumes, in hopes of making the contemporary phenomenon of ancient ascetic exploit more available for the God-seekers of today.

Most of the fathers were adherents of the "old" church calendar, zealots in their spiritual make-up, yet stood above politics while passions raged on Mount Athos, as they still do in the Orthodox world. It would be unfair to the memory of these modern-day heroes to omit this fact, because their defense of traditional values renders moral support to those who still face the same problems.

Of course, there were many more similar ascetics of Mount Athos, who still await their biographers, translators, and publishers in the modern world. For example, Fr. Ignatius the Bulgarian of Chapter 7 of this book had a Russian disciple of great spiritual height, Theodosius of Karoulia, whose cell-attendant and *sotainnik* (sharer of the monastic mystery), Fr. Nikodim, was my Athonite elder for years. When I first saw Fr. Cherubim's books in Greece I at once recognized the need to make them available to our English-speaking converts. For these texts, more than others, are essential, like daily bread, to spiritually starving modern man; and the miracle of the still living and breathing Mount Athos is the perfect oven to bake that bread in.

From the very beginning, the publishers of this book about Mount Athos dreamt of printing a book on the 20th-century Russian hermits of Karoulia, the severest "desert" of Athos, who were instrumental in inspiring the brotherhood of St. Herman to move into the deserted "dry places" of California's wilderness. From the very day of my conversion, a humble monk, Hierodeacon Vladimir of the Holy Trinity Monastery in Jordanville, gave me the address of a monk on Mount Athos, stating that every true son of Holy Russia must always have contact with some Athonite monks, sending them donations and requests for prayers for those in the world. He said that monks living high up the Mount, close to God, are more easily heard by God than us lowly ones languishing in the heat of this world. Giving me the name and address of a Mt. Athos monk, Fr. Nikodim, he said that he would be an especially good monk to correspond with, because he could send me rare patristic books in exchange for a few dollars, which he would pass on to some abandoned hermit to help him with the essentials of life. For monks of this caliber need very little to sustain them, and their prayer is potent to instill a true understanding of spiritual life, the art of prayer, and general spiritual welfare in an Orthodox Christian of the 20th century. I took his advice; being very new to the Church, still in my teens, I sent a letter to Fr. Nikodim, asking him to pray for me, living in the tumult of the affluent hedonistic society of materialistic America, and to guide me on the spiritual path.

Then, having just become aware of the monastic world, I saw clearly the path which was so attractive to my soul. Very shortly afterwards I received from Fr. Nikodim a kind little note and an icon of my patron saint—my first actual contact with Mt. Athos!

Soon afterwards, a package of the complete works of Ignatius Brianchaninov arrived at a time when I was spiritually hungry; my appetite for Patristic wisdom was almost unbearable. Intensively reading the first volume of the great writings of one of the major

Church Fathers of our times, St. Ignatius Brianchaninov, the world of spiritual reality opened to me on the level of classic literature. Through the pages of Ignatius Brianchaninov I breathed into my inner world the fragrance of Mt. Athos. The impression of that Holy Father's writings was so strong, that after hours of hearing the exalted, noble narrative of this ascetic of the 19th century, the world of the 20th century did not become distasteful as I thought it would, but on the contrary I understood exactly what age we live in, what is meant by apostasy from the truth, and what is the path of an Orthodox Christian—a path to paradise through the hell of modern nihilism, of which St. Ignatius was so well aware.

Fr. Nikodim kept sending me volumes of priceless patristic literature: the complete set of the *Philokalia* of St. Theophan the Recluse, twelve volumes of Br. Nikodim's *Russian Ascetics of the 18th and 19th Centuries*, published by Mt. Athos, writings of St. Tikhon of Zadonsk, and many more. These books not only opened wide the spiritual horizon of the Orthodox worldview, but they all seemed to me to be breathing into my soul the air of Mt. Athos. As the years passed, I was drawn closer and closer to Fr. Nikodim. The world of his books developed an unquenchable thirst for Athonite wisdom. For merely the few dollars that I would send to him as donations, I received access to paradise. But to go myself to Mt. Athos on a pilgrimage was too distant a reality, because it involved great sums of money. For a poor college student the prospect of going to the other side of the globe was unthinkable; and after all, I had my Mount Athos right there in my room on the quiet streets of Boston.

When I received from him both volumes of the *Athonite Patericon* and an almost complete set of magazines that St. Panteleimon's Monastery published from the 1870's to 1914, *Soul-Saving Conversor*, then the army of Athonite saints marched before my mental gaze straight from the beginning of Mount Athos 1000 years ago to modern times, ending up with men who were alive as the magazine was being published. These men were contemporary ascetics who lived the same type of life as did those saints 1000 years ago, and in my mind I automatically placed Fr. Nikodim into the same category. They all seemed to be of exactly the same spirit, with little variations, living on the same mountainsides and coastal cliffs accessible only to birds and cave-dwellers, and I imagined that Fr. Nikodim was one of them, which in reality he was.

A decade later I received a letter from him, and another from his spiritual son, Fr. Rostislav of Australia, with a request that I recopy fragmented portions of the spiritual diary of Fr. Nikodim's elder, Schemamonk Theodosius, who was for many years a semi-hermit in Karoulia, the severest geographical region of Athos, on the southern side of the Holy Mountain. I eagerly agreed to undertake the task of typing the manuscript letters, which were sent bit by bit all the way to Australia. They had been damaged by water in places, causing the ink to run, and it was very difficult to decipher the Athonite monk's handwriting. At times the task was beyond me, as the water damage prevented me from understanding the content of the extremely refined text. The original journal from which these letters were copied by Fr. Nikodim during World War II was still preserved by Fr. Nikodim, but he could not part with it. To ask too many obscure questions by letter proved impractical, and so, having completed the typing of the manuscript, I was compelled to go personally to Mount Athos and verify the text with the original journal. Meanwhile, the influence of the books from Athos had created in me a desire for monastic life. Since I couldn't afford to seclude myself in a monastery and was pressured by the pastoral need of conducting missionary activity through the spreading of the printed word, I not only founded a Brotherhood that enabled me to publish Orthodox texts, but also eventually created my own desert in Northern California, whose terrain recalled Mount Athos. There, in the silence of the Platina Mountains, in the company of a few struggling brothers, we were able to write and print ascetic texts designed for contemporary God-seekers.

By the time I finished the manuscript, the situation was ripe for me to go to Mount Athos, after twenty-five years of longing to do so. God granted me an unforgettable pilgrimage to Fr. Nikodim on Mount Athos who by this time became my dedicated instructor in areas where only he could give me proper advice.

I spent a week on Mount Athos right after Pascha. I visited most of the monasteries of the Holy Mountain and served in my beloved St. Paisius' Skete of St. Elias, and spent unforgettable time with my dear Fr. Nikodim, laboring over the wonderful spiritual journal of his elder, the great zealot of modern times, Theodosius of Karoulia. Knowing that our parting would be for ever, my dear elder Nikodim gave me priceless spiritual advice, loaded me with boxes of manuscripts which the Mt. Athos government graciously allowed me to take out, and fortified me by his touching farewell homily as I parted from him forever. Not long after that, he went to the Lord, and before that his cell-attendant, Fr. Seraphim, also died, leaving in my heart not a sense of loss and negative emptiness, but on the contrary a sense of deep enrichment, making me an inheritor of a bit of their spiritual treasures.

Fr. Nikodim also blessed our brotherhood to found St. Xenia's Skete for women, giving for the nuns his mantle and monastic kamilavka, so as to have a bit of the Athonite spirit wafting in Northern California.

On my way back, as I stopped in Piraeus, I was searching the religious book stores for books on recent ascetics of Mount Athos, since Elder Theodosius was in contact with great Athonite Fathers of his time. And great indeed was my pleasant surprise when I discovered the little volumes of Archimandrite Cherubim's Lives, *Contemporary Ascetics of Mount Athos*. I vowed to bring all that treasure into the English language and make them available to those young monastic aspirants for whom Fr. Nikodim prayed all these years and whom he had in mind when he blessed me to found a skete for women in the wilderness of Northern California. And it is precisely the sisters of this convent who translated and edited the work of Fr. Cherubim, which we have finally been able to publish. We ask the reader for prayers not only for the repose of the soul of Fr. Cherubim

Fr. Nikodim climbing a near-vertical "path" of Karoulia with the aid of chains. *Fr. Nikodim holding the skull of his Elder Theodosius.*

but also for the struggling monastics who made these English-language volumes a reality.

But that is not all. The world of Fr. Nikodim, his Elder Theodosius, his spiritual son Seraphim, and others, is yet to be presented in the English language. The diary of Elder Theodosius is especially significant for serious God-seekers. It is a candid narrative of an old Athonite struggler who recorded for his own use the condition of the soul when the heart prays the Jesus Prayer ceaselessly. The revelations, temptations, and allurements are at times exalted beyond our mortal understanding, and are, I thought, too much for the neophyte mentality of us inexperienced, pampered, and whimsical converts. But when I mentioned my doubt of the propriety of publishing this material, fearing that it might mislead people lacking sober experience, Fr. Nikodim said, "No, no. Print it as it is. If, having such a spiritual treasure, they go astray, let them. Those who know its value can pray out those who get lost."

It is the publishers' desire to print also a third companion volume to Fr. Cherubim's books: *Karoulian Ascetics of Mount Athos*.

VI

ELDER SABBAS
THE FATHER CONFESSOR

*I am made all things to all men,
that I might by all means save some.*
(I Cor. 9:21-22)

ELDER SABBAS' KALYVE,
dedicated to the Resurrection of the Lord.

Author's Prologue to the Greek Edition

We feel special satisfaction in handing over the sixth volume of *Contemporary Ascetics of Mount Athos* to the publisher, because the wonderful figure of the Athonite Hieromonk Sabbas the Confessor (1821–1908) was in danger of drowning in the sea of oblivion. It would have been a great pity had this bright star of the Athonite heaven remained in obscurity.

I remember that when I came to the Holy Mountain at the age of eighteen, the atmosphere was laden with his holy presence, even though he had reposed thirty years before. I was always hearing: "Over there, on the hill, in Little St. Anne's, in the kalyve of the Resurrection, lived the famous confessor Fr. Sabbas"; "Fr. Sabbas said this..."; "Fr. Sabbas did that..."; "he commemorated so many names, he served Liturgy like this, this is the way he healed the possessed..." and so on. In my young mind Fr. Sabbas stood forth like a wonderful hero, a wide-winged eagle soaring at unattainable spiritual altitudes.

If the compilation of Fr. Sabbas' life had been delayed any longer, it would have been too late, because the old monks who knew him personally have one by one departed to the next world. Glory to God that we were in time to lock this precious treasure in the pages of this volume. It is a treasure which should enrich many souls who amidst the spiritual poverty of today seek for strong food and to "receive the things of the Spirit."

Fr. Sabbas was accounted a great ascetic, an angel-like liturgist, an incomparable confessor and guide of souls. His work of spiritual fatherhood had unprecedented success; it was astonishing, and was reminiscent of the God-bearing *startsi* of the Orthodoxy of the North (Russia). In times of difficulty and trouble, innumerable suffering souls found through him the harbor of salvation, the paths of life, the water of refreshment.

In the first pages of this book we have also preserved the figure of Fr. Sabbas' elder. This was the Georgian Hieromonk Hilarion, a wondrous man, a holy branch from which budded a sacred flower, an Elias the Tishbite who raised up a great Elisha.

We received information for this biography from a multitude of aged Athonite monks, many of whom had close ties with him, and also from the books *Lausaicon of the Holy Mountain* and *The New Evergetinos* by Archimandrite Gabriel of Dionysiou. Most of all we were helped by the excellent book by the ever-memorable Athonite Archimandrite Joachim Spetsieris, Doctor of Theology and national preacher, *Memoirs, Vol I: Holy Mountain—Jerusalem*, published in Athens in 1931.

At the end of this book, completely spontaneously, we express the wish and advance the idea that the Church would enroll Fr. Sabbas among the choirs of the Saints. The competent ecclesiastical authority should ascertain that in the conscience of all Athonite monks there was and is an indisputable, unquestioning belief in his sanctity. We would feel great joy if he is worthily honored who himself honored God, who illumined Athos, quenched the thirst of great multitudes of people, returned the hearts of the sons to the Father, was a Spirit-bearing Confessor, *a rushing river, glorious in a thirsty land* (Isaiah 32:2), a lily fragrant and peerless in the sacred garden of the Theotokos.

Archimandrite Cherubim
Oropos, Attiki, July 1, 1972

I

The Children of the Desert

1. THE MODEL

It was evening. In the enclosure of a kalyve of Little St. Anne's Skete, next to a parched and rugged hill, two monks were talking: an elder and his disciple. The evening stillness was emphasized by the unceasing roar of the sea washing the foot of the hill—an ideal accompaniment to the prayers of the ascetics who with their raised hands support the world. The two monks talked, until finally the younger one was seen to rise. He made a prostration to the elder and turned towards the kalyve, where another monk was waiting.

"Are you finished, Fr. Onouphrius?"

"Yes, I am finished, Fr. Hilarion."

"Then I will go."

With light step the young monk drew near the elder. "Bless, Elder."

"Well, Hilarion! Well, my little angel! Sit here." Not many days had passed since his tonsure. His love for God had taken him from his country and his relatives in Vriola of Smyrna and brought him to the land of ascetics. For three years (1879–1882) he had been a novice. From the moment that he put on the angelic schema, he felt wholly changed. He was not George Hadjitasou any longer—he was Fr. Hilarion of Little St. Anne's Skete. He belonged not to men but to God, and was flooded by divine grace. This evening he prolonged the discussion with the elder, delighting in his grace-filled words.

A little time passed in confession of thoughts.

"Hilarion my child, do you like the name I gave you?"

"Very much, Elder."

"Do you know why I chose it?"

"How could I not know? You gave me the name of 'Grandfather', your blessed Elder Fr. Hilarion."

It was not the first time that Fr. Sabbas' eyes brimmed with tears when thinking of his venerable spiritual father.

"May his prayers support us, may we have his prayers. And for you, my child, I pray with all my heart that you may inherit his grace. As a rule, grandsons resemble their grandfathers. See that you imitate his virtues. May you remind me of him both by your name and by your life."

"May God grant it by your blessing, Elder." A little silence followed.

"May you resemble him, Hilarion my child, in the purity of his life. His whole soul, his thoughts, desires, and determinations, shone in the light. In his sweet, joyful face you saw the reflection of the Lord's face. In his gaze you saw the light of Paradise. Oh, what a gaze he had! Many times I dared not directly meet it. His eyes literally flashed with light. He had the eyes of a prophet!"

"Elder, you have told us he had the gift of foresight."

"Yes, my child. That was to be expected. Those who are pure in heart acquire prophetic eyes. What does our teacher St. Basil the Great write? 'The grace of prophecy increases in them whose souls are immaculate and pure of all spot.' Where there is a pure heart, there the Holy Spirit 'speaks through the prophets,' raising His tabernacle."

"It appears, Elder, that he had exceedingly great love for the Lord."

"My child, his heart burned with divine love. What else made him set out from the distant Caucasus and come to the wilderness of the Holy Mountain? Without the thought of Christ he could not live. Oh, that you could have seen him when he served Liturgy, when he received Communion! He did not pass a single day without Holy Communion! 'Christ is my life,' he said. And on Friday, every Friday, he suffered at the foot of the Cross together with the Theotokos and St. John—so intensely did he participate in Christ's Passion. Never on that day did he eat or drink anything, out of devotion to the Saving Passion."

The elder continued, unfolding before the eyes of the disciple the virtues and graces of his own blessed elder. And the young monk listened insatiably. His soul was shaken with divine yearning like a sea churned by a strong wind.

"Your 'grandfather' was a true saint, my child Hilarion. Let him be your model."

That evening, as soon as his eyes had closed, an angelic vision of Elder Hilarion greeted the newly-tonsured monk.

Now it is time for us also to meet this earthly angel, this 'tree of glorious fruit' that produced the holy and inimitable Fr. Sabbas the Confessor.

2. HILARION THE IBERIAN

At the southern feet of the Caucasus Mountains, above Armenia, lies Iberia (modern Georgia). This is where the mythical Argonauts found the golden fleece. It is a mountainous land, picturesque and fertile, rich even in its subsoil. For ages it has been inhabited by the Iberians, one of the most beautiful races in the world.

The Iberians, being a people responsive to the higher spiritual callings, embraced Christianity early, at the end of the 3rd century. Even up to today, in spite of all their difficulties and changes of fortune, they have not betrayed the treasure of Orthodoxy.*

---

*Even in 1439, the representative of the Church of Iberia at the Council of

Iveron Monastery

The Iberians have always been lovers of monasticism. Its first missionary and enlightener, St. Nina, was a monastic. The effects of the Iberians' intense love for the monastic life extended as far as Palestine, Sinai, and Mount Athos. The Athonite Monastery third in seniority and importance was built by the Iberians, as its name, Iveron, indicates. How many saints matured in the Iberian monastic establishments! A great multitude of rare flowers grew in them, carrying their fragrance to Heaven, *on the mountain of spices* (Song of Sol. 8:14). The holy soul of Hilarion the Iberian, one of those flowers from the Iberian soil, enchants us with its wonderful fragrance.

It is now more than a hundred years after his repose, and the dwellers of the Holy Mountain still have not forgotten Fr. Hilarion

---

Florence proved steadfast in Orthodoxy and did not succumb to the pressures of those trying to institute the "Unia." He even feigned foolishness, thus managing to escape signing the inadmissible "terms of union."

the Georgian. The surname "the Georgian" refers to his nationality, for Iberia is also called Georgia. He was generally acknowledged to be "a venerable man, a perfect keeper of the monastic life," a wonderful and renowned father confessor who reached the heights of virtue.

About his life in Iberia we know very little. What could have brought him to abandon his fatherland? Surely the longing for high spiritual ascents, to which the hesychastic, other-worldly, and ascetic Mount Athos is preeminently devoted. Perhaps also the political climate of his land: when in 1807 Tsar Alexander I forcibly annexed Georgia to Russia, a disturbed, agitated situation was created. Perhaps he even left Georgia to escape the honor everyone awarded him for his virtue. Apparently his fame had spread over all Georgia, for even the king came to him for confession.

Coming to the Holy Mountain, Fr. Hilarion naturally went to the Holy Monastery of Iveron. The lover of silence turned his attention to the nearby Monastery Kathismas,* finally going to live in the Georgian cell of St. John the Theologian. This was an ideal arrangement. Hilarion, the loving disciple of Christ, came under the protection of the Apostle of Love. It was not long before he was joined by a young disciple, Sabbas.

Fr. Sabbas came from eastern Thrace. He was born in 1821, in Athira, an important town on the shore of the sea of Marmara. Twenty-five years later, the Saint of our century, Nectarius of Pentapolis, was born in the neighboring region of Silyvria.

The God-enlightened Fr. Hilarion foresaw his future progress and unhesitatingly took him under his spiritual protection. He had wished for a Greek disciple to help him master the Greek language, for "although gracious to all, he did not hide his preference for everything Greek, desiring to converse and live together with the Greeks, to pray, read, and liturgize in their language" (Archimandrite Gabriel of Dionisiou, *Lausaicon of the Holy Mountain*, pg. 35).

---

*i.e., outlying cells. Kathismas are usually a little smaller than Kalyves.

The radiance of his virtue and his renown did not allow him to live quietly in his new abode. Bees always discover nectar-laden flowers. Many sought his acquaintance, marvelling at his spiritual greatness. All were deeply moved by the story of his life. He who had been so wealthy in Georgia now accepted no money in his kalyve. When confessing the king of Georgia, he had worn, as prescribed by court ceremonial, a splendid mantia glittering with rubies, pearls and 750 diamonds. Now he was clothed in the cheapest monastic clothing. Naturally all this deeply affected the Holy Mountain fathers.

The Russians importuned him much. He knew their language well and could help them with all their spiritual needs. They would ask him to come to the Monastery of St. Panteleimon to give confession. They finally made him the permanent father confessor of the Monastery and honored him as a Saint.

The Kathisma of the Theologian evidently did not provide him with the silence he longed for. The words of the Psalm, *I have fled afar off and dwelt in the wilderness* fanned the zeal of the elder and disciple. Fr. Sabbas, then very young, from time to time would enthusiastically bring up the question.

"My Elder, let's flee; let's go far away; let's dwell in the wilderness and find holy stillness."

Thus they fled from an Apostle and came to another Apostle. The Theologian delivered them over to the Brother of the Lord. The wilderness Kathisma of Dionysiou dedicated to St. James the Brother of the Lord, gave them all they longed for. According to handwritten records of Fr. Sabbas, they moved in the year 1843 and a wonderful period began for them.

They left their name behind them and their praises are still sung (Wisdom of Sirach 44:8).

3. THE PURSUIT OF GOD

The History of the Monks of Syria* tells the story of a certain general who went hunting in the mountains with his horse, dogs, weapons, and retinue. Suddenly an ascetic appeared in front of him.

"What are you doing here, Abba?" asked the general.

"And what did you come here to do?"

"I? I came here to hunt. I am hunting."

"I am doing the same thing."

"What? You're also hunting?"

"Certainly! I am pursuing my God. I pursue God day and night, striving to see Him, seize Him, and lock Him in my heart."

The general was amazed at these words. "This," he said, "is a true ascetic."

By general acknowledgment, the wilderness is the most suitable place for the pursuit of God. For this reason, our two ascetics leapt for joy. Their new dwelling was a true Mount Carmel, and they were Elias and Elisha; that is to say, souls burning with love for God.

The Kathisma of the Brother of the Lord is situated some distance above Dionysiou Monastery in a quiet, deserted, and isolated region. To the right are shrub-covered hillsides and the fearful ravine of Aeropotamou where the winter winds moan and roar. To the left where there is abundant water is a dense forest of huge trees. Above the Kalyve is a bare rocky mountainside. The cell was obviously very old. Who knows how many hermits it had sheltered?

Men did not pass through that area. They dealt not with men, but with the desert: the sun and wind, the trees and shrubs, birds and reptiles, the demons, the angels, St. James, the Lady of the Mountain, and God—God before all, for it was Him they were pursuing. For twenty-one years they climbed the ladder of Jacob, never giving

---

*A book similar to the *Lausaicon*. It was written by Theodoret, Bishop of Cyrrhus by the Euphrates River in Syria (393-460). He wrote wonderful accounts of the ascetic exploits of many ascetics of Syria and Mesopotamia.

in to faintheartedness or despair. The voice of the Prophet called to their hearts: *Come ye, and let us go up to the mountain of the Lord, to the house of the God of Jacob* (Isaiah 2:3).

They had their weapons of the chase: Asceticism that mortifies the flesh—temperance, fasting, and vigils. For a sharp two-edged sword they had the study of the Word of God and of the patristic texts that hold an inestimable wealth of spiritual experience. Other weapons were the ceaseless invocation of the Name of Jesus and the almost daily Communion of the Cup of Life and the Heavenly Manna. All of this was made possible by holy and sacred silence which carried them to the heights. To silence St. Basil the Great dedicated these immortal words:

> Silence is the beginning of purity of soul. The tongue speaks not things about one or another man, nor do the eyes turn to bodily beauty, nor do the ears cripple the vigour of the soul with sensual melodies or idle talk of light-minded and comic men. The mind, when not scattered in external matters and not diffused in the world by the senses, returns to itself. From itself it ascends to the concept of God. Drawing near to God, the mind receives richly the radiance of the divine beauty and forgets even itself. (Epistle to Gregory)

With scientific precision, the Holy Father describes the ascent made in hesychia. The final ascent is to God, the most delightful Good. The mind, being enlightened by the good, forgets even its nature. Enraptured, carried away, captivated, it is outside place and time and loses its own self.

Blessed and thrice-blessed are the souls who are counted worthy of such heavenly ascents. Blessed are you also, Fr. Hilarion, and your disciple: souls ascending, becoming refined and purified, pursuing God in the midst of silence. We foresee that you will catch Him and taste Him and will offer Him even to us wretched ones who are "exceedingly poor."

4. THEIR DESERT LIFE

For twenty-one years, Fr. Hilarion and his disciple Sabbas struggled together in the desert. Frugality and temperance naturally ruled in everything. Dionysiou Monastery and some fathers they knew would send them food. Needless to say, comfortable beds, sheets, mattresses and things like that are unknown to ascetics. Water was abundant in the forest, and every so often Fr. Sabbas would carry some to their cell.

Although the main emphasis was given to the contemplative life, they also had plenty of labor to do—cleaning the cells and especially the church, putting the surrounding land in order, caring for some olive and other trees, keeping the invasive wild shrubbery in bounds, building some low stone walls, gathering firewood against the fierce winters, and so on.

They spent much time studying; books are ever the dear friends of hermits. The disciple helped his elder learn the Greek language well, both the spoken language and the Greek of the sacred books. So many holy texts are written in Greek that it is a sin not to know that language. Of course it is difficult to learn and requires much labor, but by his diligence Fr. Hilarion succeeded in fully mastering the language.

Only rarely did they leave their hermitage. Sometimes the elder would go to St. Panteleimon's Monastery for a few days to confess the monks. Then Fr. Sabbas, all alone, experienced intensely the majesty of the desert. He did not fear the demons of the wilderness who delight in creating strange noises and disturbances at the time of prayer. He had grown used to them, and he also had a strong protector beside him, St. James.

Occasionally, on Christmas, Pascha, Pentecost, and other great feasts, the Brother of the Lord was left by himself. They would go to the Monastery for the all-night vigils, bringing with them the breath of the desert. Fr. Hilarion, stately, beautiful like all Iberians, tall, with a venerable beard, stood in one of the "elders'" stalls. He remained upright the whole night. No one ever saw him sit down or leave the church even for a little while. Even during the break before Liturgy began, he would wait in the narthex. His son in spirit unfailingly imitated him.

For a while, at the beginning of their stay there, the silence of the Kathisma was disturbed by construction workers who completely rebuilt it. The building was in ruinous condition, and if Fr. Hilarion had not suggested to the abbot that it be reconstructed, some winter it would have completely collapsed. It was excellently rebuilt. On the east side was a small church, on the west the elder's cell, and below it his disciple's. A little while later the church was consecrated.

The rest of the time, silence reigned. Only occasionally would they hear the sound of a water-driven saw working in the nearby forest. It made a rhythmical, agreeable noise and blended with the diverse sounds of the wilderness.

Every year, as the evening of October 22 fell, sweet melodies burst forth everywhere. The mellifluous singers of the Holy Mountain movingly chanted the praises of St. James:

Thy priesthood was adorned with the blood of martyrdom, O Hieromartyr and Apostle!

Their patron Saint was being celebrated, who was not only the Brother of the Lord, but also an ascetic, a hierarch, and a martyr.

St. James was a great support for the two hermits. A "pillar," as the early Church called him, he especially helped and strengthened the young disciple in the struggle of prayer. However much the enemy battled him, the Brother of the Lord, this giant of prayer, supported him. Ancient Church history tells us that the knees of St. James were hard like a camel's from endless prayer and prostrations. He constantly bent them in the worship of God, asking forgiveness for the people.

5. BETWEEN HEAVEN AND EARTH

The desert life of the two hermits unfolds before us like a blossoming bough, each sweet-smelling flower being a holy incident in their life. We will see miracles of blessed obedience, prophecies, living revelations of the supernatural world assuring us that in the wilderness the dark curtains are drawn aside and the gates of Heaven open.

* * * * * * * *

Their hearts especially trembled before the Paschal mystery of the Divine Liturgy. Soon Fr. Sabbas was also wearing the robe of the priesthood, and the liturgical rhythm beat more strongly. Little incidents from their lives that have been preserved for us give us to understand that, "soaring above all created things," they served together with the celebrants of the heavenly altar. We will relate these incidents in a later chapter.

* * * * * * * *

To meet a rabid dog with savagely glowing eyes, barking strangely and tearing at everything its path, is a terrifying experience. Since he runs wild over the countryside it is possible to encounter him anywhere, even in such an unlikely place as a hermit's Kalyve.

Once such an undesirable visitor came to the Kathisma of the Brother of the Lord. And what did Fr. Hilarion decide to do?

"Fr. Sabbas," he called, "Do you see that dog? Quickly catch him and bring him to me."

Here the virtue of discipleship, blessed obedience, was put to a grievous test. Would the "prize-fighter" give way? Perhaps another would have, but not Fr. Sabbas.

"With your prayers, Elder. Bless me."

Without fear, armed with faith in miracles of obedience, he made the sign of the Cross, invoked his elder's blessing, and walked towards the dog. "Obedience can tame even wild beasts," write the Fathers. And truly, not only did he not suffer the slightest harm, but even the rabid animal was healed.

* * * * * * * *

One time Fr. Sabbas fell gravely ill. For many days he was tortured by a high fever, and his condition did not improve. Then the elder decided to resort to the weapon of monastic saints, the prayer-rope. He was inwardly assured that the Lord would not disregard his request. Nevertheless, he also wanted the "virtue of discipleship" to contribute to the healing. What did he think to do?

In their hermitage they had some olives, onions, beans and other vegetables. He took some of these and approached the sick man.

"Fr. Sabbas," he said to him, "eat what I give you and you will become well."

Fr. Sabbas almost laughed at the "medicine," but he soon understood the significance of the action and as a faithful child of obedience consumed it all. Not only was he not harmed (a doctor who was informed later of the incident rubbed his eyes with amazement), but he was completely healed of his illness.

* * * * * * * *

John Remoundos, a young student from the Polytechnic who was born in Andros, came with his brother George to Dionysiou Monastery to become a monk. After a few days they accepted him, telling his brother to go to another monastery. The day following the sad parting, John, going to work at the mill in the forest, thought to visit the two hermits in order to meet them and receive their blessing for his new life.

"Come here, my child," he heard an unknown voice say. It was Fr. Hilarion, who was sitting outside the door. "Welcome." After greeting him, he said:

"You must be patient, my child, patient and obedient. Don't grieve over the separation from your brother. Today he will go to live the coenobitic life in the Holy Monastery of Xenophontos, and later he will even become Abbot."

The young novice was filled with wonder at the strange things he heard. He thought he was speaking with some biblical prophet.

"Come here, my child, and venerate St. James. Make three prostrations and kiss his holy icon."

And striking him on the shoulder with fatherly love, Fr. Hilarion said to him:

"You must love this Apostle whose name you bear. He will be your best protector."

"But holy Father, I am not called James."

"Yes, my child John, but you will become James. And take care that until your tonsure no one but you knows what I, a foolish elder, have told you today."

When John was named Fr. James and when his brother became Abbot of Xenophontos Monastery, Fr. Hilarion was in no danger of vainglory, for the dead are not exposed to such temptations.

* * * * * * * *

For Russia, 1854 was a year of hardship and disturbance. Having provoked the Ottoman Empire to war, it was now suffering reverses. It had to fight not only the Turks, but also the English and French—a large enemy army. The Crimean peninsula had become a field of violent battle, with Sebastopol undergoing a cruel siege. The future looked dark.

In such situations the Tsars of Russia did not forget the holy elders, but they had recourse to them as did the Kings of Israel to the prophets. On this occasion, a sailing ship with officers of Tsar Nicholas I came in search of a man of God. It steered for Athos and dropped anchor outside Dionysiou Monastery. They were looking for Fr. Hilarion. When the officers came to him, they asked to be told the outcome of the war. The elder, a child of humility, did not want to be honored as a prophet; but the officers, knowing the man's spiritual power, did not give way. The more he refused to tell them anything, the more they implored. For three days the ship remained at the Monastery's wharf. Finally he gave in. Taking in his hands the wonder-working prayer-rope, he turned to God, the Lord of time and eternity, praying to Him about the matter.

"Russia will endure hardship; she will be defeated in the end, but will not suffer any territorial losses."

This is what the Tsar learned about the outcome of the Crimean War (1854-1855) and the future justified the "Starets" of the Athonite desert.*

6. THE PARTING

As he advanced in age, Fr. Hilarion grew white both in body and in soul. He was white-haired, sweet in his manner and speech, gracious to everyone, overflowing with holy, angelic grace. His snowy hair and beard and his pure white soul reminded one of the Gospel passage, *Lift up your eyes and see the fields, for they are white already for the harvest.* (John 4:35)

He had struggled for many years, enlightening his own mind and, by his work as a confessor, the minds of others. He had brought up his disciple to the heights of virtue, he had glorified the name of the Lord, and supported the world by his prayers. He emitted a spiritual fragrance *like cinnamon and aromatic balm.* (Wisdom of Sirach 24:15) Now nothing remained but for the ripe cluster of grapes to be harvested and placed in the bosom of the Church Triumphant.

At the beginning of Great Lent he went to the Monastery of St. Panteleimon (the Russian Monastery) to confess the fathers. There death met him on February 14, 1864, and conducted his soul to the bright country of joy on high.

---

*See Appendix 1 for a further account of Elder Hilarion's views on the Russo-Turkish War, told in the words of Elder Sabbas himself.

But parting is always grievous. Great pain seized the soul of Fr. Sabbas, who was present at the Russian Monastery, as well as all the monks. They had lost their father. The death of such a spirit-bearing Father creates an unfillable void; it brings not only grief, but sometimes even despair. Loud outcries were heard:

"Why have you abandoned your children, Father, whom you always showed such love and paternal sympathy?"

Like all God-bearing men, Fr. Hilarion had foreseen his end. He had also foreseen that the Russians would honor him as a saint, and would place his mortal remains among the holy relics. Because of his profound humility he took steps to prevent this; he had commanded Fr. Sabbas to prevent him from being buried in the Russian Monastery. He was to bury him in his first place of repentance, the Iveron cell of the Theologian.

The elder, as he had foretold, reposed in St. Panteleimon's Monastery and Fr. Sabbas did not know how to carry out his last request. The fathers of the Russian Monastery were adamant. Not knowing what else to do, one night when all was quiet he took the relics of his elder from the Monastery without being observed, and buried them in the quiet Iveron cell of St. John the Theologian. Now the grace of Christ's beloved disciple overshadowed the holy remains of the blessed Hilarion. Resting peacefully in his ascetic arena, he reposed where his ascetic sweat had sprinkled the ground, now watered anew by the unrestrained tears of his disciple.

In 1867, after three years, the whole Monastery of Dionysiou was moved by tender emotion. With much ceremony and magnificence, the relics of the ever-memorable Fr. Hilarion were placed in the Monastery cemetery.

"When my bones are disinterred, carry them to the cemetery of Dionysiou Monastery and mingle them with the bones of the other fathers," he had commanded Fr. Sabbas.

The servant of humility did not want his bones to be displayed and honored, but to be mingled with the others and not set apart. And so the venerable relics of the holy fathers welcomed into their midst the precious treasure. There, together with the relics of more recent strugglers, they await the time when the trumpet of the Archangel will resurrect them. *And your bones shall flourish like an herb* (Isaiah 66: 14).

* * * * * * * *

In concluding our account of the wonderful Fr. Hilarion's life, we have to note that Athonite tradition surrounds him with glory. Many aged fathers tell anecdotes which make you wonder whether they belong to the realm of history or legend. Some of these, like the following, tell of the intensity of his ascetic struggles.

One time Elder Hilarion shut himself up in a tower, one of those built on the Holy Mountain as a protection against pirate raids. He wanted to completely shut out the outside world and occupy himself only with the inward life. He had made himself a rule never to raise his eyes and look out of the window. No external thing was to distract his mind from prayer and sobriety.

But the evil demons, the age-old enemies of ascetics, contrived to make him break his rule. While he traveled mentally in heavenly, spiritual spheres, they gathered at the base of the tower, outside the door, and suddenly assaulted him with voices, calling: "Where are you, Elder Hilarion?" They screamed, struck the door, and in general made commotion and mischief. Then involuntarily the ascetic, thinking that there was some emergency, interrupted his prayer and anxiously looked out of the window. Immediately the demons shouted with delight, applauded, and cried, "We defeated you, Elder Hilarion! We defeated you!"

Their aim was not merely to defeat him in this matter, but to destroy him completely, which they proved unable to do. In the end he completely defeated them, as did also his worthy disciple.

Right background: the tower in New Skete where Elder Hilarion lived in seclusion for three years.

The towering coenobium of Dionysiou.

II

The Ascent

1. TOWARDS THE LIGHT

After the repose of his elder, many things changed in the life of Fr. Sabbas. At first he was obliged to abandon his beloved hermitage and live in Dionysiou Monastery. It is not known whether he did this by his own desire, in obedience to the fathers of the Monastery, or at the command of the departed Fr. Hilarion.

With pain of soul, he gathered his few possessions. Reverently he collected the things his elder had left him, setting aside a large, heavy metal cross that he had worn on his breast, and also a wonderful wooden crucifix that he had brought from Georgia, the work of an ancient Georgian artist.

His eyes overflowing with tears, he prayed to his protector, St. James, asking for his farewell blessing. Bidding farewell to the desert, he descended to the Monastery, shaken by emotion.

It is said that St. James spoke to him, that he heard the final words of his Epistle echoing in his ears: *He who turns a sinner from death shall cover a multitude of sins.* Fr. Sabbas could little guess what a holy life-work lay before him, how many souls he would put on the road of repentance. Many, many lost ones would through him find salvation.

For the Dionysiou Coenobium Fr. Sabbas was a God-sent blessing, a source of spiritual fragrance, a flower of divine grace full of heavenly nectar. Everybody wished to be near him and profit by his spiritual wealth. But for him, things were different. Accustomed to stillness from his youth, he found no repose in the populous community of the coenobium. The atmosphere there oppressed him, and he was consumed by the yearning for silence. His soul thirsted for some desert hermitage.

When he revealed this desire to the abbot, he met with opposition from both him and the brethren, for they greatly revered and loved him and no one wanted to be deprived of his presence. In the end, however, they gave way in order not to quench the love of silence. Moreover, the Lord had other plans for him which they could not prevent.

High up in Little St. Anne's Skete, opposite the Skete of the Foremother of God, was a barren Kalyve then dedicated to the great Saints Onouphrius and Peter of Mount Athos (later, as we shall see, it was dedicated to the Resurrection of the Lord). It was everything Fr. Sabbas was seeking. The whole region exerted a charm over him. Every Kalyve, every rock and cave had its own wonderful, holy history. Below his Kalyve was the cave where Agapius Landos, the renowned monk from Crete and great evangelizer of the enslaved Greek nation lived for a time in asceticism in the 17th century. In that cave he attained holiness, and there also he wrote his celebrated and well-known book *Sinners' Salvation*.

A little further away was another cave where the first inhabitants of Little Anne's Skete, the Studite monk St. Dionysius the Orator and his disciple St. Mitrophan, struggled in asceticism at the end of the 16th century. Fr. Gerasim the Hymnographer of Little St. Anne's Skete calls them "bright lamps illuminating all the wilderness of Athos by their angelic way of life."

But in Fr. Sabbas' time also there were virtuous monks living in Little St. Anne's. For example, in the Kalyve of the Dormition of the Theotokos lived the famous confessor Fr. Gregory from

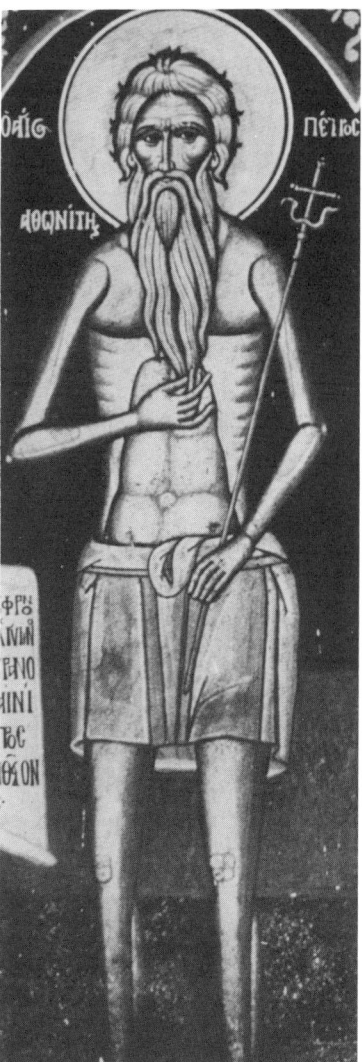

STS. ONOUPHRIUS AND PETER OF MT. ATHOS.
The icon of St. Onouphrius is from the Monastery of St.
Onouphrius in Poland; that of St. Peter, from a fresco in the
refectory of Docheiariou Monastery, Mt. Athos.

Little St. Anne's Skete, the vicinity of Fr. Sabbas' kalyve.

Messolonghi, the "Basil the Great of the Desert," as they called him. The eminent and much-laboring Patriarch Joachim III, during the twelve years (1889-1901) that he rested on the Holy Mountain, in picturesque Milopotamou, had him as his confessor.*

Needless to say, such an excellent spiritual climate filled Fr. Sabbas' soul with joy. But although he imagined his new abode to be a quiet and isolated Mount Carmel, the Lord planned to change it to a much-frequented pool of Siloam. May the foresight of the Good Shepherd, Who knows best how to use His brightest lamps, direct all things according to His will.

2. FATHER SABBAS' COMMUNITY

Souls attracted by the monastic life search for a suitable director, and when they find one they run to him eagerly. Thus many thirsting souls came to Fr. Sabbas for spiritual refreshment, and a community quickly formed around him. This was something that he also desired, because when he was alone he could not celebrate the Liturgy. In all, five disciples are mentioned: Onouphrius, Hilarion, Peter, Anastasius, and Sabbas.

The first one, Fr. Onouphrius, who came from the environs of Constantinople, received the name of one of the two patron Saints of their Kalyve, so that he would be inspired by his ascetic struggles. Indeed, he closely resembled him in his asceticism. The only thing in which he did not resemble St. Onouphrius was his thin little beard. This, however, was of no importance. What was important was his great virtue, piety, struggles, and also his education, intelligence, and varied talents, from artistic to culinary. He learned the art of icon-painting, and in this way brought in an income for the support of the community. He was the right hand of the elder, the general caretaker

---

*The Patriarch also confessed to the famous Father Confessor Fr. Abraham of Kavsokalyvia. Probably he chose him after the repose of Fr. Gregory.

of the business of the Kalyve, and later, when Fr. Sabbas was absorbed in purely spiritual work, a second elder. This first disciple was a God-sent blessing for Fr. Sabbas.

The arrival of the second disciple to the Holy Mountain is connected with a moving story. In 1879, twenty men from Vrioula of Smyrna, longing for spiritual ascents, made a courageous decision. One night, without being observed, they bade farewell to worldly vanities and set sail for the Garden of the Mother of God, in order to increase the ranks of earthly angels. Fr. Hilarion was then twenty-five years old. In this group was also the future famous Abbot of Karakallou Monastery, Fr. Codratus.

The spiritual development of Fr. Hilarion was as wonderful as his beginning. In him not only the name of Fr. Sabbas' elder lived again, but also his virtues. He was tall, slender, rather blond, and in his face was seen the essence of cheerfulness, sweetness, and peace. His exceeding simplicity and kindness, the expression of his face, his glance, reminded one of the world of angels—immaterial and grace-filled. His devotion to his elder knew no bounds, and for his sake he was ready to sacrifice anything. Every now and then you could see him with a sack on his back, carrying what was necessary for Divine Liturgy, food, supplies, and whatever else the Kalyve needed.

Fr. Anastasius, who was the brother of Fr. Sabbas according to the flesh, came late to the Holy Mountain, and—this is certain—reposed before his brother.

The two others, Peter and Sabbas, did not progress far in the monastic life. We know that one died prematurely (on February 14, 1907) from a serious illness. The second one, to whom Fr. Sabbas showed special love, even giving him his own name, left the Holy Mountain and ended up in another monastery.

The presence of the ever-memorable Elder Hilarion was very much felt in the community. Fr. Sabbas mentioned him so often and portrayed him so vividly that to the eyes of the disciples he seemed fully alive. If Elisseus could have forgotten Elias the Tishbite, then Fr. Sabbas could also have forgotten his elder. By his legacy, commands, and rule of life, he filled the atmosphere of the Kalyve. Even after many years his presence was clearly felt.

When the service of the deposition of Fr. Hilarion's relics in the Dionysiou cemetery was completed, Fr. Sabbas warmly begged for one favor from the abbot: that he might take his honorable skull. They did not object, and with immeasurable joy he carried it to his Kalyve. How they trembled with joy, and daily prayed before it with tears! Now the Kalyve was enriched and beautified, and filled with spiritual fragrance.

3. SPIRITUAL NOURISHMENT

For a man to gain spiritual wealth, study and degrees in theology are not enough. He must struggle ceaselessly, breast to breast against the "old Adam" within him, and against the powers of darkness. Only thus are true spiritual guides and teachers cultivated.

Some time ago, a hieromonk who is a friend of ours wrote to us these noteworthy words on the subject of inexperienced men meddling with deep spiritual questions: "I humbly believe that their work failed in the end because they did not have training in sobriety and did not know the ascetic tradition. You see, beloved, science is one thing and traditional asceticism is another; learning is one thing and experience another, the student's desk one thing and obedience another. Tradition, I humbly believe, is the presence of the Holy Spirit, the succession of the Spirit."

It is not difficult to see the importance of these thoughts. The "student of divinity" is at a low degree. The student and *lover* of divinity is at the summit of the pyramid. If Fr. Sabbas became a source of great spiritual nourishment, it was due to the great experience of spiritual life he obtained by his personal struggles and sweat. For twenty-one years he struggled as a disciple in the Kathisma of the Brother of the Lord, and before that for several years in the Iberian Skete under the supervision of an experienced spiritual father, a living bearer and continuer of tradition. Thus he also could become an "honorable teacher of the law to all the people," rich in spiritual experience.

We can imagine what treasures of ascetic wisdom would come from his lips during his discussions with his disciples, what wonderful descriptions of his struggles, perils, ascents, and illuminations.

"My children," he said to them, "beware of temptations from the right hand. They allure us with desire for excessive asceticism, severe fasts, a lofty contemplative life, absolute seclusion and isolation. Put down the thieving wolves clothed in righteous thoughts. Do not be trapped by them, for they are plotting our destruction. The grace of God does not bring forth such premature fruits. I have had bitter experience of the demon from the right hand."

"'My Elder,' I once begged blessed Fr. Hilarion when we lived in silence in the Dionysiou Kathisma, 'I want very much to have perfect solitude and seclusion. I want to be alone with God, alone before the Alone. Give me your blessing to find some cave higher up the mountain and to live there in asceticism.'"

"I besieged him with such requests, thinking that my longing was very God-pleasing. He, however, being experienced and enlightened by God, saw the deception in this, understood that it was a dangerous fascination of youthful enthusiasm—premature and unripe. However, he did not want to oppose my flaming desire.

"'You may go, my child,' he said to me. 'Since you desire it so much, you may go. Christ will show His will.'"

"That evening, settled in a secluded cave high on the bare hillside, I sent up prayers and thanksgiving to heaven. 'This night,' I thought, 'I will enjoy prayer!' Lower down, however, in the cell of the Brother of the Lord, my Elder was praying with his prayer-rope to God to give me a good lesson, as befitted my youthful presumption and hastiness.

"It became quite dark. Immersed in prayer, I enjoyed the quiet. But I did not enjoy it for long, because an unexpected storm broke loose. Rocks were crashing everywhere, the wind was roaring—it seemed like the end of the world.*

"Overpowered by terror, I was in danger of losing my mind. I didn't know whether I could ever make my way back to the cell of St. James, to my spiritual father. May such hesychia be far from me!

"It is fortunate that God heard the prayers of my elder and allowed the demons to terrorize me, for if I had remained there I would have suffered more serious harm. It was an unforgettable experience and lesson!"

In time, many were nourished by Fr. Sabbas' rich storehouse of spiritual experience. When he was raised to the dignified position of father confessor, even more people tasted of the fruits of his wisdom. The void that Fr. Hilarion had left was now more than filled.

Even though the silence of the Kalyve was continually disturbed and many visitors needed to be cared for, even though the artistic Fr. Onouphrius was compelled to work intensely at his icon-painting in order to meet their economic needs, even though they had much labor and trouble, it didn't matter. Above all, "God's will be done." Could the disciples of the Lord have grown tired feeding the five thousand? But about how Fr. Sabbas became established as a father confessor, how, like another Joseph, he *opened all the storehouses and fed all the Egyptians* (Gen. 41:56), we will speak in greater detail.

4. A LIVING PILLAR OF VIRTUE

Even if Fr. Sabbas had never said a word about the spiritual life, if he had maintained absolute silence, his daily life would have spoken eloquently. In him, like in a living pillar, were engraved all the virtues of the saints.

---

*In the lives of hermits, demons often cause such temptations. For those who have questions, we recommend that they study the life of Anthony the Great, written by the authentic and God-moved hand of Athanasius the Great.

He assiduously cultivated temperance and self-control. Many times he would set himself a "rule of temperance," as is said in ascetic language, which he observed faithfully and steadily. And remarkably, he did not abandon these ascetic exercises even in deep old age.

A very aged monk of New Skete, Elder Simeon (who has since reposed) three years ago told us the following:

"Sometimes the father confessor would set a rule for himself that, from the food he was brought, he would leave a little as a gift of abstinence 'for the Lord,' for the love of God. What then, by the allowance of God, did the enemy do? Elder Onouphrius, his disciple, seeing that the elder left food and bread, supposed that he was not able to eat it all, so he diminished the portion. The elder, not wishing to break his rule, continued to leave a little. Elder Onouphrius again cut the portion, thereby risking to kill the elder with hunger. The elder, however, said nothing to them about this. Then it happened that I went to the father confessor, and since he regarded me more than the others and loved me very much, he confessed to me: 'Now, Simeon my child, I am close to death.' He told me in secret what had happened, enjoining me not to tell anyone. I, however, thought it good to inform someone, and when I left I revealed the matter to Elder Onouphrius. Thus he corrected his mistake, and the father confessor lived until his natural death."

By means of such heroic ascetic exploits, Fr. Sabbas learned to rule over himself like a king. He was always at peace; no wave of anger, agitation, sorrow, or melancholy could disturb him. Those who knew him confessed that they never saw him angry, agitated, upset or despondent. He had arrived at the summit of passionlessness.

If someone happened to hurt, injure, or grieve him, it did not cause him confusion or distress, or lessen his love.

One time a group of merchants arrived at his Kalyve.

"We're from Sikia of Chalkis," they said. "Down by the beach we have a load of the highest quality honey. Here is a sample. Do you want to buy some?"

Honey on dry bread was a fasting food they used in their Kalyve, so Fr. Hilarion finally bought a crock of this choice honey. But when he opened it, he found that they had cheated them. They had given them a tasteless thick syrup that was not like honey at all.

"Let's go to church," said Fr. Sabbas peacefully, "and say a prayer-rope for them, so that God will have mercy on them."

After some time, the swindlers replaced the crock. They had had great hardships at sea, and ascribing it to their fraud against the holy elder, they decided to rectify their sin.

Fr. Sabbas was very circumspect in his judgment of others. He systematically avoided blaming anyone, and in speaking about people would take care to praise and extol them.

"What kind of man is he, holy Father?" people would ask.

"A good man, very good. He is a holy man," he would answer them.

In almsgiving also he was unequalled. As we will see below, the multitude of monks and laymen coming to him for confession would leave him many gifts, even if he would refuse them. He gave away almost everything. Thus, when one time the church needed some repairs and alterations, he did not have the money for it. Many wondered at his disregard for money.

5. PROPHETIC GRACE

When I was fourteen years old, the following story impressed me:

A very pious young woman in a neighboring house in Piraeus exchanged the tumult of the world for the monastic state. Her relatives, and even her brothers and sisters, headed by Dionysius, the eldest, searched for her everywhere. Fiercely agitated and angry, they breathed fury against her and also against the monastery that had received her. For a long time, however, they could not discover where she was, until they turned their attention to the region of Parnithos. They learned that their sister was in the Holy Monastery of St. Paraskeva, and there they went.

They passed through the gate. On a balcony facing them was an aged monk. Naturally, they had never seen him before, nor he them. They did not know that he was named Hieronymus or that he was the Monastery's father confessor, or that he was unable to see. The elder, however, surprised them. Rising from his seat, he turned to their party and welcomed them:

"Welcome, Dionysius. Come, come over here to me. It's good that you have come. We have your sister here."

All that was needed to add to their astonishment was to discover that the elder was completely blind. They were thunderstruck and didn't know what to believe. They trembled before a holy mystery. The blind man had not only seen them, but had even known why they were there and called them by name! Their souls were filled with piety and fear, for they realized they were in the presence of a prophet.

And what was the result? Not only did they not trouble their sister or make a scene in the Monastery, but they were changed from irreconcilable enemies of monasticism to its advocates. They could not find enough words to praise this wonderful man of God.

I remember how everyone in the neighborhood discussed this unexpected change. As for me, I was completely carried away by this event, and lofty longings were kindled in my soul. My admiration for the blind Fr. Hieronymus was boundless. That was the first time I learned that there exist men with the gift of clairvoyance.

Fr. Sabbas also received this grace to a high degree. Many who came to him for discussion, advice, or confession were filled with astonishment, seeing how his spiritual gaze penetrated the depths of their hearts and read their secret thoughts. He brought to light their hidden sins, recalled forgotten transgressions, revealed demonic snares, foresaw what the future had in store for them.

"You will leave the Holy Mountain," he once said to Fr. Gregory of Grigoriou, "but you will come back. This will be repeated, and finally you will again go away."

And in fact, Fr. Gregory saw the words of Fr. Sabbas come true to the letter. The last time that he left the Mountain, he ended up in the Holy Monastery of Bulkanou in Messinia.

What can it be that occurs in the mind of a prophet? Do truths and revelations appear in a mystical manner? Have his spiritual eyes been purified and strengthened by his holy life? How much is the action of natural purity, and how much of supernatural illumination? Can the prophet have ties with his prophecy afterwards?

Generally speaking, I think that a bearer of prophetic grace is like a man who has ascended to the top of a mountain, and from there naturally can see more and farther than others. When he speaks about what he sees, he expresses himself with great naturalness and certainty, with no hesitation. The great luminary of the Orthodox Church, St. Gregory Palamas, expresses this truth beautifully. "Inasmuch as he is become a receptacle of the power of the Divine Spirit, he sees by means of it" (In Defense of the Holy Hesychasts, 1:3). That is to say, he has received the gifts of the Holy Spirit. These gifts are given to those who struggle to purify and set in order the receptacles of their souls.

As Fr. Sabbas ascended to the highest spiritual peaks, he was not only illuminated by "the abundant and brilliant rays of the divine sunbeams," but he also experienced indescribable states of spiritual joy. He was warmed by an unquenchable divine warmth, and refreshed by the sweet breaths and gentle winds of the Holy Spirit. He was transported by otherworldly melodies and hymns; intoxicated by indescribable beauty, by visions of the angelic hierarchies, by heavenly and divine fragrances, by inaccessible mystical visions of what lies "behind the veil," by the superessential brilliance of the light of Tabor. Thus illuminated and inundated with divine brilliance, he himself could shine and enlighten the deluded, leading them from darkness to light, and from light to yet greater light. "He who is enlightened can, like the sun, also enlighten all who draw near him." (St. Symeon the New Theologian)

III

The Renowned Father Confessor

When a tree is given fertile soil, light, and coolness, it grows and bears fruit and becomes a "tree of shady leaves by which many are sheltered."

This is an image of what happens with an elect confessor. Souls tormented by the scorching heat of evil run to him for refreshment. They are washed, cleansed, their garments are made white. And when the confessor is a God-bearing elder of exalted virtue, overflowing with illuminating grace, then the days and nights will not be long enough to confess all who flock to him. They also will grow weary, waiting hours and even days for their turns. If he is the elder of a community, his disciples must abandon all hope of stillness and repose. They also have to endure a constant stream of mailmen bringing mountains of correspondence.

All this happened to Fr. Sabbas, whose fame as an outstanding physician of souls grew day by day. Those coming to him for confession never stopped recommending him enthusiastically to everyone, until his renown had spread to the ends of Orthodoxy.

His mercy, forbearance, and sympathy, his skill in diagnosing spiritual illnesses and helping his patients reveal their wounds; his ability to console, encourage, and instruct them—all this, together with the holiness of his own life, made him an incomparable spiritual father. "Many of the monks and laymen who used to go to him for confession," wrote Abbot Gabriel of Dionysiou in 1953, "are still alive. They all hold in reverence the memory of his kindness, fatherly love, and compassion, and especially his gentleness towards penitents burdened with heavy sins. Nobody left the small, crypt-like confession-room of the gentle spiritual father without consolation" (*Lausaicon of the Holy Mountain*, p. 36).

If we compare the confessors of the Holy Mountain with the great hierarch-saints, then Fr. Sabbas would correspond to St. John Chrysostom. Even the other fathers of Mount Athos, so sparing in their praise, did not hesitate to call him "the Chrysostom of confessors."

In presenting the labors of this famous spiritual father, we feel powerless to do him justice. We fear to make him seem less than he was. But the wonders that God worked through him should not remain in oblivion, so we will report them in a poor brief manner, and let the mind of the reader do the rest. First we will speak of his methods, and then we will relate a few characteristic anecdotes that are still talked about on the Holy Mountain, and that show forth Fr. Sabbas' skill in the healing of souls.

1. *I AM BECOME ALL THINGS TO ALL MEN*

The Christ-bearing soul of Fr. Sabbas trembled with boundless love for every Christian. Everyone who came to him for confession was the person for whom Christ, moved by infinite love, poured out His blood. This love was the driving and guiding force of the loving spiritual father's soul.

No sacrifice was too great to save the lost, scattered, wounded, enfeebled, sick sheep of Christ from the wolves and robbers. The words of Scripture, *I will seek that which was lost, and bring again that which was driven away, and will bind up that which was broken, and will strengthen that which was sick* (Ezekiel 34:16), were ever in his heart in his work as confessor.

Perhaps the most difficult thing in the world is to abandon a broad, comfortable thoroughfare of sin and return in humility and repentance to the path of God. One must struggle with oneself, with the world, and with those dark powers that prevent souls from reaching the light. This makes the work of a confessor very difficult, sometimes to the point of despair.

Fr. Sabbas knew very well how difficult it is to confess one's faults, disclose one's inner wounds, reveal the abscesses and foul odors of guilt. He also knew that there can be no healing, repentance, or absolution without this revelation of one's sins. To effect this, therefore, his love and compassion for his wounded brethren led him to marvelous contrivances. When he first met a visitor, regardless of what day or hour he arrived, he disarmed him with an onslaught of kindness, warmheartedness, and joy. It does not need much thought to perceive that a gloomy, frowning face is unfitting for a healer of souls. When hearing confessions, he did not hurry at all, or take any account of himself and his own weariness. All that concerned him was the work of confession—the diagnosis of the disease and its healing, the penitent's repentance and resolution to correct his life. The Gospel words *sin no more* were always his main emphasis.

Many times you would see him leave the room where he heard confessions and go outside. Someone would be walking around in the Kalyve, hesitating to make some soul-saving decision. In order to help him at that critical moment, he had to inspire his confidence, persuade and encourage him, and guide him to the harbor of salvation.

When he saw that someone had difficulty revealing his sins, he would use all kinds of means and contrivances to give him courage. We will describe some of these in the following pages. Even though some hearts would seem to be locked shut, he would manage in the end to unlock them.

He did not hesitate to place himself on the same level as a deeply sinful penitent. In order to give him the courage to uncover his deep wounds, he would lead him to believe that he also had fallen into similar sins. Thus he could rightfully say with the Apostle, *To them that are without law, (I became) as without law, that I might gain them that are without law. To the weak became I as weak, that I might gain the weak. I am made all things to all men, that I might by all means save some* (I Cor. 9:21-22).

As he knew how to lower himself in the eyes of the penitents, he also knew how to reveal his spiritual greatness when this was appropriate. He was a bearer of the Holy Spirit, and he used his gifts of clairvoyance and prophecy for the salvation of souls. Then the penitent would find himself confronted by the flames of Pentecost. Before this force no device of the enemy could stand, and the penitent, filled with wonder, would cry: "Is this elder a man or an angel?"

3. ARTIFICES OF LOVE

Several years ago we visited Elder Symeon, who was living in the Kalyve of the Meeting of the Lord in the beautiful New Skete, which is near the Holy Monastery of St. Paul. Ninety-five years old and bed-ridden, he was hourly expecting the death that was to lead him to God. By his side was his disciple, Fr. Panteleimon, a loving son and guardian angel.

"Elder, do you remember Fr. Sabbas the Confessor?"

"Oh, the confessor! The holy Fr. Sabbas! May we have his prayers! How could I not remember him? I confessed to him; I was always at his Kalyve. Many, many times I helped him during Liturgy with the singing."

"Tell us something about him. We have heard very much, and we are thinking of writing his life. They say that he was a famous spiritual father."

"He had great grace upon him. He could give courage to everyone, especially the young monks. As soon as he saw them in the room where he heard confession, he would smile and say, 'Well, little angels! Good, good, my angels are here. I regard these young monks as angels, because they have left the vain world and come here to the desert for the love of our Sweetest Christ.' He also encouraged all who were disheartened. 'Do not drive anyone to despair,' he would say again and again."

"They say, Elder, that he was very skillful in hearing confessions."

"Very skillful and very loving. He did not want people to hide their sins from him. If he saw some young monk or novice who was ashamed to tell all his sins, what would he do? He would think up tricks, artifices of love. 'Don't hesitate to tell your sins, my child. I am an old man—I might even fall asleep, but you just continue. Christ is present and hears all. Confess everything fearlessly, and you will purify your soul and make it white as snow.' The monk would begin to speak, and the confessor would seem to grow sleepy. Soon his head was down, and he was snoring. Then the monk would confess his most serious sins. 'My child, stop a moment. You just mentioned a certain sin. What did you say? I didn't hear well. Say it more clearly, and cleanse your soul.' The monk would take courage and say it clearly. Then his soul was relieved. God rejoiced and the devil was wounded."

"Oh, Elder, thank you. You have given us precious information. We are amazed by the skill of this great spiritual Father. Such a trick! We never heard of one like that before."

"I told you—he was very skillful and very loving. Today there is no one like him."

* * * * * * * *

In a Kalyve of St. Anne's Skete lived another hieromonk who was also a confessor, but who did not have the experience and discernment of Fr. Sabbas. One time a man who had committed terrible sins came to confess to him. The priest had never met anyone like this man before. A true "bruised reed," he began to confess. Hearing him, the confessor was horrified and sickened. "My God, what atrocities! What am I hearing! What kind of devil is he?"

Before the unfortunate man could finish, the confessor interrupted him, full of agitation:

"Stop, I am horrified! I will lose my mind! These are not human sins, they are satanic. Get out, you have no absolution! I won't hear any more! Go away!"

The only thing in the world he had left to him had been the mercy of God. When even this door was closed, nothing remained. Looking down at the sea, he thought his only solution was to drown himself, to put an end to the tragedy of his life.

But God is great. At this moment, an acquaintance of his who lived in St. Anne's Skete happened to see him.

"How are you? What's going on? What's the matter?"

He did not speak.

"Eh, what's the matter? Why won't you speak?"

With great difficulty he succeeded in learning the details. His soul was distressed and grieved. How could he help him? He could think of only one solution: to bring him by any means to Fr. Sabbas. To this end he quite exhausted himself, and finally he succeeded.

As soon as Fr. Sabbas saw him, all was clear to him. "My brother is in an abyss. In order to bring him out, I must climb down to him."

"Father, is there salvation for me?"

"For you, my brother? There is salvation for everyone. The mercy of God is wider than heaven and deeper than the abyss."

"No, not for me! A sinner like me can't be saved. It's impossible!"

"*You* can't be saved? What a joke; you seem to think that *I* can!"

"What sins can you have committed?"

"Great sins, very great sins."

"What 'great sins'! Who can be as guilty before God as I, the wretched one?"

"Nevertheless—you see, once I wasn't careful. I was carried away, and fell into the following sins."

Here Fr. Sabbas related a certain serious sin. The other one seemed to come to life.

"Oh, Father, that's exactly what I did!"

"You too? Don't worry, God will forgive you. It is enough that you have confessed it."

Fr. Sabbas continued in the same way. The artifice had complete success. The unfortunate man took courage and brought forward with all sincerity the whole grievous list of his sins. The thought that even the confessor was like him gave him courage.

"I repented and wept bitterly," Fr. Sabbas said to him in the end. "It's been two years since I changed my life. They gave me an obedience to hear confessions. I did this. I also gave alms and fasted, and I became another man."

"I also repent with all my soul, my Father. I will fast, and do anything else you tell me."

"Since you have resolved to change your life, bow down, and I will read the prayer of absolution. God will blot out all your sins."

When he left him, the man was almost flying from joy, for he was relieved of an insupportable burden. Meeting his friend in St. Anne's Skete, he said to him:

"You saved me. I am a new man!"

"Give God the glory."

"He is a good father confessor; good, tender-hearted. The poor man is the only one who has done worse things in his life than I."

The other one understood immediately.

"Worse things than you? I must laugh a little! Christian, my friend, he has lived on the Holy Mountain from childhood and is completely an angel. That is why he was counted worthy to be made a priest."

The man was dumbfounded—what had happened? His friend, however, explained everything to him, and he understood the artifice of love. Great was his astonishment. Indeed, after the blow that the previous confessor had given him, there had been no other way to save him from the edge of the abyss. From this moment he was filled with an infinite wonder and love for this excellent physician and healer of souls.

We should note here that some of the fathers of the Holy Mountain did not approve of these "tricks." They were not in the right, however, for Fr. Sabbas was discerning enough to know exactly how and when to use them, so that there never occurred the slightest harm or scandal.

4. HEALING REMEDIES

Fr. Sabbas knew well when to be lenient, when moderate, and when to be strict and exacting. Grieving and humbled souls he encouraged with gentleness and indulgence. When he saw that someone was obstinate and resistant, however, he would make no concessions. He gave penances when necessary, but always in a gentle way, and therefore they were received without indignation. Like an experienced camel driver, he knew exactly what burden each camel could bear.

He dealt severely with those who injured their neighbors.

"Father," a pilgrim said to him, "there is something else I must tell you. I was passing by the kalyve of an elder I know, who happened to be away. I was bold enough to pick some oranges from his garden."

"Ah, my child, take care! God forgives all your other sins through me, but you must return the oranges. Otherwise you will not be forgiven, and your other sins also will remain unabsolved."

He was very strict and uncompromising in matters regarding the priesthood. If a candidate for the priesthood was hindered by some sin, he would under no circumstances give him any recommendation or approval. Again, if a cleric suffered a serious fall, he would tell him:

"Father, in order not to burden your soul even more, you must hang up your epitrachelion."

When he first became a confessor, he used to travel through the monasteries every Great Lent and hear confessions. Once in Iveron Monastery, however, it happened that he had to strictly punish two priests who had gone astray, which led to unpleasant consequences. He was very grieved by the attitude of these priests, and from then on he did not make these tours, but confined himself to hearing confessions in his own Kalyve. In any case, he would not compromise the dignity of the priesthood.

* * * * * * * *

He knew that an appropriate, well-chosen penance has great educational and healing value. As we will see from the following incident, he was unrivaled in selecting penances.

Many years ago, in the quiet month of October, we set out for the Holy Mountain. In a few days we arrived at the unforgettable St. Anne's Skete, our spiritual birthplace. In its holy atmosphere we could meet holy monks who, under the protection of the Foremother of God, preserved the flaming torch of Orthodox asceticism.

"See, there is Elder Anthony," a hieromonk who was our friend said to us one day. "He is there below picking olives. He is ninety years old. Take the opportunity to speak with him—he remembers much about the old fathers."

That was exactly what we wanted, and we approached him without delay. He was tall and weakly. His clothes were shabby, and because of his age his vision was poor. He was as cheerful as a little child.

"Do you remember anything about the father confessor Fr. Sabbas?"

"Fr. Sabbas! How could I not remember the holy father confessor? I used to go to him for confession."

"Then you will have many things to tell us."

"Sure, I can tell you something that will make an impression on you! It made an impression on this tongue that speaks to you!"

What could this be, we wondered? How could it make an impression on his tongue? But he solved the riddle for us.

"I was a young monk, and I had not yet forgotten the bad habits of the world. Also, I was a little quick-tempered by character. One time in the garden of the Kalyve I had a difference with a neighbor. It was a temptation. He said something rather sharp to me, and I also got carried away. I opened my mouth, and without thinking I said to him...."

Simple and humble as a small child, Elder Anthony told us the truly bad phrase that had escaped from his mouth.

"A little while later I was climbing up to Little St. Anne's Skete. My Elder had sent me to Fr. Sabbas to confess my sin. As soon as he saw me, the father confessor perceived my inner agitation.

"'Father, I have come to confess a great sin.'

"'You should confess it—it is good that you confess it. But don't hurry. Sit down and have a little cake. Hilarion!' he called his disciple, 'bring the treat!'"

"He asked me about my elder, our handiwork, and our Kalyve. He wanted to dispel my anxiety before receiving my confession. It was necessary that the Sacrament be performed in a peaceful atmosphere.

"I grew calm, and we went to the room where he heard confessions. It was a tiny room, small as a crypt. There I confessed my great sin. I remember that he said wise, fatherly words. He cleared away the dark clouds from my soul.

"In the end he said to me, smiling: 'We must place a little penance on your tongue, my child.' 'Yes, Holy Father.' 'Not a great thing. See, when you return to St. Anne's, go to the Kyriakon.* Stick out your tongue and draw it along the floor from the door-step to the icon of Christ, and ask Him to forgive you. Agreed?' 'Agreed.' At the time it did not seem to me a very serious penance.

---

*Besides the small churches in every kalyve, in the sketes there is also a large central church, the "Kyriakon." All the monks of the skete gather in it for the celebration of the Liturgy, mainly on Sundays and great feasts.

"A few hours later I was again in the Kalyve of Fr. Sabbas. "'Father,' I said to him, 'Come and see how my tongue is from the penance you gave me. It's all skinned, swollen, red like a *tsarouchi* [a kind of peasant's shoe].'

"I showed it to him, and he smiled a little. 'Eh, my child, what can we do? A tongue like that, that's what it needed.'

"From that time on, I can't remember that ugly words ever again came out of my mouth."

5. TRANSFORMATIONS

For someone to come to Little St. Anne's Skete, he must disembark at the harbor of St. Anne's Skete and follow a narrow, steep footpath. When Fr. Sabbas was alive, this footpath had much traffic. During Great Lent especially, it turned into an endless chain of Christians going for a spiritual bath.

"There was an endless stream of people," we were told by old monks of St. Anne's Skete. "There were people from everywhere—monks from every corner of the Holy Mountain and from outside monasteries, priests, laymen, employees from Karyes and Daphni, people from the neighboring region of Chalkidiki. No pilgrim to the Holy Mountain would lose the opportunity of going to Fr. Sabbas for confession. There was not enough time for them all! Every evening the Dikaios (the monk who administered the Skete) of St. Anne's Skete gave shelter in the Kyriakon to those who had to wait their turn the following day."

Another astonishing phenomenon was the facial expression of those leaving his confessional. It was an amazing thing. "What goes on in there?" one would think. "What kind of transformations happen in there?"

Two fathers of St. Anne's Skete who were blood brothers told us something about this. Their old father visited them from Arfara of Messinia. When the discussion turned to confession, they recommended that he visit Fr. Sabbas and make a general confession of his life, in order to refresh his soul with the grace of God.

View along the path followed by penitents going to Fr. Sabbas for confession.

How could he despise such a rare spiritual baptismal font? He went to Fr. Sabbas and stayed with him quite a long time. When he came out, he was leaping from joy. A bright peace was on his face, and he felt a mystical transformation within himself: "a strange and glorious change," to use the phrase of the hymnographer. He took a deep breath and cried out: "O my children! How light my soul feels! I am not walking on earth, I'm flying. The whole world seems changed. Glory to Thee, my Christ!"

Only God knows how many similar sighs of relief, joyful tears, and exclamations of praise resounded in the region around this pool of Siloam.

* * * * * * * *

Once in Athens, in 1896, Archimandrite Joachim Spetsieris, the Rector of the Holy Sepulchre Metochion, was talking with his friend Theophanes Troungas, a factory owner.

"Dear Theophanes, I am thinking of going to Mount Athos. I must breathe a little of the fragrance from the Garden of the Mother of God."

"I would be very happy, Fr. Joachim, if I could go with you."

"Why not? 'Two are better than one,' as the Scriptures say."

Soon they had arrived on the Holy Mountain as humble pilgrims. One of their main priorities was to visit the holy confessor Sabbas. Fr. Joachim had confessed to him before in the Holy Land, seven years ago, and could not praise him enough to his friend. He was hoping to persuade Mr. Troungas to approach this spiritual bath.

When they came to the Kalyve of the Resurrection in Little St. Anne's Skete, they were surprised—especially the factory owner—by the crowd of people they saw there.

"They are all waiting for confession," observed Fr. Joachim. "Fr. Sabbas is a great guide of souls. He is a God-enlightened shepherd, and the sheep of Christ run to him as to a place of grass and refreshing water. I don't see when my turn will come to cleanse my soul from all the harmful poisons. My spirit is exhausted from the atmosphere of Athens."

All that Mr. Troungas saw and heard impelled him to make a resolution: to settle his accounts with God, so to speak; to seek forgiveness and make peace. His conscience was suddenly revolted by his way of life. This was the time to approach a confessor and receive Communion.

Surely he was tempted by contrary thoughts that tried to dissuade him from this saving resolve. Finally, however, helped by the grace of God, he conquered his doubts and went fearlessly into the confession-room. His friend Fr. Joachim had visited the confessor before him.

Mr. Troungas stayed for a long time in the spiritual hospital. He had many wounds to heal. What happened to him? Perhaps he had experienced wonders before in his life, but this time he was dazzled and thunderstruck. "My God," he said, "where am I? What am I hearing? Are my ears deceiving me?"

"First I went to confession," wrote Fr. Joachim later, "and then my friend Theophanes.... He remained with Fr. Sabbas for a long time. When he had come out and we were walking to Katounakia, my friend Theophanes said to me: 'What kind of man is Fr. Sabbas? Is he an angel?' I asked him what had happened. 'Well,' he answered, 'during confession he told me everything I have done for the past twenty years and more, without me saying anything to him. He told me old deeds which I had forgotten. How could he know what I did?'

"'Dear Theophanes, don't be astonished,' I told him. 'Fr. Sabbas is clairvoyant!'"

"'What does *clairvoyant* mean...?'"*

Fr. Joachim resolved his perplexity. On that day, Mr. Troungas' soul was transformed.

That was Fr. Sabbas the Confessor!

---

*Archimandrite Joachim Spetsieris, *Memoirs,* Vol. I, pp. 21-22.

IV

The Pilgrim

1. THE JOYS AND SORROWS OF SION

The Passion and Resurrection of the Lord were the daily delight of Fr. Sabbas. Dearest to him of all places on earth were Golgotha and the Holy Sepulchre. If only God would grant him to travel there as a humble pilgrim! It would be a great refreshment for his soul, wearied by his labors as a father confessor.

His state of affairs was favorable for the pilgrimage to the Holy Land, and so his deep longing was satisfied. The Orthodox believers there were also gladdened by the presence of the elder from the Holy Mountain. Times were very difficult in the Holy Land, and they needed such visits.

He arrived at the holy city of Jerusalem in 1889. From his contacts with the Orthodox believers, he soon learned of the situation there. It made him very sad. Jerusalem! A city of holiness and joy, but also of sin and turmoil.

For six years Nicodemus of Cyzicus had been Patriarch of Jerusalem. He had many virtues: he was moral, upright, just, and generous. He was also an imposing man, energetic, and a skillful administrator. The times, however, were very difficult. A few years before, the ship of Orthodoxy had been shaken by the Bulgarian schism. Now the consciences of the Arabic Orthodox were thrown

A view of Jerusalem from the Mount of Olives.

into confusion by the so-called "Arabian question," and the "Palestinian Confederation" was quickly developing.

The Patriarch, who formerly had been Exarch of the Holy Sepulchre in Moscow, was accused of being a Russophile. The finances of the Patriarchate were in a critical state. For the second time, the Theological School of the Holy Cross was closed down. To show how confused and electric the atmosphere was, we may mention that the year before (March, 1888) the Patriarch was narrowly missed by four gun-shots.

Thus, the arrival of the Spirit-bearing Elder was a great relief for the afflicted Greek Orthodox believers. Weary and scandalized souls saw him as a God-sent angel of consolation, as "dew from Hermon." Here we give the words of an eyewitness, Fr. Joachim Spetsieris, who at that time was at the Monastery of St. Sabbas.

> Archpriests, priests, monks, nuns, and all classes of men came to him for confession. According to the words, *Whoever comes to me I will in no wise cast out,* he received everyone. He said to me:
>
> "I came to Jerusalem to worship at the holy places and to be quiet for a little while, and look! They all run to me, the humble one."
>
> "They have need of a confessor," I said to him.
>
> "Yes, I see the need also," he answered, "but in a little while I will be going back."
>
> "Now they have found a physician and want to be healed of their wounds. When he goes away, the most merciful God will send them another to treat them."
>
> At that moment his face shone with pleasure, and he said to me:
>
> "Truly, my child, the Lord will not leave His creation to become prey to troubles and disappointments." (*Memoirs,* vol. 1, pp. 19)

Now that he had been vouchsafed to worship at those places from where our redemption had come, Fr. Sabbas experienced the mystery of Confession even more keenly.

What indescribable tender feeling he experienced as he approached the blood-soaked hill of Golgotha! In that place, human sin had offered to his beloved Lord a most bitter cup of torments. Barely could his lips pronounce: "...nailed to the Cross and pierced by the spear, Thou didst pour forth immortality to men. O our Saviour, glory to Thee."

Again, what heavenly feelings flooded his heart when he worshipped at the Life-Giving Tomb! From here came the victory against the three lords of evil—the devil, sin, and death. From here dawned forth a new world, flooded with divine light and triumphant alleluias. In memory of his pilgrimage to the Holy Sepulchre, he dedicated the chapel of his Kalyve to the Resurrection of the Lord.

2. ST. SABBAS THE SANCTIFIED

Among all the other holy and glorious Saints, St. Sabbas the Sanctified shone like a star in the life of Fr. Sabbas. This hero and instructor of the desert, adornment of monks and luminary of the inhabited earth, was his most beloved Saint. Not only had he given him his name, but until the very end of his life he surrounded him with his special protection and favor.

"My St. Sabbas," he now called to him, "I am longing to make a pilgrimage to your holy school, sanctified by your prayers and labors."

The famous Lavra of St. Sabbas is a three hours' walk from Jerusalem. One walks southeast, following the valley of Josaphat, which begins at Gethsemane and ends at the Dead Sea. All around is hopeless desert; the wind is scorching, the sky seems made of bronze. As one walks, the vale deepens into a steep-sided gorge.

The Monastery, situated high on the right side of the ravine, fills one with wonder. Amidst the wild, majestic nature one sees huge buildings, towers, and walls, all ancient, and countless caves and hermitages. The air is filled with the smell of brimstone and sulphur, the fragrance of incense, bird-song, and the ringing of bells. The Monastery of St. Sabbas rules supreme in this lonely kingdom.

The Monastery of St. Sabbas.

Approaching this holy place, Fr. Sabbas cried out together with the hymnographers: "O godly-minded Sabbas, equal to the angels, citizen of the desert, pure receptacle of the Holy Spirit...."

The fathers of St. Sabbas' Monastery welcomed him with joy.

"Bless, Holy Father! It is good that you have come to the Saint, and brought us the blessing of Mount Athos."

He stayed at the Monastery for two days, getting to know it a little, wondering and delighting in it.

"Holy Father Confessor," said the abbot to him, "the fathers want to come to confession to you. Do not deprive us of this grace."

How could he refuse an offering of love? The sixty fathers of the Monastery came to confession, being refreshed under the epitrachelion of the God-bearing Elder.

The time that remained he used in becoming acquainted with the Lavra. There was much to see—the Saint's sepulchre, the cell of the golden-penned St. John Damascene, the relics of the fathers slaughtered by the Saracens. The whole place was filled with the unutterable fragrances of the holy relics. What sweet-scented lilies God had planted amid these rocks!

In the beautiful Church of the Annunciation was the ancient wonder-working icon of the Saint. On the rocks above, a proud ruler, stood the tower built by the Emperor Justinian. Down in the deep ravine was the Saint's holy spring, where water gushes from the rock. To the north was his mother's cell, and also a date-palm planted by him. To the south was the cave of the great and wonderful John the Hesychast (6th century). The main thing missing was the relics of St. Sabbas himself, which at that time were in far-away Venice. God be praised that they have since been returned to the Monastery! (They were returned on October 30, 1965.)

3. THE DESERT BIRDS

God consoles His faithful servants in many different ways. In this dry and hot place, He provided the monks with a unique diversion: flocks of marvelous birds.

In all probability, Fr. Sabbas made his pilgrimage to St. Sabbas' Lavra at the end of Great Lent, and so was there in time to see this wonder. (This was not the only one; there were many extraordinary phenomena to be seen in this holy place, which we cannot enlarge upon now.) As is reported in the monastery chronicles, more than two hundred wild birds, black with yellow beaks, like blackbirds, lived with the monks from September to April. When they saw an open window they would fly into the monks' cells, bringing gladness and cheer. In the morning when the fathers took their coffee, they would perch on their rassas and feet, looking for crumbs. When a monk called them, they would come and sit on his head or shoulders, and with unusual boldness pick bread or raisins from his hand. They would never come near worldly men, or strange monks or priests—only the fathers of the monastery. Apparently, however, they had discretion. If a monk were very devout, like Fr. Sabbas, they would come to him even if he were a stranger.

Fr. Philotheus Zervakos, who was at St. Sabbas' Lavra on April 28, 1924, reports the following incident:

When I was preparing to drink the coffee I had been given, seven or eight birds suddenly came. Some sat on my shoulders, others on my hands, and the rest sat around me in a circle, calling and chirping. It happened so suddenly that I was startled, but I soon recovered. The fathers were amazed that they had all come to me, and they said, smiling, "Here are the birds you wanted to see." Filled with astonishment and happiness, I put down my coffee and picked up some bread, which I offered to the birds. The fathers also brought me figs, which I cut into small pieces and gave to them. The blessed birds ate from my hands; when they had consumed everything, they expressed thanks with sweet chirps, then flew away.*

A contemporary monk in Palestine.

Like the birds, the monks also have sweet voices, and as they increase in holiness their spiritual songs become ever more melodious. Among these reason-endowed birds, three holy fathers were distinguished at that time. In their presence Fr. Sabbas was spiritually refreshed.

One of these was the venerable Elder Barnabas from Mathitos, seventy years old. After ascetic struggles on Mount Athos and in the Jordan desert, he had come to St. Sabbas' Monastery. In his face one saw the ancient anchorites live again.

"Contemplating his face, one was inspired with reverence, for his countenance was full of virtue. He died in deep old age, having

---

A Great and Wonderful Pilgrimage to Palestine and Sinai, Sirus, 1935, pp. 142-143.

foreseen his end many days in advance." (*Memoirs*, Vol. 1, pp. 57-58)*

Then there was Fr. Callistratus from the Peloponnesus, a great worker of virtue, wise and clear-sighted. In the past he had labored in ascetic struggles for three years (the Patriarch had not permitted him any more) in a cave located in a frightful cliff, under Nebo, the mountain where Moses was entombed. The Arab Orthodox believers of the small town of Koriakon would lower him bread and water by a rope, in exchange for garments which he sewed for them. His lips and mind ever intoned the divine song: "Lord Jesus Christ, Son of God, have mercy on me."

The third was the fifty-year-old Hieromonk Germanus from Kerkyra. He is described as "simple, innocent, guileless, kindly, and humble—an example of a true monk." When serving Liturgy he would be enraptured by divine grace, and his face would become angel-like. He used to repeat: "If we knew what glory and spiritual delight the Communion of the Holy Mysteries gives us, we would sacrifice everything, including this life of ours, in order to communicate worthily."

4. PILGRIMAGE TO THE JORDAN

Fr. Sabbas' plans included a visit to the holy river Jordan, the place where "the worship of the Trinity was made manifest."

In those days there were no comfortable means of transportation like there are today, and it took a laborious journey to arrive at

---

*Fr. Joachim Spetsieris wrote the following about Elder Barnabas: "He did not even have a straw mat in his cell, but only an old coarse rug, a small pitcher for water, and some worn-out garments. He did not have a mattress, or books, or any furniture. He did not sleep at night, but kept vigil, praying and conversing with God. At night he was heard to cry, 'Flee, evil spirits, Christ rebukes you!' Often he was heard quarreling with someone. A monk named Cornelius had a cell next to his, and one day I asked him what had happened to Elder Barnabas to make him cry out and quarrel. 'The evil spirits were harrassing him,' answered Fr. Cornelius, 'and he was answering them back like the great desert fathers, like we read in the Patericon....'

The Monastery of St. Gerasim of the Jordan.

the site of the Lord's baptism. Walking east and a little north from Jerusalem to the elevation of Jericho, the journey took between five and six hours. The countryside was rough, scarred by deep ravines and torrents, making the walk even more difficult. Devout pilgrims, however, took no account of the toil.

The Monastery of St. Gerasim, that great ascetic who tamed the wild beasts of the desert, provides a welcome stopping-place for weary travelers. Nearing the holy place at the end of their journey, Abbot Anthimus of St. Sabbas' Lavra, who together with several other fathers had accompanied the Elder, explained what the ruined buildings that they saw next to them were.

"There, Holy Father, is the ancient Monastery of the Holy Forerunner, built by St. Helen and endowed by Justinian. Pray that we will be able to restore it."

"May the Holy Forerunner grant it."

Glory to God—in the last few years it has been restored by the Patriarchate. Today Liturgies are celebrated there, and it gives a little happiness to pilgrims.

Five minutes past the ruined Monastery, they could hear the roar of the Jordan.

Trembling seized the soul of Fr. Sabbas. He had been counted worthy to live for a short time in the Monastery of his patron saint, St. Sabbas. Now he was in the land of that great unique ascetic and protector of all monks, the Holy Forerunner. He could almost believe that somewhere he would meet his immaterial figure and burning prophetic eyes.

Involuntarily, with lips trembling from tender feeling, he stammered:

"O Holy Forerunner, do not cease to intercede for us."

To his mind came the living narrative of the Gospel:

Thereupon Jerusalem and all Judea, and all those who dwelt around Jordan, went out to see him, and he baptized them in the Jordan, while they confessed their sins (Matt. 3: 5-6).

This place is indeed holy. Here was the pulpit of prophecy; here was the way of the Lord prepared. Here was established a holy place of confession where sins were remitted; here was accomplished the "bath of regeneration." And one time, like one among many, the Son of God came to this very place and was *baptized by John in the Jordan* (Mark 1:8).

Holding on to a willow branch so as not to be carried away by the strong current, Fr. Sabbas received the baptism of the Jordan. Then he saw something like a dove and heard a voice of thunder: *This is My beloved Son, in whom I am well pleased.* Unrestrained waves of prayer ascended from his breast to the Most Holy Trinity, the worship of Whom had been revealed in this holy place.

The area around the Jordan River was created only for prayer. It has never been without elect, holy dwellers of the desert, the successors of the Forerunner. What joy Fr. Sabbas felt when he learned that in the trans-Jordan desert, amidst the endless expanse of shrubs and reeds, the hermitess Photini* had lived in asceticism in

---

*Archimandrite Joachim Spetsieris has written a book, *The Hermitess Photini of the Jordan Desert* (S. Skinas, Volos, 1955), in which one can make the acquaintance of this holy ascetic and her wonderful life.

Pilgrims receiving the baptism of the Jordan.
A 17th-century engraving.

his lifetime. She had lived there for five years without anyone knowing of her, perfuming the air with ceaseless prayer. Thus, "the Confessor was greatly pleased. Worshipping, he bent his knee to the Heavenly Father and blessed His All-Holy Name. Then he returned to the Monastery, from which he walked back to Jerusalem" (Spetsieris, *Memoirs*).

Finally, with the blessing of Patriarch Nicodemus, he set out to return to the Garden of the Mother of God, the Holy Mountain. He did not feel the grief of the Israelite exiles when he left Jerusalem to return to his own land. At the Holy Altar of his Kalyve's chapel there awaited him the light and glory of the New Jerusalem. There he was surrounded by the prayers of the saints, and the blessings of the Mother of God, the Lady of the Mountain.

V

War with the Demons

1. GRACE TO OVERCOME DEMONS

By His economy in becoming incarnate, the Lord overcame sin and death and abolished the rule of the devil. To His followers He gave authority to tread on *snakes and scorpions, and all the power of the enemy* (Luke 10:19). This authority is the possession of all His truly God-bearing followers.

We see this often in the lives of the Saints. Those who fight and overcome the old man with the weapons of light, who are crucified and resurrected with Christ, are flooded with spiritual gifts. Among other things, they become fearful to the invisible enemies. They can undo the workings of Satan and heal those bound by him.

In the *Spiritual Meadow* it is written about a certain monk: "Truly, O Christians, the devil is great and terrible. However, those who came here troubled by the spirit of uncleanness were granted healing by him."

These words apply perfectly to Fr. Sabbas also. By his ascetic labors, fasting, vigils, and prayers, by his intense sacramental life, by study, sobriety, and contemplation, and by the power of his blessed elder's prayers, he completely overcame the power of the devil. In his battles against the evil spirits he was always victorious.

From something that Fr. Sabbas confided to Fr. Joachim Spetsieris, we can catch a glimpse of his strife with the powers of darkness. "Many times he told me that he saw with his eyes the evil spirits that were coming to disturb him. Whenever he perceived the importunity of the evil spirits, he immediately bent his knees and prayed. All the workings of the evil spirits would disappear" (*Reminiscences*, Vol. 1, pp. 19). He flogged the enemy by his prayers, and they were burnt by the words of the Psalm that came flaming from his lips: *O Lord, fight against them that fight against me ... Let them be like dust in the face of the wind, and let the angel of the Lord drive them* (Psalm 34:1,5).

He not only saved himself from the fierce attacks of the demons; a multitude of unfortunate men and those oppressed by the devil were delivered by him. It was not unusual to see them come to his Kalyve so that he might sign them with the Cross, read the service of exorcism over them, and rebuke the unclean spirits. Many times, when a sufferer was unable to come to the Holy Mountain, he would read the exorcism from afar. Those bound by the demons would leap from joy, feeling the fearful chains falling off them.

2. THE BOOK OF MAGIC

Somewhere in Chalkis, the relationship between a man and his wife had become very strained. The husband did not lead a normal life, but lived in a strange, obscure manner. His face took on a repulsive expression. He had broken away from the Church; he wanted nothing to do with Church life, and especially not with the Sacraments. His unfortunate wife tried in every possible way to bring him back to God, but he was unyielding. Finally she understood that she must take a hard position.

"Listen to me. You have made my life unbearable. If you won't come to receive Communion on Pascha, I am going to have to leave you. It will be impossible for us to live together. I want Christ to rule in our family."

The persistence, pressure, threats, and heartfelt prayers of this good Christian woman were not in vain. The husband saw that by his behavior he was in danger of irreparably destroying his home, his future, and the future of his children. His soul was shaken, and he resolved to return to the light.

Great was the darkness hidden within him, for the unfortunate man had descended to collaborating with the demons; he had trained himself in magical arts. This is what had kept him so stubbornly away from the Church. He understood that he first of all needed a confessor. The Holy Mountain was not far away, and there he went, seeking the right person. He found Fr. Sabbas.

How different was his return journey! He was renewed inside. Instead of confusion, chaos, and darkness, he saw a new regenerated world. Relief and tears of joy shone on his face as he finished his confession. What peace he felt, what a lightening of his burden! But there was still something else to get rid of. He stretched out his hand, holding a certain book.

"Take this book also, my Father. This was the cause of my catastrophe."

It was a Solomoniki (a book of magic), the essential manual of all who study magic.

"Why are you giving it to me? It wants burning. Take it and burn it somewhere away from here."

On his way from the Kalyve to St. Anne's Skete, he saw a large hole in the rock. In this cavity the Solomoniki was soon reduced to ashes. The Evangelist Luke wrote about a similar incident: *Those who followed magic arts made their books into a heap and burned them* (Acts 19:19). Fires like these are a joy to the angels, a wounding of demons. Such books of darkness and stench should not circulate among us.

Still more relieved, the man continued on his way. He happened to meet Fr. Hilarion, a disciple of Fr. Sabbas.

"Convey my respects and boundless gratitude to the father confessor. And tell him that the book was burned in the cave above here."

Fr. Hilarion continued heedlessly towards the Kalyve. But when he reached the cave, showers of great boulders fell around him, thundering and rolling down the hillside. Terrified, he reached the Kalyve and told the elder what had happened.

"It was the work of satan, my child."

When he had recovered from his fear, he remembered to convey to the Elder the words of the man he had passed on the road. He remembered about the burning of the book. When Fr. Sabbas explained who the man was and what book he had burned in the cave, he understood what had happened.

Not only Fr. Hilarion experienced the stoning, however—it happened to everyone who passed by that place. In the end the road became impassable, for nobody dared to come near that place. Disturbed, the fathers sought the help of Fr. Sabbas. He fasted, prayed, sprinkled the cave with holy water, and the evil spirits retreated. He advised the fathers to place an icon of the Theotokos and a lampada within the cave. Thus the road became peaceful as before.

Today, those who pass by there often stop and sing "Meet it is..." to the Theotokos, with no danger. Some fathers have told us, however, that occasionally there is still demonic activity in that place, mainly when a disciple who has broken obedience passes by it.

3. THE STRANGE SHOWERS OF STONES

A young pastry-cook from Thessalonika, Athanasius, felt aversion for worldly life, and resolved to take the monastic schema and live in the Holy Monastery of Dionysiou. As a novice at Dionysiou he was sent to Monoxilitis, a Metochion within Mount Athos, to receive monastic training.

In the meantime, his parents in Thessalonika were embittered by the decision of their cherished only child. They moved heaven and earth to "save" him, to bring him back to the world. They did not even hesitate to seek the help of satan, resorting to magic and sorcery.

Athanasius suddenly began to feel pressure, as though there were a heavy weight on him. He himself in his former life had dealt in magic, and so was not uninitiated in such matters; therefore he correctly guessed what his parents were doing. He felt an anguish that became more and more intense. Something very unpleasant was hanging over him. From inner need he prayed more frequently, painfully emphasizing the phrase in the Lord's Prayer, "Deliver us from the evil one."

The other brothers of Monoxilitis suspected nothing of this. One morning after the service as they were preparing for their work, stones suddenly began falling on them from the forest above. Luckily for them and for the property of the Metochion, they suffered no harm. They waited a while—some passers-by, apparently, had an appetite for jokes. But when they began their work again, stones started flying from behind them. Then they understood that something serious was happening, and they took refuge in the church. They did not dare to leave it, for as soon as they did so the stoning would start again. Stools, wooden forms for monastic skoufias, and other objects were hurled through the air. Their dog was thrown three meters down from where he had been lying.

Soon some policemen who had been notified came from Karyes. They searched the area and shot volleys in the direction that the stones came from. Finally they realized that this was not the work of men, but of unseen enemies.

Then the novice Athanasius came forward and explained the cause of the mischief.

"To completely persuade you," he finished, "let me go by myself over there to the little church of St. Artemius, and you'll see that the stones will follow me."

That is what happened. The stones fell all around him, but without hitting him.

After this demonstration they isolated him in the church. The steward of the Metochion, Fr. Porphyrius, sent a letter asking for a boat from the Monastery. From the moment that Athanasius left the church until he disembarked at the harbor of the Monastery, terrible things happened. It is a wonder that the boatmen did not faint from terror. "The stoning did not cease on the sea, even though they were a distance from the shore. The stones kept falling, but fortunately around the boat, without doing any damage" (Gabriel of Dionysiou, *The New Evergetinos*, p. 65).

Between the shore and the courtyard of the Monastery, all was quiet. This encouraged several people to call it an illusion. A sudden shower of stones from a nearby tower, however, silenced them.

The Council of Elders, which assembled immediately, made the decision "to send the novice to the God-bearing Elder, Fr. Sabbas ... so that he may deliver him." The general conviction of the fathers was that the prayers of Fr. Sabbas could flog the evil spirits.

The Kalyve of the Resurrection underwent a week of hard trials. There was an atmosphere of war—an open war between the powers of light and darkness. There was continuous, deafening noise. Enormous boulders came loose from the nearby cliffs, flying by and over the Kalyve, and hurtling with terrifying crashes down the nearby precipice into the sea. Fierce voices uttering blasphemous words disturbed and sullied the area. And there were insults—unwonted insults against all monks, and especially against the confessor. All the stench of Hades revealed itself.

The man of God, disregarding his deep old age (he was then in his last years), gave himself up to great struggles. For a whole week he kept a complete fast, praying continually. *This kind goes not out but by prayer and fasting* (Matt. 17:20). His compassionate heart could not endure seeing God's creation undergoing such tyranny.

At the end of the week, the elder, with steadfast, unwavering faith in the Resurrected Lord, approached the sufferer. The evil spirit became agitated.

"I banish thee, ...O unclean spirit ... by God Who created all things by His word, and by our Lord Jesus Christ ... Fear, begone, flee, depart from the servant of God Athanasius ... Depart to the dry, deserted, uncultivated places...."

And thus it happened. It seemed as though something came out from Athanasius' mouth. The undesirable occupant disappeared, *like smoke vanishes*. The words uttered by the Spirit-bearing mouth of Fr. Sabbas struck the demon like a flaming sword. Instantly the novice became calm and quiet, sighing with relief. Out of boundless joy and gratitude he fell at the feet of the confessor, kissing them and moistening them with tears.

"O Saint of God, you have saved me, you have taken away the horrible weight. Oh, thank you! You rescued me from the dreadful serpent. Glory be to Thee, my God!"

Athanasius stayed with his physician for several more days. By his advice, he went to the Skete of Koutloumousiou, where he remained. Fr. Habbakuk—the name he received at his tonsure—is distinguished among the fathers by his austere ascetic life. He never forgot the unforgettable elder who had saved him from the power of the devil.

4. THE FALSE ANGEL

Among the spiritual children of Fr. Sabbas was a certain Romanian deacon. He was still young, and lived in silence in the desert around Little St. Anne's Skete.

"My Father," said the deacon to Fr. Sabbas one day, very sorrowfully, "I beg you, do not forget to commemorate my mother during Liturgy tomorrow. She died three days ago."

To Fr. Sabbas' mind these words seemed to indicate a victory of the devil. The discerning elder was troubled. Here, he thought, the enemy is doing something ugly. The cunning one! He stops at nothing to deceive and darken God's creation.

Without showing his concern, he tried to probe into the matter a bit further.

"Tell me all about this, my child. Tomorrow is the third day after your mother's repose—that means she died the day before yesterday. She died in Romania. How could you learn about her death in two days?"

There was a little silence.

"How? How did I learn?" the deacon began timidly. "Well, he told me...."

"Who told you?"

"My guardian angel told me."

"Your guardian angel? You saw your angel?"

"I have been granted to see him, not just one or two times. It has been for two years now. He appears to me and joins me in prayer. We sing the Akathist together and make prostrations, and we have spiritual conversations...."

This "two years" grieved Fr. Sabbas very much. Two years of demonic deception are no light matter. To allow the enemy to work undisturbed for your destruction for two years is indeed grievous.

"And why, my child, did you not tell me anything all this time?"

"The angel told me it was not necessary."

Fr. Sabbas understood that he had a great struggle on his hands. First he had to persuade the poor deacon that it was not an angel that was appearing to him, and then he had to be prepared to face the rage of the demon. "Lord Jesus Christ, Son of God, have mercy and save us!" he prayed secretly and fervently.

"My child, are you sure it was an angel that appeared to you?"

"I am absolutely sure, Elder! Really, we pray together and make thousands of prostrations every day. We talk about the future life and paradise. He is my guardian angel!"

The deacon seemed set in this belief. However, he also had confidence in his God-enlightened elder, and this made him think again. But, he said, how could a demon encourage him to pray? The devil fights those who pray.

Finally they agreed to test the "guardian angel."

"As soon as he comes to you again," said Fr. Sabbas, "ask him to say the 'Theotokos Virgin, rejoice...' and make the sign of the Cross."

But it was not so simple. When the evil one has had you wrapped in deception for two whole years, then even your eyes and ears are deluded. He can make you imagine that you hear the "Theotokos Virgin" and see the sign of the Cross.

At his next visit, the deacon, with concealed inner gratification, said to the confessor:

"Elder, everything was done as you said. It is an angel of God, my guardian angel. He both said the 'Theotokos Virgin' and made the sign of the Cross."

Fr. Sabbas understood it well—two years of service to the cunning enemy could not be undone easily. But even though the devil knew many tricks, he could not prevail against the wisdom of God that shone in the God-bearing Elder. He turned to the deacon.

"Listen here, my child. Pay heed—we will make one final test, which will clear up the matter. The angels of God can know everything, because it is revealed to them by God. But the demons cannot, and many things are dark to them. Do you agree?"

"I agree."

"Since you agree, pay attention to what you must do. At exactly this moment, I will think of something"—and he thought something against the devil—"and I will leave it hidden within my mind. This evening, ask the angel to tell you what I thought. If he answers correctly, then he undoubtedly comes from God. Come and inform me what happens."

When he returned to his Kalyve, the deacon felt a certain anxiety, an unpleasant foreboding. At the same time, however, he marvelled at the elder's excellent idea. Now the affair would come to a crisis.

When the deacon asked the angel that night to solve the problem, a faint disturbance furrowed his bright face. He seemed confused.

"But my beloved Father, why should you, a superior man, be interested in the thoughts of a mortal? You are lowering yourself—it is an unworthy desire. Would you not prefer that I show you tonight hell, paradise, the glory of the Lady Theotokos?"

But the deacon, who had begun to suspect something, insisted.

"I am being obedient to my confessor. Tell me what he thought."

The angel twisted and turned, trying to change the subject, but the deacon persistently brought him back to the question. Besides, this evasiveness did not make a good impression.

"You must tell me what the confessor was thinking. It's a simple thing. Don't you know?"

"Take care, deacon. By this pettiness you are in danger of losing my good-will."

"I don't know, I am asking you something easy. For the last time, do you or do you not know what Fr. Sabbas was thinking?"

At that moment the shining appearance was cast aside, revealing a frightful form. It gnashed its teeth, and with a voice like a rabid wild beast, cried:

"You are lost, wretch! Tomorrow at this hour you will be in the fire of hell! We will burn you, we will destroy you!"

With that, the deacon was alone, alone and in ruins. All the sweetness of his two years of visions could not compensate for this present grief. If he had not been supported by the prayers of his confessor, who at that moment was keeping vigil and supplicating for him, he would have given up his spirit. Several hours passed before he could pull himself together and stand on his feet. He could not stay in his Kalyve. He saw no safety anywhere but with the confessor. All the time the threat was roaring in his ears: "Tomorrow at this hour you will be in hell!" Terror pierced him to the marrow.

Somehow he reached the Kalyve of the Resurrection. He seized hold of the elder's rassa, and would not let go for a moment.

Even when the elder had to sleep a little, next to him was the terrified deacon!

"Don't be afraid, my child. Be calm."

"How can I not be afraid, my Father, when the hour is coming? Oh! The hour is coming when they will take me. O my Christ, save me!"

And indeed, at the appointed hour there came a violent attack of the evil spirits. From the deacon came cries of terror and despair:

"Save me, my Father! I am lost, they are taking me! Save me!"

Fr. Sabbas prostrated himself, and with pain and tears he prayed to the Lord to take pity on His servant and rebuke the evil demons. His supplication was heard, and the unhappy deacon was rescued "from the mouth of the lion."

Thus ended that tragedy—a very instructive tragedy. Truly, visions and apparitions conceal many dangers! When we do not fully reveal our inner world in confession, the enemy can do whatever he likes with us. How precious is a skillful confessor!

But the story is not quite over yet. With time, and with the instructions of Fr. Sabbas, the deacon became calm. His spiritual life developed well. Later he was ordained to the priesthood, and was always distinguished for his piety. Nevertheless, those years of demonic delusion left unpleasant traces. The devil, you see, had acquired a certain right over him. Was it for free that he had given him such delightful visions? Thus, even though he had come to the Holy Mountain in his youth and had grown up in angelic surroundings, as they say—in spite of all this, for the rest of his life he was tormented by various troublesome temptations. All the discerning fathers saw in this the remnants of the two years' cooperation with the false angel.

VI

"Make Known to Me the Ways of Life"

1. AT THE FOUNTAIN OF LIFE

Like the earth with its abundance of herbs and fruits, the fruitful soul of Fr. Sabbas was watered by never-failing fountains. By continual prayer and an intense life of worship, he attracted the waters of grace, and became like *a tree planted by the streams of the waters* (Psalm 1:3).

He would keep vigil almost the whole night long, sacrificing sleep on the altar of prayer. He would stand upright like an unshakeable pillar, and holding a 300-knot prayer-rope in his hand he would elevate his mind to the heavens, hymning the Most Holy Trinity together with the light-bearing angels. If the weak flesh protested and was ready to fall and surrender to sleep, it was restrained by straps that Fr. Sabbas passed under his armpits, which were tied to ropes hanging from the ceiling of his cell. This method was invented by the great lovers of God, that they might remain upright and alert in the battle of prayer.

What heavenly moments these were, when his mind was "taken captive to divine and heavenly things, to things infinite and past comprehension," which, as St. Macarius the Great writes in his wonderful Eighth Homily, "no human lips can express."*

---

*To those interested in cultivating the higher spiritual life and tasting the "bread of angels," we recommend the wonderful *Spiritual Homilies* of St. Macarius of Egypt. The whole text is imbued with the fragrance of the Holy Spirit.

Fr. Sabbas' liturgical life was correspondingly intense. The Paschal Mystery was performed every day in the Resurrection Kalyve. His many faithful spiritual children were present at these Liturgies, as well as several monks who desired frequent Holy Communion.

Much is said about the height to which Fr. Sabbas brought the life of prayer in his church. He preserved complete orderliness, attention, and solemnity. As an indication of this we will relate one detail: he never wore his normal shoes in the church, but would put on a special pair of "sirtes," or monastic slippers, which he kept for use in church. Also, he was exceedingly careful about the Holy Altar, avoiding even touching it. "What a fearful place this is!" he would cry.

"When you saw him in his cell," we were told, "he looked like a poor and insignificant monk, as he was very small in stature. But when he served Liturgy, he looked majestic, and his face shone like the face of an angel."

Fr. Onouphrius, who had a very beautiful voice, also contributed to the solemn liturgical atmosphere. Fr. Hilarion also, even though he was illiterate, was gifted with a good memory, and from hearing them had learned many hymns and psalms by heart, as for example Psalm 118 and the Six Psalms.

What can we say about the heavenly, indescribable tremors Fr. Sabbas experienced before the Holy Altar? We need only remember that he was the disciple of Fr. Hilarion the Iberian, and the heir of his liturgical spirit. Fr. Joachim Spetsieris writes: "Fr. Hilarion, engaged in exceedingly great ascetic struggles, would, when he liturgized alone or with Fr. Sabbas and when he chanted the 'Holy, holy, holy, Lord of Sabaoth,' violently smite his chest and weep." Who can say what his clear-sighted eyes beheld at that moment? Surely he saw the angels liturgizing with fear before the blood-stained and slaughtered Lamb. What could he do but strike his breast and dissolve into tears?

We will relate here a similar example. Some years ago the hermit Fr. Tikhon lived in asceticism near Stavronikita Monastery. It is said that when he celebrated the Liturgy he would often fall into an ecstasy during the Cherubic Hymn, gazing upon the cherubim and hearing the Trisagion Hymn. Full of awe, the chanter would wait for half an hour, an hour, until the celebrant recovered from the divine rapture. These were angelic, paradisal hours of liturgical life!

The liturgical life of Fr. Sabbas also moved on these levels. Together with the six-winged seraphim, he sang: *Worthy is the Lamb that was slain to receive power, and riches, and wisdom, and strength, and honor, and glory, and blessing* (Apoc. 5:12). Every day the Crucified and Risen Lord nourished him with His Body and Blood, and for him He became "paradise, tree of life, pearl, crown, builder, husbandman, sufferer, incapable of suffering, man, God, wine, living water, lamb, bridegroom, warrior, armor..." (Macarius of Egypt, 31st Spiritual Homily).

Thus, with prayer and daily Liturgy, he was continually watered by the fountains of life and immortality, and he became *like a thriving tree by the waters* (Jer. 17:8), sending forth flowering branches and sweet fruits of righteousness. In the following chapter we will offer another view of Fr. Sabbas' liturgical life that clearly shows his love of his neighbors.

2. "REMEMBER, O LORD..."

The rivers of grace flowing from the Bloodless Sacrifice benefit not only the living, but also the dead. That is why the celebrants at the Altar continually supplicate: "Remember, O Lord, thy servant...," "grant health to thy servant...," "grant rest to the soul of thy servant...." The greater their faith and love, the longer is the list of names for whom they pray.

Fr. Sabbas commemorated numberless names. He began the Proskomedia alone, and for two to three hours he would take out parts from the prosphora, ceaselessly commemorating names. He

The hermit Father Tikhon.

used a very large paten, which bore also a representation of the Nativity.

"Holy Father," some fathers would say to him, "you are very tired. Why read so many names and stand for so many hours?"

"I'm not tired," he answered. "On the contrary, I am very happy. The ones who are commemorated receive great benefit, and that is my joy."

Occasionally he did not hide from them that God had once given him a certain revelation of the great benefit the souls received by being commemorated. Once when he was still a young priest in the Kathisma of St. James, he had seen an angel in the form of a priest who washed and blotted out sins in "the blood of the Lamb." He did not tell anyone what he had seen, however, and all asked: "What can the confessor have seen? What makes him commemorate so many names?"

Just before his repose, he deemed it unnecessary to keep back the mystical revelation any longer, and so he recorded it in his manuscript. In 1925, Fr. Joachim Spetsieris found it as he was searching through his belongings, and copied it. The text is as follows:

> To those who ask whence I was inspired to commemorate names and take out parts in the Proskomedia of the daily Liturgy.
>
> In 1843 we came from Iveron to Dionysiou Monastery, living in silence above the Monastery in a Kathisma whose church was dedicated to St. James the Brother of the Lord. This is the one that my Elder requested the abbot to rebuild from its foundations. The bishop came to consecrate it, and in the evening a hieromonk from the Monastery came and sewed the cloths for the Altar and Proskomedia tables, and prepared oil for the consecration.
>
> In the morning, after the consecration and the Liturgy, the bishop said to my Elder: "Please let me give some names to Fr. Sabbas for commemoration since he will be serving Liturgy for forty days." My Elder said, "Give him as many as you wish." And the bishop wrote sixty-two names on a piece of paper, and in the end he gave some alms to Fr. Stephen.

When I had commemorated these names for thirty-nine days, on the fortieth day I was leaning on the analogion, waiting for my Elder to come so that I could start the Liturgy. I fell asleep, and in my sleep I saw that I was wearing priestly vestments and standing in front of the Altar table, on which was the diskos, full of the Blood of Christ. I also saw Fr. Stephen come and take from the Proskomedia table the paper with the names and a pair of tongs. He went to the Holy Table, and holding the paper with the tongs, plunged it again and again into the diskos containing the Blood of Christ. Each time he dipped it, he blotted out a name, until finally the whole paper was cleansed.

I awoke. My Elder came in, and I told him what I had seen. He said to me: "Didn't I tell you not to believe in dreams?" After the Liturgy he told me: "It is not by your worthiness that these peoples' sins are forgiven. By faith we receive the forgiveness of sins."

This is the reason I commemorate so many names.

With time, the number of his acquaintances grew. He obtained more and more spiritual children, and many people asked for his prayers. Thus his list of names grew longer, until finally he had thousands of names. How could he find time to commemorate them all? Finally he devised a system: he divided them into three parts. He copied them with beautiful, large letters into three books, and read through one each day. The fathers of Koutloumousiou Monastery, who venerated the old confessor exceedingly, took care to obtain one of these books from his disciples, and they keep it as a holy text.

May the example of Fr. Sabbas encourage us to reflect on the abundant gifts that pour forth from the sacrifice of Golgotha through the Divine Liturgy. Much has been said on this subject by St. Cyril of Jerusalem (4th century) in his *Fifth Mystical Catechism*.

3. A HELPER AND COUNSELOR

A monk named Fr. Arsenius, who had come from a monastery in Chios to St. Anne's Skete, once came to him for advice.

"My Father, what should I do? I very much feel the need for frequent Holy Communion, but some of the fathers have told me that I should receive Communion only every forty days. Tell me what I should do."

"Come here to our Kalyve, and I will give you frequent Communion," answered Fr. Sabbas.

Later, as a more permanent solution, he advised him to change his abode.

"Go and live in the Skete of Kavsokalyvia. There no one will say anything to you."

Other spiritually thirsty monks besought Fr. Sabbas to initiate them into the secrets of mental prayer. If he could ascertain that they were sufficiently trained spiritually to control that powerful and intoxicating wine, he would satisfy their desire.

Many monks cultivated mental prayer under his supervision and guidance. We know that among them was the fool-for-Christ Theophylactus of Kavsokalyvia,* who reposed in 1927 at the age of seventy-two.

That which happened to the *startsi* of Russian Orthodoxy happened also to Fr. Sabbas. He did not restrict himself to offering assistance only in purely spiritual matters, but would give advice on a

---

*There is a variety of ascetic practices in monasticism. In the ancient practice of "foolishness for Christ," the monk feigns foolishness or madness, and thus conquers the summits of humility of wisdom and dispassion. Some renowned fools for Christ are St. Symeon (Syria, 6th century), St. Andrew of Constantinople (9th-10th century), and St. Isidora (upper Egypt, 4th century).

wide variety of problems that men brought to him. This is clearly shown in the following incident.

During Fr. Sabbas' lifetime, the Holy Mountain was under the suzerainty of the Turks. It was not unusual for serious confrontations to arise between the monasteries and the Turkish authorities.

One time, some monks from Koutloumousiou Monastery came to him troubled.

"Holy Father, we are in a serious position. We're in conflict with the Kaimakan (the Turkish governor). Our Monastery may be destroyed. What should we do? Save us!"

In this critical situation, Fr. Sabbas gave them some astonishing advice.

"In front of the Monastery gate you must place the English crown, and from the corners of the walls and the towers fly English flags. The Turks will not dare to fire at them if they think there are English ambassadors there."

His advice was followed; and indeed, the fury of the Turks was checked by this unexpected sight. They gnashed their teeth, but could do nothing. Finally they withdrew, for they had no wish to create a diplomatic problem and come to a confrontation with Great Britain.

Fr. Sabbas received many letters from people who had heard about him but were unable to come to Mount Athos. As the years passed he received more and more letters, some from very far away— from Jerusalem, the fathers of St. Sabbas' Monastery, Russia, and even from Orthodox people living in America. People who visited the Kalyve of the Resurrection were astonished to see that his cupboard was completely full of letters.

In order to answer all the letters, Fr. Sabbas had to stay awake at night and write. What else could he do? To be a spiritual father means to expend oneself for one's children. In his beautiful letters (he was distinguished in calligraphy) he offered to the people of God consolation, joy, peace, and divine wisdom. He took no account of the labor; he only took care to heed the voice of the Great Shepherd: "Sabbas, son of Hilarion, lovest thou Me? Feed My sheep."

4. A LETTER-RELIC

Among the things left to us from Fr. Sabbas is one very important letter. It is dated December 12, 1907, and addressed "To Russia, to Katherine." We don't know who this Katherine was. It is not very likely that it was Katherine Dolgoruki, the wife of Tsar Alexander II. However, it is clear that this Katherine did have close connections with the royal family.

When this letter was written, the Russian Tsar was passing through a time of tragedy. The atmosphere in his land was unquiet and agitated. There were many evils: atheistic and nihilistic ideas, unsolved social problems, popular protests, revolutionary movements, conspiracies, political assassinations, anarchy. In such difficulties one naturally seeks support. Thus, we see the pious Tsar Alexander III (1881-1894) accompanied in his hours of tribulation by the holy priest St. John of Kronstadt.

At that time, the fame of our confessor of the Holy Mountain had reached the Russian royal palace, and a member of the royal family, the aforementioned Katherine, sent him letters asking for his prayers. Truly, the souls of men are drawn to the radiance of holiness independently of position or rank, nationality or distance! Let us attend to the answer Fr. Sabbas sent to the "most honorable and pious Katherine."

IC XC
NI KA

To Russia, to Katherine.

In the Name of the Father and of the Son and of the Holy Spirit:

Beloved! I received your honorable letter with the twenty-five Karpoboulas [a coin—trans. note], and I rejoiced greatly at your good health, which I very much wish for you. I pray for this day

SABBAS THE FATHER CONFESSOR 451

and night, both in our daily services and my all-night vigils, together with my brotherhood, my spiritual children, Monk Onouphrius (an icon-painter), Monk Hilarion, and Monk Sabbas, who love you as brothers. Therefore I say to you together with the Apostle Paul: Rejoice in the Lord always, and again I say, rejoice. Rejoice, blessed Katherine, that God has vouchsafed you to offer to Him, as a choice gift from your chaste womb, your two beloved children.

Furthermore, you will receive a great reward from Christ in His Heavenly Kingdom, because your beloved children do not serve a corruptible and temporal kingdom, but the heavenly Kingdom of Kingdoms and Lord of Lords, whose representative is the most Orthodox and Christian Monarch of blessed Russia and all Christendom, the Lord Nicholas.* Today only the Lord Nicholas is Emperor of our Orthodox Faith, anointed by the Holy Spirit in the image of Christ—he alone, and no one else under the sun. He who does not pray day and night for him, and for all his Court and Army, thinks in vain that he is a Christian. Beloved, every day I perform the fearful and holy Liturgy, and I never do so without praying to God and taking out a part especially for Tsar Alexander,** uniting it with the Holy Blood of our Savior Jesus Christ, and then always for the court and its guard. I must write this to you, my child, not because I want everyone to know of it, but because you have written to me once, twice, and three times to pray to God for your beloved children, who are prepared to die for the Orthodox faith and the love of Jesus Christ. For this reason, not wishing to grieve you, I have written even more than is my wont. Wherefore, I beseech God for you all, that you may be vouchsafed the Kingdom of Heaven and rejoice eternally in the

---

*In the years 1894–1917, the Monarch of Russia was Nicholas II Alexandrovich, the last of the Tsars. In 1918, the family was assassinated by the Bolsheviks in Ekaterinburg, a city of the Urals.

**This refers to Alexander III Alexandrovich (1881–1894), who was a powerful Tsar and endowed with outstanding attributes. He was a lover of peace and a protector of Orthodoxy, but he died prematurely at the age of thirty-nine.

most sweet light and beauty of the holy and life-giving Trinity, before the face of Jesus Christ with all the saints. Amen.

     December 12, 1907
     Humble Hieromonk Sabbas,
     Confessor of Little St. Anne's Skete,
     Church of the Holy Resurrection of Christ.

I embrace you, my spiritual children.

This letter is a valuable spiritual text. If studied with care, it can open many windows for us into the wondrous spiritual heaven of Fr. Sabbas. For example, how much exalted humility is contained in the phrase: "I must write this to you, my child, not because I want everyone to know of it, but because you have written to me once, twice, and three times...." And the ending phrase: "to rejoice eternally in the most sweet light and beauty of the holy and life-giving Trinity, before the face of Jesus Christ with all the Saints...." is an exact and concise summary of the whole treasure of Mystical Theology.

5. PASCHA IN HEAVEN

Great Lent of 1908 found the aged confessor weak. His physical powers had forsaken him, his body was giving way. The only thing that kept him alive was the Holy Altar. Archimandrite Gabriel of Dionysiou reports that he continued to celebrate the Liturgy daily "until deep old age, only tasting bread and lenten food once a day. In his last four or five years he was sustained only by holy water and a cup of coffee in the evening." Nevertheless, his inner man was vigorous, and the goodness and sweetness that shone in his face made an impression on everyone.

The feast day of his Kalyve was the Resurrection. Many who came to him for confession during Holy Week stayed to celebrate Pascha with him. Washed by the sacrament of absolution, they were prepared to meet Christ risen from the tomb. In this poor Kalyve, they could perceive all the blinding greatness of the feast of Pascha.

In 1908, Pascha fell on April 23; on that day, Fr. Sabbas celebrated his first Pascha in Heaven. He had borne on his back eighty-seven years of spiritual labor, and the time had come for him to enter into rest.

God often takes His saints to Himself on significant days. On Friday, April 14, the eve of the Resurrection of Lazarus, the aged confessor concentrated his weak powers to perform the Presanctified Liturgy. He knew it was the last Liturgy he would ever serve, and he was filled with tender emotion. This was increased by the readings at Vespers, which spoke of the death of holy men: "The reading from Genesis... *And Jacob gathered up his feet into the bed ... and Joseph said unto his brethren, I die...*" It was a fitting time to depart. Had not Fr. Sabbas wrestled like Jacob to win God? Had he not like Joseph nourished God's starving people?

"After Divine Liturgy he sat down, like one tired, and said to his two disciples, Onouphrius and Hilarion, 'Come and read for me the prayer of forgiveness, for in a little while I will die'" (Spetsieris).

He blessed them, bid them farewell, gave them his final admonitions, spoke to them of the reunion in the Heavenly City. It was a holy moment, full of mourning, silence, and mystery. With infinite peace in his face, he anticipated the visitation of the angels, while his lips ceaselessly glorified the Lord of life and death.

At the ninth hour Byzantine time, three hours before the sun set behind Mount Athos, amidst the tears of his disciples, the fragrance of the April flowers, the springtime songs of the desert birds, and the incense of the evening prayers, the soul of the elder flew to the heavenly chambers, to the world of incorruptibility. It departed full of the hope of resurrection, while the Church glorified Him Who vanquished death and granted resurrection to Lazarus, four days dead.

The Lord Jesus awaited the loving soul by the shore of the heavenly Tiberias, in order to give it "the palace of beauty and the diadem of comeliness." He addressed it with the words of the Song:

Thou art beautiful, O my love, comely as Jerusalem, ... as a palm tree (Song of Solomon 6:4, 7:7).

Many souls were filled with grief at the repose of this holy and fruitful palm tree. A power, an irreplaceable personality, had departed "from the hosts of Israel."

* * * * * * * *

The footpath that ascends to Little St. Anne's Skete is untrodden, the mailman brings no more letters, the Kalyve of the Resurrection is sunk in silence. Only a few pious pilgrims occasionally go there to sprinkle the grave of the Confessor with their tears and beg a priest to read a Pannikhida.

Elder Arsenius of the community of Fr. Charalampus told us the following:

"In 1909 I departed from the Caucasus Mountains, crossed through Palestine and Egypt, and came to the Holy Mountain. In Alexandria, my Patriarch gave me some money. 'Go,' he told me, 'to Little St. Anne's Skete and say a Pannikhida at the grave of Fr. Sabbas. He was a Spirit-bearing man, and I had him for my confessor. I knew him in Jerusalem.'"

The Patriarch still bowed before Fr. Sabbas! (This was Patriarch Photius, who came from Tinos. He was a virtuous man, a beautiful and strong preacher, and he came from the bishopric of the Patriarch of Jerusalem.)

When in the course of time Elder Onouphrius departed for eternity, Fr. Hilarion became the elder of the Kalyve. Together with one selected disciple, Emmanuel Papadovasilakis, who came from Crete, and who received the name of Fr. Onouphrius, he designed and carved prosphora seals and spoke continually of the ever-memorable confessor, the monk's "grandfather."

To the visitors who came to the Kalyve, Elder Hilarion continually spoke of the greatness of the blessed Elder. If they asked, he would show them his manuscripts. He had no photograph to show them, for "the ever-memorable and renowned ascetic and hermit

avoided photographs" (Paul of the Great Lavra, physician). He would also allow them to kiss his venerable skull, which he guarded in the church as the apple of his eye.

"In the Kalyve of Little St. Anne's Skete where Fr. Sabbas the Confessor resided," writes Fr. Joachim Spetsieris, "his skull was preserved. When I kissed it, I received the impression that it was the skull of a holy man" (*Memoirs*, Vol. 1, p. 22).

From reading his life, how can we avoid the impression that this was a holy man? The multitudes that visit the Kalyve express it in this way: "We are going to confess to St. Sabbas." All that remains is for his holiness to be officially recognized by the Church. We desire this with all our heart. Fr. Sabbas was, by general acknowledgement, a bright meteor of virtue, a flourishing vine of the holy Vineyard, merciful, consoling, "mighty in battle," clairvoyant, saintly, blessed, a man of God, beloved and witnessed to by God and men.

VII

Elder Ignatius
the Father Confessor

A God-sent blessing for all,... a sea of love and patience.
          —an aged monk of Mount Athos

ELDER IGNATIUS THE CONFESSOR

I

His Spiritual Formation

1. A SACRIFICE TO GOD

The monastic settlement of Katounakia is situated on the southern foot of Mount Athos. About thirty Kalyves are scattered across this steep and rocky area, which is divided into two sections by a deep ravine. High up on the eastern section, next to a huge cliff, the Kalyve of the Dormition dominates the area like the watchtower of the Prophet Habbakuk. The whole area, boulder-strewn and barren, relieved only by a few wild evergreen oaks, is full of otherworldly grandeur.

If you sit for a little while on the low wall enclosing the yard and look six hundred meters below, you will face the sea with its unceasing roar. A massive cliff, like a section of the Great Wall of China, blocks your view to the east. Because of it, the rising sun comes late to the Kalyve. Yet this cliff has its own enchanting majesty, and every morning, in the deep dawn, the desert birds that nest in it fill the air with their warbling songs.

The Dormition Kalyve can be justly proud of its location. If Katounakia were a kingdom, the king would surely build his palace on that spot, both to enjoy the magnificent view and to oversee his subjects.

View of Katounakia. The Dormition Kalyve is on the upper left.

This Kalyve, which even in our days is well preserved and has regular Liturgies, shone like a beacon in the first decades of our century and earlier. The presence of Hieromonk Ignatius the Confessor made it a wonderful spiritual beehive, where souls found the nectar of the Holy Spirit.

* * * * * * * *

Father Ignatius was born in Serrai in 1827. His parents were Orthodox; his father was Bulgarian, and his mother Greek. As John (his name in the world) grew, he *grew in wisdom and age and grace before God and men* (Luke 2:40). As a youth he was distinguished for his physical beauty, and even more for the beauty of his soul. Courteous, sincere, sober, filled with prudence, love, and industry, he was his parents' only child and their secret pride. Naturally, therefore, they fashioned around him all kinds of beautiful dreams.

The Heavenly Father, however, had other plans for him, even higher and more beautiful. He had prepared for John the angelic schema, the garment of the priesthood, the grace of the prophets and the monastic saints.

At the appointed time, the voice of God called him to his high destiny, whispering in his heart like a gentle breeze. And he proved worthy of the heavenly call, crying out eagerly, "Behold the servant of the Lord!"

We must not think, however, that this was an easy reply for John to make. He had mighty obstacles to overcome. If his parents had had other children, it would have been easier. But he was their only child, their only hope, their support and joy. The thought that he was abandoning his parents and plunging them into unbearable grief was a fearful martyrdom for him. His sensitive and tender personality made the martyrdom even more painful.

In this cruel struggle, he was preserved unwounded by the breastplate of faith. What did the trumpet of faith call out to him? The greatness of God's love. It assured him that God Himself would care for his parents. He would pour on them the balm of consolation and calm them. He would change the storm into peace, and would satisfy their every need. In this way John triumphed and, like the great Patriarch Abraham, exiled himself from his land and his relatives. *This is the victory that overcometh the world, even our faith.* (I John 5:4).

His flight to the Holy Mountain was of necessity secret. One can imagine the heart-rending laments of his parents and relatives when they learned of his departure.

Thus the twenty-year-old John went bravely forward on the road of the consecrated life. Every carnal inclination and desire he slew on the altar of the Spirit. Every earthly love he sacrificed for the love of God. Such sacrifices are inconceivable for most people, especially for men who are *flesh* (Gen. 6:3).

St. Symeon the New Theologian, the glory of Orthodox mystics, said: "Not thus the lovers of the world, not thus the lovers of (their own) life, the lovers of glory, the lovers of the flesh, the lovers of pleasure and the lovers of riches" (Moral Homily No. 12). John, however, lived in the Spirit.

His sacrifice ascended before the throne of God like "the sweet smell of the spirit." His offering was acceptable, like Abel's, and immediately, as a first reward, God gave him a rare gift: a righteous spiritual director. His steps were guided to the virtuous hermit, Elder Neophytus the Hadji-Georgite (*i.e.*, the disciple of Hadji George) who resided at Katounakia, in that lofty solitary watchtower we described above.

The very name "Hadji-Georgite" was an indication of the Elder's greatness. The approximately forty disciples of Hadji George, his spiritual scions, were the brightest diamonds that shone in the land of the Holy Mountain.

Elder Neophytus came from the area of Olympus, and was a model of genuine asceticism. A prayer rope and the book of St. Isaac the Syrian were his only possessions. He was entirely indifferent to the earth, aflame for Heaven. His mind dwelt continuously in Heaven and the Heaven of Heavens. As the hymnographer says, he was "a heavenly man and an earthly angel." He glorified God unceasingly, offering sacrifices of praise, and his every prayer was like a flame of fire.

Living with this strict hermit, John found all the conditions he needed to ascend the mountain of virtues, "like Moses the God-Seer to Sinai."

2. DISDAIN OF MAMMON

When John was established in his new abode, he had something particular to tell his spiritual father.

"Elder," he said, "before I left the world, by working and saving I gathered some money, which I thought I should take with me. I must give it to you. It is a fairly large sum: three hundred pounds!"

Elder Neophytus was the only one who did not laugh, hearing the news.

"Three hundred pounds! ... And what do we need it for here? You want to become a monk. If you really want this, you must get rid of this burden. Pay attention to what you must do! Take the money and start travelling around the Mountain. Wherever you find needy monks, give some of it to them and get a receipt. When you return you will have to show me the receipts—otherwise I will not accept you back."

John had not yet entered into the school of asceticism. Now he was given a generous lesson, which was at the same time a serious test. Now he would take an examination in self-sacrifice, obedience, and contempt of all earthly wealth. He would learn that the word "monk" means one who is not weighed down by material burdens. "A possessionless monk is a high-flying eagle" (St. Nilus). If he would receive a good mark in this contest, he would make good progress in the monastic life.

Aflame with the love of Christ, the young novice went bravely into the arena. Would the money hinder him, when he was not held back by the love of his parents? He knew that he would sacrifice greater things than money. Fearlessly, therefore, he began his work. When was ever a monastic candidate given such a task—to go around and distribute money?! He had imagined his mission would be easy, but he quickly realized how difficult it would be. Many monks, in spite of their poverty, did not want to take any money. With some, therefore, John had to "wax eloquent."

"Take a little money, Father," he would say. "You are a poor man, and you can use it for your needs. Take some, and do me a good deed also, so I can quickly finish distributing it all. If I do not give it all away, I cannot go back. Please have compassion on me, and accept some money."

This business plagued him for four months. But what could he do? Obedience is above all. And because he was obedient, God sent him a great blessing, for he was given the opportunity to meet the most virtuous monks of the Holy Mountain. The poorer were the kalyves that he visited, the more outstanding they were for their spiritual wealth. He gave the monks perishable gold, and they gave him imperishable. Not only their spiritual words, but also the sight of their immaterial figures encouraged and strengthened him.

At last! With the receipts in his hands he returned to Katounakia. The three hundred pounds were all given away. He had only kept a little and bought one book, St. Isaac, and a thick overcoat for winter. The elder rebuked him for this and demanded that they be returned, but finally he yielded and let him keep them.

Now that he was free from the money, he could quietly and undistractedly give himself up to mastering the monastic science. Money would never again disturb him—so he thought. Nevertheless, after some time mammon again troubled his peace.

In Serrai he had a certain aunt, extremely wealthy. Her property was estimated at eight million gold drachmas. She was childless and elderly, and could not bear the thought that her enormous property would fall into the hands of strangers. Because of this, her designated heir was her beloved nephew. Learning that he was on the Holy Mountain, she sent men to meet with him. They came to Katounakia and dramatically described his aunt's situation.

"Your aunt will lose her mind!" they said to him. "She has so much wealth, so much money, and no one to leave it to! Go back and inherit her enormous property, and also your parents'. After that you can do what you like. You have to go back or your aunt will go mad with distress. Eight million gold drachmas, and it will all be lost!"

They said more besides to the nephew, urging him to have pity on his aunt. At the same time, the unseen enemy whispered to him of all the good he could do with the inheritance. Fierce was the attack, but John was not alone. The shield of his elder helped him repel the arrows, for the wise counsel of Elder Neophytus settled the matter very satisfactorily .

"I understand your aunt's situation," he said to John. "I realize one must take care to settle such great wealth in a responsible way. Therefore you should write her a letter, thanking her for her great love for you and suggesting the following solution: she should divide her property into three parts. One she should give to her poor relatives, another to widows and orphans, and the third part she should offer to various churches. In this way the poor relatives will be aided, the widows and orphans will bless her, and in the churches her name will be continually remembered."

The elder's suggestion resolved the difficulty. A more God-pleasing solution could not be found. We also confess our unreserved admiration for the wisdom of this simple and uneducated hermit. It recalls a certain incident connected with St. Anthony the Great:

In Alexandria there was a shoemaker who lived very virtuously. He had attained the heights of humility, and saw himself as worse than all the inhabitants of the city. He certainly did not have great possessions, but the little that he earned from his daily labors he used in a very God-pleasing way. He divided it in three parts. One he kept for his personal needs, another he gave to the poor, and the third he dedicated to the Church. And one time God revealed to St. Anthony the Great that this shoemaker was higher in virtue than he.

"Anthony," He said to him, "you have not yet reached the measure of this shoemaker of Alexandria."

Let us pray that there will be some Christians who will dispose of their wealth in this way. Then men will thank them, God will bless them, and their consciences will feel great peace.

3. ASCETIC LABORS

It was no small thing to become a disciple of Elder Neophytus. Usually those who came to him were obliged to find another elder. In order to stay with him they had to cut off their own opinions, learn writing, do heavy manual labor, be men of sacrifice, and above all have boundless patience. From their very first days he gave them hard trials by which their fate was decided. John's trial, as we have seen, was to travel around the Holy Mountain for four months, giving away his money and collecting receipts.

John's endurance signified to the elder that this youth was capable of high spiritual attainments. The other Fathers of Katounakia, who knew his methods well, also foresaw this.

The elder's ascetic life was extremely hard. He faithfully observed the typicon of Hadji George, without any deviation or relaxation. His trapeza never had oil, eggs, cheese, or fish, even on Pascha. His little boat crossed the sea of Great Lent with the sole provision of salt, dry bread, and olives. They could have no more than ten olives a day, which were eaten with the pits, according to their typicon.

They had no time to care for their bodies, for bathing, washing, combing, etc. The other ascetics also observed this rule, as we saw in the life of Callinicus the Hesychast.

In clothing also he followed his elder's rule. To be a "Hadji-Georgite" meant going barefoot and having only one cloak. He did no business with the shoemaker, although in that area untrained feet wore woolen stockings. His clothing consisted of one tunic, which he dyed black once a year.

From the little that is mentioned, you can see under what a hard yoke John had to place his neck. Elder Neophytus further described to him the difficulties and hardships of his life, but John was determined to endure everything. In his mind echoed unceasingly his elder's words: "Give blood and receive the Spirit." (Abba Longinus)

Around the Kalyve there was an acre of olive trees that belonged to Elder Neophytus, and it took much hard labor to care for them. Consider the work that went into those trees, especially the seedlings they planted. The soil also demanded much labor. The infertile, sloping ground had to be enriched with good earth and secured with stone retaining walls. And this was not all, for they also had to help other aged or feeble ascetics who were unable to build their own walls. Later, as we shall see, came the need to build a church. All this, together with the shortage of water, the fasting, vigils, the rule of prayer, and the temptations of the enemy were like a *pit of misery* (Psalm 39), from which only the strength of God could raise them up, provided they had indomitable patience.

Many times, because of their great weariness, they did not wake up exactly at midnight for their nightly service. After the service they had to pray individually in their cells, at which time it would still be dark, even in summer. The novice thought it a serious sin when he overslept and confessed it, troubled and uneasy, to the elder. He calmly reassured him:

"My child, there is no reason to be upset. Close the windows, and it will be night again. The dark of night and the light of day are both of God. How says the Psalmist? *Thine is the day and Thine is the night*" (Psalm 73).

In these labors, Elder Neophytus kept in mind a passage of Scripture that his elder often quoted: *He who struggles exercises self-control in all things, those indeed therefore that they may receive a corruptible crown, but we an incorruptible.... I keep my body and bring it into subjection...* (I Cor. 9:25-26). The vision of incorruptible crowns inspired the hearts of the strugglers.

The daily services were performed according to the eremitic rule—that is, not with books, but with prayer-ropes. For example, the nightly service began; they each said five or six prayer-ropes, one after the other. When they had spent exactly three hours, an alarm clock rang, and with "Through the prayers..." the elder ended the service.

Elder Neophytus was not an eagle with one wing. He was not limited to bodily labors and rules of prayer, but he joined action with contemplation. He zealously cultivated the contemplative life, and his spirit withdrew to fish for pearls in the depths of holy contemplation. The continual reading of St. Isaac helped him in this, and in the cultivation of the Jesus Prayer. Fortunately, some decades before, the wise clergyman Nicephorus Theotokis had published the Ascetic Homilies of St. Isaac the Syrian. Thus it was available to every struggler in the desert. For a hermit there exists no more precious companion, guide and consoler than this wonderful book, "the most exact rule of the hesychast life."

Both the elder and his disciple had their own copies of St. Isaac—John had taken care to buy it when he distributed his money, as we mentioned above. Thus they both could refresh their souls with the spiritual and life-giving breezes of this holy book. In times of weariness, affliction, cruel attacks and temptations of the enemy (men who live in the world cannot even suspect these attacks), St. Isaac armed them with invincible faith and courage:

> So let us shun the body with all our strength, surrender our souls to God, and in the Lord's name enter into the arena of temptations. May He that preserved Joseph in the land of Egypt... and Who kept Daniel unharmed in the lions' den and the Three Youths in the fiery furnace, and Who delivered Jeremias from the pit of mire ... and Who brought Peter out of prison while the doors were shut, and saved Paul from the synagogue of the Jews ... may He give us strength also, and rescue us from amid the waves that encompass us. Amen (Homily 45).

Little by little, John made progress in the study of St. Isaac. Before he could learn the harder lessons, his elder had to teach him the simpler ones—the elementary monastic education, so to speak. According to the Apostle, milk comes first, then vegetables, and in the end the solid food of meat (cf. Hebrews 5:12, Romans 14:2).

4. THE MYSTERY OF OBEDIENCE

When a man comes to a large, unfamiliar city in a foreign land, his first concern must be to find a guide and interpreter; otherwise he will wander aimlessly, not knowing where to go. It is the same in monasticism—one entering the vast, boundless land of monastic life needs first of all a spiritual guide. The monastic state is a chamber full of hidden mysteries, into which the teacher must introduce his student by degrees. Fundamental and most important is the mystery of obedience. If the monk does not understand it rightly, he charts his own spiritual shipwreck.

Without delay, Elder Neophytus had to initiate John into this fundamental mystery. Therefore he began, like a hierophant, to guide his disciple into the Holy of Holies of the mystery of obedience. Let us imagine that we hear his voice in the secluded silence of Katounakia, amidst the incense of prayer, tears of compunction, and the ceaseless murmuring of the sea, six hundred meters below.

"My child! Obedience is a holy path that leads a monk to salvation. Obedience is the door to Paradise. The monk who acquires it tastes Paradise; he has already attained the angelic state. The angels in Heaven are filled with humility, while Satan and his battalions lost the glory of Heaven by their pride. Losing humility, they lost also their place of light. O humility! It places us in Paradise! How shall we find it? Only in obedience do you safely find humility. Only in obedience do you safeguard the blessedness of Paradise. By their disobedience our First Parents lost Paradise, while Christ, 'becoming obedient until death,' opened Paradise again. 'Obedient until death!' These three words hide the whole extent of the mystery of obedience. Obedience equals life; disobedience equals death."

The elder's words, his voice, these holy truths, were like a mystical wind laden with the breath of continuing tradition.

He handed on to the young desert-dweller what he himself had received from his own elder, Hadji George, through his words, but mostly through his life. And Hadji George also had received this tradition from his elder, Hieromonk Neophytus of Kavsokalyvia. And Hieromonk Neophytus from his elder, and so on. Thus we reach the Abbas of the Egyptian desert in the first centuries of Christianity, when the Holy Spirit first began to deliver to the Church the treasure of monastic life. This tradition, its development from generation to generation, its enrichment and unity, owes everything to the unseen activity of the Holy Spirit.

Elder Neophytus turned his thought to his elder, the preceding link in the tradition of the Spirit.

"John, my child," he continued. "My elder excelled in spiritual struggles, and in obedience he was unrivaled. Before their disobedience Adam and Eve tamed the wild beasts. My elder also attained to this measure—in the name of obedience he could also tame wild beasts."

Elder Neophytus took the opportunity to mention a moving incident in the life of his spiritual father. Even before he finished, he was shedding tears, while to the novice's soul was revealed the paradisal beauty and power of blessed obedience. Today, a half-century later, the Fathers of the Holy Mountain still tell this story. Let us also attend to it.

To the south of the Skete of Kavsokalyvia there is a wild deserted territory. There, near the sea, is located the cave of the angelic ascetic St. Niphon (14th century). In that area, Fr. Neophytus, the elder of Hadji George, lived in solitude in the beginning of the last century. He must have been advanced in virtue, if we judge the tree by its fruit. His disciple, Fr. George (he was later called Hadji George because he visited the Holy Land and received the baptism of the Jordan), developed into a wonderful monk, exemplary in obedience.

To feed themselves in that barren place, they made a small garden, watered with rain they collected in a small pit like a cistern. However, in the wild and impenetrable forest above their Kalyve lived wild boars, and one of these would occasionally come down and ransack the garden.

This boar was a great temptation! How could they get any harvest? Various thoughts came to Fr. Neophytus. In the end, he saw that this trial had a certain meaning. "God is using this boar," he thought, "to give me the opportunity to test my disciple in the lesson of obedience. Now he will show what he has learned." Before this bold venture he prayed long, seeking inward confirmation; and in fact, a voice encouraged him to proceed. The crucial hour arrived.

The Kalyve of St. George near Kavsokalyvia, where the young Elder Hadji-George lived as a disciple of Elder Neophytus.

"George," he said authoritatively to his disciple, "you will keep watch in the night. When you see the wild boar come to the garden, lead him to me bound with your belt."

Fr. George immediately caught the spiritual significance of this command, and fearlessly went forth to the contest. He knew that with his elder's prayers he would be in no danger.

In various Lives of the Saints we read about disciples crying out, "By the prayers of my Elder..." and subduing wild animals. And now again this miracle of obedience came to pass. That evening the wild boar, bound and tame as a lamb, was led to the elder. He signed it with a priestly blessing and commanded it to go away and not come back.

Let us examine this incident thoughtfully. Fr. George led the beast to the elder. At that moment, the devil furiously struggled to throw the disciple and his elder into the abyss of pride. But the two of them put him to shame. "I," said the disciple, "did nothing. Whatever happened was due to the prayers of my elder." "I," said the

Elder in turn, "did nothing. The humility and obedience of my disciple attracted the grace of God."

O holy obedience! You lift a monk to the heights, and also shield him from precipices. You win divine grace, and also safeguard it. What deep divine wisdom you conceal! Blessed are they who seek you. More blessed are they who taste your holy fruits. In truth you are invincible strength, "fearlessness of death, a safe voyage, a sleeper's progress" (Ladder, Step 4:3).

5. OBEDIENCE AND PRIESTHOOD

Today one can still visit the Church of the Dormition in Katounakia, because it has been preserved in very good condition, untouched by the decay of all-conquering time. It is of solid construction, with its north side wedged above in rock. It is not as poor as the churches of some other Kalyves, but neither is it rich or showy. Its semi-darkness leads one to compunction and prayer. From the two windows in the southern wall one can see in the distance the rocks and the restless Aegean Sea.

The iconostasis is adorned with simple wood-carvings. It has five icons—the four usual ones and a fifth of the Transfiguration. Even though painted in the popular [western] style, they draw forth grace and reverence. From above, a depiction of the Crucifixion, the Theotokos, and the Theologian holds sway as a work of rare art, with beautiful painting, rich gilding, and excellent woodwork. An inscription below the Crucifixion, "The year 1862 after Christ—September," tells us the exact year of its creation.

The narthex, lighter and relatively spacious, can easily shelter ten people. Later, when Fr. Ignatius had developed into a well-known confessor, people would wait there for confession.

If we betake ourselves a century back, to the time when the church was being built in this harsh, waterless, rocky place, we can imagine the great hardships that the builders, together with Elder Neophytus and his disciples, had to face.

Until then there had been no church in Katounakia, and therefore the Lavra encouraged Elder Neophytus in this work. A church was needed in this desert settlement to serve the spiritual needs of the ascetics. It was consecrated and dedicated to the Dormition of the Theotokos. This pleased John greatly, because the church of his parish in Serrai was also dedicated to the Dormition. As a secondary feast it was dedicated to the Transfiguration, a feast especially beloved by Elder Neophytus.

The church needed a priest, and this would be none other than John. In monastic tonsure he received the name of the God-bearing father Ignatius, the saint who felt perceptibly in his breast the grace of the Holy Spirit. This name was also a reward for the moral purity of his life.

The monk Ignatius was a model and example in everything. In his relations with his elder, he was very careful to confess his thoughts exactly, and to keep undiscriminating obedience. They tell us that he preserved obedience to a hair's breadth, even though his elder was very strict. This is also confirmed by the way in which he became a priest.

Fr. Ignatius had been tonsured a monk for six years. During this whole time he observed the strict rule of his elder faithfully. Thus, among other things, he had never cared for his body—he had not washed, bathed, or combed his hair. He had become accustomed to this rule, not feeling it difficult or imagining that he would ever break it.

One morning his elder astonished him by saying:

"Fr. Ignatius! Today you must wash and comb your hair and clean yourself up as well as you can."

Although astonished by such an unusual command, being a child of obedience he did not contradict. A great struggle began. He busied himself with lye and desperately tried to settle the matter. His hair tormented him most of all, until he had washed it, untangled it, and subjected it to a wooden comb.

The next day, without any explanation, his elder announced that they were going to the Lavra. They arrived there after two or three hours of walking, and Elder Neophytus went on into the Monastery while Fr. Ignatius waited outside. After a little while he also was led in to make a prostration to the elders. Then his perplexity was resolved.

"Now, when you have received the grace of the priesthood, you must remember us also and commemorate us in the Proskomedia," the elders of the Lavra said to him.

Fr. Ignatius was completely at a loss. He was thunderstruck, but he could say nothing. His elder had arranged everything, like Indian parents who arrange the marriages of their children without their knowledge. Naturally he had mixed feelings about it, but since it was his elder's will, and God's will, he was reassured.

The newly-built church with its newly-ordained priest gave another tone to the desert life. A little haven was created, where the hermits on Sundays and the great feasts came for common worship. They would wait decades before another such spiritual center arose; the beautiful church of the Danieloi would be built forty years later. The Dormition church was the first one there, and Fr. Ignatius blessed all the children of the desert.

The writer Moraitidis of Skiathos, in his book *By the Waves of the North*, mentions how the hermits of that area attended church. "Because the Kalyve of Elder Daniel had no church, they went on foot to the desert Kalyve of the great confessor Fr. Gregory. They did this every morning. That is to say, they went to hear Divine Liturgy sometimes in one Kalyve and sometimes in the other.... Thus they repeatedly visited the Kalyve of the confessor Fr. Ignatius."

At the Dormition Kalyve you could meet not only the wise Elder Daniel and Moraitidis, but other well-known people as well. You could meet Elder Gerasim, a great teacher of mental prayer; the hesychast Callinicus (before he became a recluse); a wonderful Russian ascetic from Karoulia; the silent Christopher the Vigilant, and others. When these holy Fathers assembled for worship, the angels indeed filled their vials with sweet-smelling prayers.

Fr. Ignatius did not serve Liturgy only at the Dormition church. He was sent for from as far away as Kerasia to perform services, Liturgies, and the Sacraments, especially when a church celebrated its feast day. These journeys outside his Kalyve occasioned a delicate problem. After the Liturgy he would be taken to the refectory, but as he was keeping to the typicon of Hadji George, he would not eat any food prepared with oil. This was an embarrassment to the Fathers, and they besought Elder Neophytus for a solution.

"Here in our Kalyve," said the elder to his disciple, "as long as I live we will not eat any oil. But when you go outside to serve Liturgy and stay for Trapeza, you have a blessing to eat it."

Thus this little question was solved by the elder's discretion. Sometimes such concessions are inevitable.

Their abstinence from oil not only strengthened their temperance, but also enabled them to give alms. Of the oil they pressed from their olives, our two ascetics saved a certain amount for the lampadas of their church, and the rest they distributed as alms. It became widely known that the Kalyve of the Dormition would give away oil, either a small quantity or a great, to those in need.

One time when their Kalyve was undergoing some financial difficulties, some poor people from the world came and asked for oil. Elder Neophytus told his disciple to go to the storage vessels and bring some. But he explained to the elder that the jars had nothing in them, and so the poor people had to depart empty-handed.

Just five or ten minutes after they had left, an unknown monk met Fr. Ignatius outside the Kalyve. Not saying much, he gave him five hundred drachmas, asked him to serve Liturgy for forty days, and went away. The elder, who was immediately told of this, asked:

"And whom did he say to commemorate?"

"Oh! I forgot to ask him. But I will catch up with him—he can't have gone more than fifty yards."

He ran outside, called out, searched for him, but the monk had disappeared. Elder Neophytus then began to think deeply: "The money came to us when we needed it. It came as soon as the poor people had left. You did not know this monk, so he had to have come from far away. But is there no priest there who could serve the forty Liturgies? And besides, how could he disappear in two minutes?" He told his conclusion to his disciple:

"It is not impossible that this monk was an angel. At any rate, he was a messenger of God. God wants to say something to us; He has been giving us a test. Indeed! Did I not tell you to go to the vessel and bring oil?"

"Yes, Elder."

"You, however, did not go, but announced to me that the oil was finished. I didn't ask you whether the oil was finished or not. As your elder I gave you a command, which you did not obey. If you had been obedient, you would have gone and found oil in the jars miraculously, just as the five hundred drachmas came to us miraculously. Then we could have had mercy on those needy people, just as God had mercy on us. By your disobedience you dismissed them with empty hands, and we also lost the reward of almsgiving. Both of us must now do a penance for this to obtain forgiveness."

After this event, the disciple began to enter more deeply into the mystery of obedience, striving to be more attentive to his elder's words. There were many things he had to view not with the spectacles of human logic, but with the mystical telescope of faith.

II

Fathers and Sons

1. THE GREAT ELDER

We will leave Elder Neophytus and the newly-ordained Fr. Ignatius for a while, in order to look into the past and briefly describe their wonderful spiritual forefather. We must look at the renowned ascetic Hadji George, the great Elder of Elder Neophytus, because we must know the grandfather in order to understand the grandson. The stock, roots, and soil tell us much about a tree's productivity.

Unfortunately, we were unable to gather many details about this great ascetic of Mt. Athos, and so our description will be poor and unworthy of him.

Hadji George's speech and pronunciation immediately revealed that he was from the East. He must have come from the region of Caesarea of Cappadocia, or from even further east, from lands where the Russian Empire holds sway.* He knew the Russian language well.

He was born between 1805 and 1810. Around 1828 we meet him as a young schema-monk, a disciple of Fr. Neophytus who lived

---

*Elder Hadji George was born in the village of Kermira in Caesarea of Cappadocia. (*Elder Hadji George the Athonite* by Monk P., Thessalonica, 1986.)

ELDER HADJI-GEORGE

The Kalyve of Sts. Menas and Demetrius.

the ascetic life in the desert of Kavsokalyvia. Later we find him higher up, at Kerasia, at the head of a large community at the Kalyve of Sts. Menas and Demetrius. Kerasia is a cross-roads where many people pass through. It was God's will for the virtues of the great ascetic to shine forth in such an eminent position. In the isolated desert of Kavsokalyvia he had struggled to win the light, and in the more populous Kerasia he distributed it to the souls that came to him.

Usually the various Kalyves in Kerasia had only three or four monks each. In Hadji George's Kalyve, however, the recorded number steadily increased, until finally his community numbered between forty and fifty monks, among whom there were several young Benjamins. Young boys from fifteen to eighteen years old, who were not yet allowed to live in the monasteries or the sketes, found refuge in his community. Hadji George, filled with love and fatherly tenderness, took them in and led them safely to the heights of virtue.

If we merely say that the rule of his community was strict, we say nothing. It surpassed even that of strict hermits. Abstinent in food, sleep, and clothes, they struggled like the heroic ascetics of ancient times. The fasting was particularly severe. To be a "Hadji-Georgite" meant to be a faster. They abstained not only from eggs and fish, but even from oil, whether it was Cheese-fare week, Christmas, or Pascha. For Easter eggs they boiled potatoes and painted them red, and with these greeted each other with "Christ is risen."

This hard rule was applied inflexibly to everyone, great and small. And amazingly, the stricter it was, the more monastic aspirants arrived. Apparently, souls are satisfied by the genuine monastic spirit, not by monasticism that is watered down with many indulgences.

The great Elder was a God-sent magnet, attracting thirsting souls. His authority and reputation spread, and those who came to him beheld him with awe. This was not only because of his great virtue, but also because of his strong and dynamic character. His mind was sharp; everyone stood exposed before his intelligence and acuteness. He was unsurpassed in debate, especially when he was defending his ascetic principles, even though he had received little education. He was also a keen psychologist. With one glance and an exchange of two or three words he could fathom and weigh a man exactly. No one could deceive his sharp eye with artifices or play-acting.

Hadji George was also skilled in medicine. He could cure many ailments with various folk medicines, ointments, herbs, massage, hot baths, and so on. He was especially good at treating the colds and frostbite that particularly plagued the monks of that district. He would light a furnace in a room, adjust the temperature, and place the sick monk inside. When he took him out, every trace of the cold had gone out together with the sweat. A quick and unique treatment! One time, however, he did not pay close enough attention to the temperature of the furnace and fired it more than necessary. When the monk came out, instead of being cured of the cold, he had burns!

Many monks thanked him for their health, and many who suffered from poverty and want praised his charity. He and his spiritual descendants were known for their generosity and charity. To be a "Hadji-Georgite" meant to be not only a faster, but also merciful. His integrity and honesty were admirable. He never cajoled or flattered great and distinguished people, nor was he frightened by unjust threats. He feared only God and His Law and the Day of Judgment. When truth and justice required it, he did not hesitate to use severe and reproachful words. When it was necessary to speak he did not keep silence, and he was not frightened by *the assaults of the wicked* (Proverbs 3:25). For him, God and his conscience were above all else.

His zeal for spiritual works was immeasureable. As a disciple he had already conquered great heights of virtue, and was his elder's secret pride. The light of God had soon found an abode in his heart.

Elder Hadji-George's furnace.

Upper Kerasia.

Even the spirit of prophecy was not slow in visiting him. Recorded prophecies of his about the future of the Ottoman Empire came true exactly. His prayer had great power, and he achieved the impossible, being made worthy of the gift of wonder-working. Even during his lifetime, pious Russians sent for his portrait; and in their land it performed miracles. Many material contributions from Russia came to the poor ascetic of Kerasia, which facilitated his charity and the building of new cells, much needed for their continually increasing brotherhood.

Like all true servants of the Lord, Hadji George also had to pass through the burning furnace of suffering. In the last years of his life he drank a bitter cup of slander, persecution, and banishment.

Thus his life conformed to the life of the Crucified Christ. Those guilty were certain Russian monks who bore malice against him because his community had attracted many of their countrymen. By means of unjust and slanderous accusations they succeeded in influencing even the Holy Governing Synod to sign his decree of banishment. Sorrowing, Hadji George had to part from his many spiritual children; he had to leave them orphans and pass the rest of his life exiled in Constantinople, far from his beloved Mountain.

However, the all-wise God can draw forth the sweet even from the bitter. His disciples dispersed over all the Holy Mountain, and wherever they settled they planted the flowers of virtue and spread the fragrance of holiness. His exile was also a heaven-sent blessing for the Christians of Constantinople in that turbulent time. The explosive situation created by Sultan Abdoul Khamit II disturbed the Christians and had brought the Patriarch to despair. The great Patriarch Joachim III was going through a hard trial with the so-called "preferential question" (1883-1884). The Elder from the Holy Mountain had much to offer the agitated and wretched Christians by his holiness, prophetic power, and gift of healing. Many miracles of healing performed by his prayers are reported. Even his belt worked miracles. A Christian woman was suffering greatly in childbirth, and was in mortal danger. They gave her the belt of Hadji George, the belt which had girded the body of the great faster, and immediately—O the wonder!—she was delivered from her sufferings.

Patiently enduring the cross of exile from his beloved Athos, and spreading blessings to the multitude of Christians of Constantinople, he fell asleep in the Lord around 1885 or 1890, full of holiness, suffering, and ascetic labors. Even in his relics his holiness was evident, because when they were removed they appeared very light, yellow as a lemon, and full of fragrance.

This was the famous Hadji George, the barefoot faster and owner of one shirt, the great Elder of Kerasia and renowned ascetic of Athos. We will not leave him yet, however, because here we will present one of his written texts which has been preserved for us.

2. A CONTROVERSY OVER FASTING

At the end of the last century Chios produced renowned ascetics, like the famous Parthenius, founder of the Monastery of St. Mark;* Pachomius, the former robber;** and many others, men and women, known and unknown. Certain of these distinguished strugglers were connected with the great Elder of Kerasia, like the ascetics Hierotheus and Macarius, about whom we will write below.

These two monks lived a hesychastic life in a certain desert Kalyve. Either they were disciples of Hadji George from the Holy Mountain, or they had from the beginning lived a desert life in Chios, following faithfully his rule and instructions.

In those years the Metropolitan of Chios was Gregory the Byzantine (1860-1877), who apparently was ignorant of this particular form of ascetic life. Unable to comprehend the ascetic spirit, he came into conflict with the two monks. They had an inviolable rule never to taste oil or condiments. The Metropolitan thought it unacceptable for anyone to fast in this way, especially on Saturdays, Sundays, and great feasts of the Lord and the Mother of God. He put pressure on them to abandon their ways. But the two monks, seeing the ignorance of the Metropolitan in ascetic matters, did not intend to yield, since they had firmly determined to keep this rule. In their

---

*It would be a great omission if someone does not write about the moving, heroic, and holy life of Parthenius. It is doubtful if such a luminous star will ever again appear in the heaven of Chios. He also had a great gift of prophecy. He prophesied and warned the inhabitants of Chios about the terrible earthquake of March, 1881, which devastated the island.

**Pachomius was delivered miraculously from the prison of Rhodes, where he was awaiting capital punishment, and came to Cyprus. Finally he became a monk and founded the Monastery of the Holy Fathers on Chios. Again and again he said to his disciples: "Struggle, my children, to inherit the Kingdom of Heaven. I was vouchsafed to see it dimly, and its beauty is beyond description."

difficulty they sought the help of Hadji George. He then sent a letter to the Metropolitan, asking him to show understanding and to accommodate the monks in their ascetic struggles.

This remarkable letter has been preserved for us, and we print it here. We have only corrected some spelling errors.

> To the Most Reverend Holy Metropolitan of Chios, the Lord Gregory:
>
> Most Reverend Holy Master, I humbly kiss your holy right hand.
>
> I entreat you and assure you that the monks, Elder Hierotheus and Elder Macarius, who live a hesychastic life in a Kalyve in your diocese, have loved and chosen the good part; may they endure in such a life, as they have vowed it for themselves. However, from today let them do so with your blessing. Let them keep their rule of fasting, because those who fast with humility as a sinner, or for the purposes of asceticism, or for the love of God, are not forbidden to do so by the Holy Fathers. We have witnesses from many places: many saints spent their whole lives eating only herbs, others legumes, like St. John Chrysostom. St. James the Brother of the Lord did not eat any animal products in his whole life. Many other anchorites have lived thus, including now my humble self. We are thirty brethren in one Kellion. I have spent forty years here, leading such a life. Neither on Pascha nor during Cheese-fare week do we break our fast. Many other ascetics live similarly, or live in silence by twos or threes, and they also spend their lives fasting.
>
> When someone fasts according to the rules, dogmatically, then he is hindered; for strugglers, it is said, there is no law, for a struggler is always abstemious. Let these monks have the prayer and blessing of your All-Holiness, that their consciences may not disturb them for being disobedient. A monk must always be a good example to the people—thus the light will shine before men.
>
> There is a great need that you be a careful pastor, which you are. You should oppose those who oppose fasting, which many Christians today ignore. With fear and admonishment you should

teach them to not transgress the laws of the Holy Fathers and Councils of our Church, because they state that he who does not keep the Wednesday and Friday fasts, Great Lent, and the other appointed fasts should be excommunicated. Therefore we must teach men to not transgress the laws of God or perform unseemly works—such transgressors you should persecute. But the brothers who desire to fast, not with a bad purpose, you should not hinder. Seeing their struggles, rejoice that you have such virtuous men in your diocese, and have them as your glory. And if a need should befall them some time, you should help them. I think you will obtain a great reward when you accommodate such men.

My Holy Master, consider well, for we also must die, judgment awaits us, and then God will judge every one according to his works. Forgive me the humble one for my audacity, for I am not worthy to open my mouth to speak a word to you. Hearing of your good renown, may your holy prayers be always with us. Amen.

Hadji George, monk
Holy Mountain of Athos
April 15, 1872

We don't know what result the letter to the Metropolitan had, but we marvel at the manly character of Hadji George. He did not hesitate to say, "My Holy Master, consider well, for we also must die, and the Judgment awaits us." He tried to turn the thought of the Metropolitan to the Just Judge, Who will not question him so much about the two ascetics who fast more than enough, as about the many Christians who despise the rules of fasting and temperance.

The Holy Mountain ascetic thus teaches us that we all, regardless of our position and rank, will one day have to face God, Who will impartially judge our every action and deed.

3. FR. IGNATIUS' FIRST DISCIPLE

There is much more to be said about the great Elder Hadji George, and we pray that someone will give us a full account of his excellent ascetic life. Now let us return to the two ascetics of Katounakia.

The elder and his disciple passed through the years together, sharing the joys and sorrows of the Lord's light yoke. Together they completed thirty-nine years of ascetic labors, and in the fortieth year Elder Neophytus finished the struggle. Faithful to his last breath to his monastic vows and the tradition of Hadji George, peaceful and calm, he exchanged the straitness of the life of Katounakia for the boundless spaciousness of Jerusalem Above.

His true and loving son, Fr. Ignatius, with his refined and sensitive nature, could hardly endure the grief of parting. Now his Kalyve was very lonely, and the plaintive words of the Psalmist came spontaneously to his lips: *My heart is dried up like grass ... I am become like a pelican in the wilderness, like an owl in a ruined house* (Psalm 101). But his loneliness was not to last long. On the fortieth day, during the pannikhida for Elder Neophytus, came Neophytus the disciple. Youth came in place of age.

He was about twenty-five years old, tall, frail, refined and courteous. He came from the Western Peloponnesus, from a wealthy family of Pyrgus, and in the world was called John Kaladzopoulos. By his countenance he showed himself to be a man of letters. He had been involved with journalism, and had studied at the Polytechnic. Burning, however, with longing for the monastic life, he had abandoned his studies (he was then a second-year student) and set out for Mount Athos.

He came to Katounakia by a round-about way. At first he was a novice at Dionysiou Monastery, and served for two years in the Metochion of Cassandra. They were going to tonsure him a monk and send him back there, but he protested, for there were serious moral dangers for a young monk at the Metochion. Unfortunately, as we must confess, the Holy Monasteries have not been careful about this. They send young defenseless monks to the Metochia, exposing them to incalculable dangers.

The presence of Fr. Sabbas the Confessor at Dionysiou Monastery (he had gone there to confess the Fathers) delivered the novice monk from this difficulty. They discussed the problem, and in the end the confessor suggested the solution:

"In the desert of Katounakia there is a virtuous hieromonk, Fr. Ignatius. If you go to him you will find relief for your soul. But he is rather austere."

"Let him be austere, holy Father. I need a strict elder, because I am easily carried away by my tongue, and need someone to restrain me."

Thus the matter was resolved, and the Kalyve of the Dormition had a Fr. Neophytus again. Having been miserable at the Metochion, where the monks mingled with the workmen, he now felt great relief in the holy atmosphere of the desert. Intelligent and sagacious, he immediately discerned that his elder was a man of high spirituality.

At first, as usually happens with beginners, he showed excessive zeal in ascetic struggles, and was even in danger of falling into prelest because of his inexperience. We will speak about this below in the chapter entitled "The Vigil Lamp."

To be honest, Fr. Neophytus' character was not smooth and even. It had some difficult qualities which fatigued both him and others. Apparently, certain types of men, unless they struggle much, are not well suited for the monastic life. He was of the kind who, if they apply themselves to politics, diplomacy, or journalism, unfailingly become famous. His skill and cleverness could open any closed door. With his nimble mind and tongue he could, as they say, show black as white and white as black.

Once he went to the Russian Monastery, which then gave plentiful, abundant alms to the hermits, in order to ask for something. The doorkeeper told him that he had a command from the

Abbot not to open to anyone that day. Then Fr. Neophytus, who with his intelligence had learned Russian well, started using his rhetoric. The outcome was that they eagerly opened to him and presented him with honor to the Abbot.

If he noticed any despondency, he could quickly change it to gladness. He was a pleasant type, and easily created a cheerful atmosphere. Once when he saw his elder upset, he said one thing after another until he had made him forget his difficulties.

He was remarkable when worldly people, wanting to appear clever, asked ironic questions. Some people from Sykia of Chalkis asked him:

"Fr. Neophytus, our town is so close to the Holy Mountain, and yours is so far away. Why do no men from our town become monks, while men from yours do?"

"My beloved ones!" he answered. "An earthly king chooses only the cream of his soldiers for his royal guard. Likewise Christ, the Heavenly King, selects only the best Christians to be His devoted servants. Who could He find to pick from you?"

In times of weakness and difficulty, however, his cleverness could cause much harm. But he had the wisdom to recognize and correct his faults. He always repented and asked forgiveness for his talkativeness, his various temptations, and his great curiosity about contemporary political news.

Fr. Neophytus had his shortcomings, but he also had his virtues. He was very consistent in his monastic obligations. To his elder he showed great love and devotion. He took more than enough care of him, and out of reverence always called him "Holy Father Confessor." His faith in God was strong; later we will even see him rebuke a demon. His piety was also evident by the feeling in his voice when he read holy texts. Because of his education and eloquence he had been made a reader. When the fathers gathered on feast days in the Dormition Church, or later in the Danieloi's, Fr. Ignatius' Neophytus (as he was called) would read the customary sermon. On Great Saturday there would resound from his lips the incomparable sermon of St. Epiphanius, "At the Burial of the Divine Body of the Lord."

"What day is this?" Fr. Neophytus would begin. "The earth is silent, silent and still, silent because the King sleepeth...." Towards the end of the sermon the emotion reached its highest pitch. The Lord, holding Adam by the hand, draws him up from the thick darkness of Hades: "Arise, My creation; arise, My form; arise, thou who wast made in My image. Arise; I will lead you hence, from death to life, from corruption to incorruption, from darkness to eternal light, from suffering to joy, from slavery to freedom, from prison to Jerusalem Above."

A reader with an expressive voice can present to the assembled Fathers the infinite compassion of God, just as the meditation of St. Epiphanius perceived it. Anyone who has been in a monastery on Great Saturday knows how moving this time can be. At such moments monks' souls are flooded with the strongest waves of grace. Eyes fill with joyful tears of compunction, and the mystical Psalmist sings the verse: *The rushings of the river make glad the city of God* (Psalm 45).

4. THE SECOND DISCIPLE

The life of Fr. Ignatius and Fr. Neophytus went on in its usual routine. Often the elder was obliged to speak to his disciple about the value of silence and self-concentration in the spiritual life. Along with spiritual matters, however, they also had to deal with practical ones, and to meet the new needs of their community.

Because the elder was a priest, he sometimes had to be absent from the Kalyve. When he started hearing confessions he received even more responsibilities. This ministry demanded much time. He had a great gift for the guidance of souls, and many came to him for confession, including many Slavic monks, as he knew their language. Thus we can see that he bore a great burden on his shoulders.

His Kalyve had its own needs. The Fathers who came for confession had to be given hospitality, as many had come long distances and were tired from the journey. Fr. Neophytus worked hard, but how could he alone take care of everything? They were continually exhausted; both of them, but especially the elder, needed assistance. And God, like a loving Father, soon showed them His good-will.

When Fr. Neophytus, the first disciple, had been at the Dormition Kalyve for twelve years, a second disciple appeared. He was a seventeen-year-old youth from Smyrna named Aristides Karidas. Handsome, of medium height, sturdily built, and with a charming character, he reminded one of Fr. Ignatius in his youth. This man was clearly a gift of God's love. At his tonsure, in order to complete the points in common with his Elder, his name was changed to Ignatius. Thus the God-bearing Elder now had two disciples in his community.

To improve the Kalyve's finances, Fr. Ignatius the younger stayed for a while at the neighboring St. Anne's Skete. When he returned, he had learned the art of icon-painting—a handiwork customary and well-suited to the monks of the Holy Mountain.

He had to carry on his young shoulders a good part of his elder's spiritual burden. Despite his young age, before he had passed four years there he was made a priest, to the great relief of his elder. This was because there was a great deficiency of priests. The young priest could serve forty-day Liturgies at the various Kalyves, liturgize on their feast days, and so on.

No matter how many Liturgies he served, his sense of the holiness of the Sacrament was never dulled. On the contrary, the more he served, the more receptive he became to the visitations of grace. He always wept from compunction when he liturgized. The elder's priestly virtues had been imparted to his disciple, and Fr. Ignatius glorified and thanked God.

After some years he also was made a confessor. Thus the Dormition Kalyve had two Fr. Ignatius the Confessors, the younger giving helping hands to the older. Affable, gracious, with a smile on his lips, yet at the same time holding strict principles, he gave direction like an elect spiritual father.

In hearing confessions he was exceedingly careful and God-fearing, as is evident from the following incident. One morning a new novice of St. Anne's Skete made his first confession to him, and received quite a heavy penance. That afternoon Fr. Ignatius came to St. Anne's Skete, searching for the novice's Kalyve. The novice, as soon as he saw him, became frightened. "What in the world!" he said. "Has the priest come to give me another penance?" But something else happened.

"My child," he said to him, "I gave you a penance of two years' abstinence from Holy Communion, but I forgot to say something to you. If it should happen (may it not be) that you are ill and your life is in danger, then you may receive Communion. That is what the Canons of the Church say. I must make this clear to you, because if you depart this life without the provision of Holy Communion I will bear the sin."

In the future, to avoid the same anxiety, when he gave penances he always finished with the same refrain:

"However, if you are in danger you are allowed to receive Communion."

* * * * * * * *

In the life of Fr. Ignatius the younger, a wonderful, unique incident occurred, which we must not fail to tell the reader.

He had gone to Karyes on some business, and because he missed the boat back, was forced to return on foot. Not only did he have to walk for seven hours, but he also had to carry a heavy bag. When the sunlight left the peak of Athos, he finally arrived at the Kalyve. Exhausted, he fell unconscious on his bed. Because of his condition, he was not aroused for any reason. After six hours, the bell rang for the three-hour-long service beginning at midnight. Fr. Neophytus tried to wake him, but he labored in vain: it was impossible. He then reported the situation to the elder, who silently reflected on how he should act.

Shortly he found the solution. He dealt with the problem in a way that might seem odd to many—but in monasticism, where the boundary between the natural and supernatural is not sharply drawn, such actions are not unusual. He said something to Fr. Neophytus, who conveyed it to his exhausted brother.

"You have a command from the elder to immediately get up, anoint yourself with oil from the lampada, and come to the service."

What would happen? He had to be obedient, so he arose, began to anoint himself with the oil, and waited for the result. And—O the wonder! A wonderful change came over his body. Every trace of fatigue disappeared. He felt rested as never before—light as a bird.

"How wonderful!" he said. "Where did all my exhaustion go? How do I feel so light?"

He was in a quandary trying to interpret the phenomenon. He did not know what to attribute the miracle to—the oil of the lampada, or obedience? Or to both? Thus his fatigue left him, but this little perplexity remained. And at the same time his belief was strengthened that his elder was indeed a man of God.

III

The Harbor of Salvation

1. THE SCIENCE OF GUIDING SOULS

Elder Ignatius was not very well educated, having never studied at a university. In spite of this, his proficiency in the monastic life was marvelous. Through this he achieved inward purification, making his soul receptive to the light of the Holy Spirit—and the Holy Spirit, the fountain of all wisdom, taught him everything he needed to know. He taught him pedagogy, psychology, pastorship, and every other science useful in his work of hearing confessions. Thus Fr. Ignatius was raised to the highest rank, and in him souls found healing, guidance, and peace. His confessional was for many people the harbor of salvation.

In giving spiritual direction he followed the middle and royal path, avoiding both too great strictness and indiscreet leniency. He knew how to use properly both the pastoral rod and the pastoral pipe. Mostly he inclined towards mercy, always taking care not to bring anyone to despair. He knew how to show understanding and how to condescend to the defects and weaknesses of his spiritual children with a spirit of constructiveness and fatherly love. His face, words, and manners had a special grace which inspired respect and full confidence.

In the performance of the Sacraments, he had been given some rare gift which astonished his spiritual children. An unforgettable impression would be made in one who came to him for the first time. A special atmosphere surrounded him, where God made His presence felt. Elder Thomas, an aged monk of Little St. Anne's Skete, talked to us especially about this. Among other things, he said the following:

"The first time you went to confess to Fr. Ignatius, the Holy Spirit spoke through him. The Holy Spirit enlightened everything he said."

The early church lost the zealous Deacon Stephen, but then gained the even more zealous Apostle Paul. Israel lost Elijah, but gained Elisha. Something like that happened also to the monks of the Holy Mountain. In 1908 they had mourned the death of the renowned confessor Fr. Sabbas; now, however, God's providence had sent them Fr. Ignatius. The waves of penitents that had flowed out to Little St. Anne's Skete, to the Kalyve of the Resurrection, now surged even further, to the Dormition Kalyve in Katounakia.

"There were other good confessors also," Elder Panteleimon, a monk of New Skete, told us. "Here in New Skete we had Fr. Cyril and Fr. Seraphim. Further over in St. Anne's there were Fr. Nathaniel, Fr. Caesarius, Fr. Ephraim, Fr. Dionysius, and others. In Little St. Anne's there were Fr. Theodosius and Fr. Cosmas. All of them were good and virtuous confessors, but we passed them all by and sought out Fr. Ignatius. After Fr. Sabbas died there was no one else like him. He was a wonderful, extraordinary confessor!"

At that time a multitude of virtuous Orthodox Slavs led ascetic lives on the Holy Mountain. In the Russian, Bulgarian, and Serbian Monasteries, and in the various Sketes and Kellia one could meet many Slavic monks. For them Fr. Ignatius was a blessing from Heaven, because he knew the Russian and Bulgarian languages well. The Russian hermits of Karoulia, among whom were former princes and generals of the Tsar's army, also revered him exceedingly. As he was not too far away, they chose him for their confessor. Two or three times a year a small Russian steam-boat took him to the Russian monastery, and also to the Bulgarian monastery of Zographou, in order to hear the Fathers' confessions. Greeks, Russians, Bulgarians, monks from the Coenobia, the Sketes, and the desert were all refreshed by the grace of the God-bearing Fr. Ignatius. He continued this work until deep old age, even after he had lost his sight. Many were the souls he relieved and enlightened.

When he heard confessions he sat in a stall of the church, wearing a completely clean rassa. Out of reverence for the Sacrament he wore also a formal mantia, and he appeared most venerable. When he became very old he heard confessions in his room, sitting in a chair next to an icon stand with the Deisis—that is, icons of the Lord, the Theotokos, and the Forerunner. Many aged Fathers remember him hearing confessions in his cell, with his white beard, his hair falling to his chest, and his bright face that radiated peace.

"Come, my child," he would say. "Come, my little Gerasim. Sit down and let's talk a little. How is it going? Does Satan throw us down, or do we throw him?"

"He throws us, Holy Father. I often neglect my rule...."

"Eh, forward now and strike down Satan! Prayer can do it. Let's make a beginning from today. Let's not abandon our rule. Are we unable to complete it? Let's at least do a little. Let's not abandon it completely. Let us strike down Satan."

In this way he would speak, strengthening souls by his great love and simplicity.

"Holy Father, I often fall into contradiction," Fr. Z. of St. Anne's Skete confessed to him. "The brothers and the elder say something to me, and I contradict them."

"Ah, my child, a great sin! When we contradict we cannot make progress. We will fall outside. Never let yourself make this a habit, and I will take responsibility for you. You must cut off contradiction."

His fatherly love made him seem punctilious and severe in serious cases, but he was never harsh or relentless. When faced with human weakness he was always ready to be merciful, when the matter permitted it.

"Well, well, my child," he would say, "since you cannot.... We don't mean for you to put a stone in your throat and choke yourself!"

In difficult, obscure cases he would speak with authority, not vacillating at all.

"In this case," he would say, "you must handle it in this way. Otherwise the following bad consequence will result."

And immediately the other one was assured that this was God's will.

When a certain monk begged to be initiated into the inner work of mental prayer, he cast a glance at his face, waited a little, and then said, slowly and firmly:

"It's not yet time, my child."

* * * * * * * *

Before we end this chapter we will mention one of his habits. After the penitent confessed his sins, he would have him read on his knees a prayer of St. Ephraim, appropriate for the occasion:

"Lord Jesus Christ, my God ... I pray Thee to forgive me Thy unworthy servant for all the sins I have committed as a man, or rather worse than a beast, my voluntary and involuntary faults, whether committed in knowledge or in ignorance, from passion, or carelessness, or indolence, or negligence; if I have sworn by Thy Holy Name ... or stolen anything, or told a lie ... or grieved or embittered my brother ... or foolishly laughed, or been vainglorious, or proud, or if I have gazed at vain beauty ... or examined curiously my brother's fault ... if I have neglected prayer, or done any other wicked thing. For all these sins and others that I do not remember, for I have done all this and much more, forgive, O God, me Thy unworthy servant, and have mercy on me as Good One and Lover of man."

At the end followed the prayer of absolution, and the penitent kissed the venerable hand of the confessor, leaving with a bright, clean soul, crowned with peace.

2. "SON OF CONSOLATION"

Fr. Ignatius' soul was like a spiritual bouquet, with many colored, fragrant flowers of virtue and grace. We will speak about these specifically later. However, we will examine here the beauty of one particular flower, since it is closely related to his pastoral art. He could be called the Barnabas of the Holy Mountain, because like the Apostle he was a "son of supplication," that is to say, a son of consolation.

The grace of consolation flowed out pure and free from his heart, which was a sea of love. All who experienced this grace remembered it with tears. Archimandrite Gabriel of Dionysiou has written about this: "This wonderful and blessed man of God had the excellent virtue of kindness and pure fatherly love towards all, especially to those coming to him for confession."

Anyone who went for confession to the Dormition Kalyve tasted his bountiful love. At first he was given bodily repose. The elder had given indispensable commands to his disciples to offer refreshment and hospitality to all their visitors. But this was only a poor prologue to the spiritual consolation which would follow. From the following incidents we will see how the souls that came to the blessed elder were rested and refreshed.

* * * * * * * *

The young Fr. Christodoulus, a disciple of the great hesychast Callinicus, was wounded in the spiritual battle by the arrows of the enemy. A great temptation came upon him. When he told his elder the situation, he sent him quickly to Fr. Ignatius.

"This is a serious matter," he said. "You need to confess it to a priest. Go to Fr. Ignatius to receive a penance."

IGNATIUS THE CONFESSOR

With a heavy heart, Fr. Christodoulus climbed up to the Dormition Kalyve and sorrowfully related the matter to the holy elder. And he, with a smile on his lips, gently calmed him:

"Don't be too upset by this temptation, my Christodoulus. It seems that you prayed a bit more than usual and wounded the enemy, and therefore he flew into a rage and attacked you. Don't be upset. Be calm, and the temptation will pass. The unseen warfare is like that."

Leaving the church, the young warrior perceived that peace had replaced the agitation of his soul. The storm-driven waves had abated.

* * * * * * * *

It was Friday, the fifth week of Great Lent, and also the feast of the Annunciation, March 25th of the year 1911. In Dionysiou Monastery, towards the end of the vigil of the feast, the 22-year-old novice George would put on the angelic Schema. Fr. Ignatius, by then quite advanced in age, was there, for he was the confessor of this Monastery also, and had decided to celebrate the Annunciation and the feast of the Akathist there. He also wanted to assist the novice who was to be tonsured, because he had special love for him.

The Matins of the Annunciation ended, and the reading of the First Hour began. Nothing indicated that a tonsure would take place. There was no preparation.

"Holy Archimandrite," asked Fr. Ignatius, "is not the tonsure today?"

"No, Holy Father, it has been postponed until the vigil of the Akathist tomorrow."

"Why? How did it happen to be postponed?"

"I will explain to you. The novice confessed to me that yesterday at noon he was in the Trapeza of the Russian Monastery and ate olives. But at his tonsure he will receive Communion, and according to our typicon he is not allowed to eat olives the day before. Therefore I told him to fast today, so that we can tonsure him tomorrow."

Archimandrite Gabriel of Dionysiou

Hearing this, Fr. Ignatius felt sorry for him. To postpone the tonsure, because the novice had forgotten and eaten two or three olives! And to have to fast on the Annunciation, the day of joy!

"...His fatherly heart was so tender," writes Archimandrite Gabriel (the former novice George), "that finding me during the Liturgy, he embraced me with tears. To console me, he said, 'I also will fast and keep vigil with you, my child.' And on this day of the Annunciation, the only day in the whole of Great Lent that fish is permitted, he did not go to the common Trapeza, but shared with me a small prosphora."*

In the afternoon he again found the novice and asked him where he would keep vigil until the time of his tonsure. He answered that he liked the chapel of St. Chrysostom, a very quiet place.

Going after Compline to this chapel, George found the venerable elder waiting for him. He wanted to assist him in his spiritual preparation. Not many monks are able to prepare for their tonsure like George. Fr. Ignatius blessed him, and at his suggestion George read three times the canon of the Tonsure to the Great Schema from the great Prayer-book. After that, he heard from the elder's lips wonderful counsels and thoughts about the monastic life. In the end, they did not forget St. Chrysostom, who had given them hospitality in his chapel.

"George, my child, take the booklet and read the Akathist to St. Chrysostom. May his intercessions support you in your new life."

---

*Archimandrite Gabriel of Dionysiou, *Lausaicon of the Holy Mountain*, Volos, 1953, pp. 26-27.

George had no idea of what was to happen after the Akathist. Apparently the golden-tongued Saint immediately answered his prayer. But we will wait to tell what George saw until the chapter entitled "Like the Face of an Angel." About what happened that day, Archimandrite Gabriel wrote later: "Alone in my life, this incident is unforgettable. It is an irrefutable proof of the man's great holiness."

* * * * * * * *

Another time, the enemy declared fierce war on a monk who had recently renounced the world. In gaudy colors he pictured to his imagination the delights of worldly life. The attacks were so violent that the struggler had to shed blood to reject them. But however much Belial tried to feed him poison, his holy confessor, Fr. Ignatius, would always console and encourage him.

"My child," he said, "the world is vain, temporary. Don't be frightened by this struggle. A small resistance wins great crowns. Reflect on Heaven, think of what awaits you where you will go. Joy and delight unutterable! Only endure, be attentive to yourself, be ready. Give your heart to Christ. Love Him Who has loved you."

By these simple words of holy fatherly love the heavy fog was scattered. This admonition, "Love Him Who has loved you," touched the finest chords of his heart. The aged monk still remembers those strengthening words, and with tears in his eyes exclaimed to us:

"How he consoled me! How he strengthened me! This man was a blessing from God. As he knew three or four languages he could comfort everyone, Greeks, Russians, Bulgarians ... innumerable monks from the monasteries, sketes, cells: he refreshed everyone. He was a God-sent blessing for everyone, he was a sea of love and patience. May we have his prayers."

The venerable confessor could not be otherwise, for he was the abode of the Paraclete (the Comforter), the Holy Spirit, Who had anointed him as a messenger of love and a "son of consolation."

3. A HERMIT'S TEMPTATION

Ever since Anthony the Great officially opened the path of the ascetic life, the devil has had no peace. He uses all his powers in his war against monks. He battles against them with rage, because they will complete the angelic order and take the place which he formerly lost. He uses his most clever tricks: when he finds it difficult to cast down a monk from the left side, he tries to do it from the right. By the attack "from the right," the ascetic is in danger, among other things, of falling into delusion.

When Fr. Ignatius was in the sunset of his life, he received one winter a visit from an unfortunate hermit, whose face showed that he had lived through a terrible experience. With a trembling voice he related his shocking adventure to the Elder. When he had finished, he sighed with relief:

"Glory to Thee, my God! Thou hast rescued me from the teeth of death. I almost perished completely!"

What could have happened to this monk? Let us attend to his story.

Aflame with zeal for the monastic life, he lived as a hermit near Katounakia. Without following a spiritual guide, as he should have, he threw himself with excessive fervor into ascetic exercises. He thought he would quickly ascend to the heights of holiness. Without even being aware of it, he began to overestimate his strength and to trust in himself. He set his ascetic goals by himself, accomplished them by himself (he thought), and gave himself rewards.

But to be precise, he was not by himself. The enemy, the lord of darkness, followed him vigilantly, preparing a pit for his fall. In short, as one could have foreseen, he fell into delusion. The wise words of a contemporary hesychast are appropriate for such cases:

> Wherever the evil demons see the desiring power of the mind incline, a corresponding spirit is sent to him by their chief, and constantly residing with him he brings the means of deception;

and with extreme subtlety he unceasingly murmurs about this desire for a long time (Joseph the Cave-Dweller).

The spirit of deception brought the means of deception, and patiently he dug the pit of destruction. Little by little, the hermit's heart imperceptibly began to darken. The more it darkened, the more the thoughts of pride increased; and the more the proud thoughts increased, the greater grew the darkness.

Time passed, and the ascetic, enthusiastic about his fasting, vigils, and asceticism, said to himself:

"The way I am going, I will reach the virtue of Anthony the Great! But I'm surprised that, with all my progress, I have not yet been worthy to see a vision...!"

And the longed-for vision soon came. A bright angel appeared to him, coming to confirm his imaginings.

"Your life," he told him, "has pleased Christ much more than any other ascetic's on the Holy Mountain."

The angel disappeared, leaving him floating in a sea of bliss. The heavenly testimony had come. His ascetic life even made the heavens rejoice! He had even been worthy to see an angel. And still there was more! One evening, as he had expected, the heavenly angel appeared again, and what gladsome messages he brought!

"Great is your virtue, my brother," he said. "A splendid crown and great glory are prepared for you. Tomorrow evening be on the summit of Mt. Athos, where Christ will descend for you to worship Him."

The ascetic's joy was unbounded—indescribable joy! What would his eyes behold tomorrow! He would taste the delight of Tabor. He didn't even notice when the new day dawned. The climb began at last. Despite the snow and freezing cold of winter, he felt nothing, for the company of angels warmed him. He advanced comfortably, feeling neither the cold nor the toil.

As he approached the summit, his joy and anticipation reached their peak. It had in the meantime grown dark. Suddenly—O supernatural and resplendent sight!—what did his eyes behold?

The lonely summit of Athos.

Torches, great light, incense, priests, hierarchs ... a wonderful welcome! And most magnificent: a glorious throne, whereon sat the King, Christ, surrounded by venerable hierarchs and other Saints. Among the hierarchs he could even distinguish St. Spiridon, beloved of hermits.

It is a terrible thing, dear readers, for the devil to acquire power over us. Then our imagination and senses submit to him, and he can make us imagine, see, and hear whatever he wishes. Then only God can deliver us.

But let us continue the description of this satanic snare. In a moment the majestic voice of the King was heard:

"Spiridon, bring hither My chosen servant to worship Me."

Obediently, St. Spiridon, in a slow and reverent pace, approached the ecstatic monk.

It was a critical moment. If the hermit would worship the false Christ, he would either be demonized, as has happened in other cases, or he would fall and be crushed; for probably under the imaginary throne there would be some frightful abyss. But apparently the heart of the unfortunate ascetic had some room open to the mercy of God. In the final moment the Divine Mercy saved him.

As the false St. Spiridon approached, he observed that he was not wearing the usual skoufia. This surely was not so important. Something else, however, was more important. By Divine Mercy, he espied on his head two devilish horns!

Instantly came out a heart-rending cry:

"Lord Jesus Christ, Son of God, save me!"

That was all. The grandiose satanic fantasy dispersed *as smoke vanisheth* (Ps. 67:3). And high up on Mount Athos, alone at night, amid snow and wilderness, was one solitary ascetic....

Thus he related his dramatic adventure to Fr. Ignatius.

"Now," said the confessor to him, "glorify God Who has saved you from such demonic wickedness. From now on, do not remain alone in your isolated Kalyve. Go and live in Dionysiou Monastery, where you will be safe."

Thus he was saved. The enemy could have completely won the game if the deception had been of an advanced form, as had happened some years before to a monk of Little St. Anne's Skete. He imagined that the Mother of God spoke with him, and that he had reached the heights of humility, even kissing the feet of the other fathers. This unfortunate man ended in being possessed. Trying to fly from the roof of the Kalyve (he imagined he could fly like an angel) he broke his legs. Later he even committed a crime in Xeropotamou Monastery, and ended up in a state prison. This miserable man, before he was demonized, had applied himself to exceptional ascetic labors. To mention a characteristic detail, in the beginning of Great Lent, when the others in the community kept the three-day fast, he ostentatiously fasted for six days.

What terrible snares the devil prepares for strugglers! Even by means of asceticism, fasts, vigils, and prayers—these means of sanctification—he is able to destroy us. Therefore it is a blessing of God that there are God-bearing Fathers who destroy the works of the enemy. The need for holy elders, and the misery of those who fall into the hooked claws of the devil, will be confirmed by the stories in the following three chapters.

4. THE VIGIL LAMP

In Orthodoxy, the spiritual element is in wonderful harmony with the material. Spiritual truths have corresponding tangible expressions. This is confirmed by dogma. According to the God-inspired definition of the holy Fourth Ecumenical Council, both the human and the divine element are preserved entire in Christ. He is perfect God and perfect man: invisible, immaterial, and indescribable, but also visible and describable. This truth is reflected in all aspects of Church life.

When we are baptized, our souls are cleansed by unseen spiritual grace; at the same time, our bodies are bathed in the holy water of the baptismal font. When we pray, our fragrant prayers ascend to the heavenly throne; at the same time, the fragrance of the

Vigil lamps over the *Axion Estin* icon of the Mother of God in the altar of the Protaton (the main catholicon of Karyes).

incense wafts upward. When we enter an Orthodox church at night, the faces of the saints are illuminated by the vigil lamps that burn in front of them. The material light symbolizes the spiritual light that the saints radiate, "the result of the saints' ceaseless illumination by the Holy Spirit" (St. Symeon of Thessalonica).

How many contrite prayers and holy tears these little lamps with their cheerful light have witnessed! In the little desert church of the Dormition the gentle light of the vigil lamps flickered every night in front of the holy icons. It was a godly joy to pray at night before the icon of the Dormition, facing the sad countenances of the Apostles and the peaceful face of the sleeping Virgin.

So far all is good and blessed. But even here the wicked serpent tried to insinuate his poison. He tried to ensnare the monk who was in charge of lighting the vigil-lamps. The treacherous scheme was sure to work; it couldn't possibly fail. There was only one danger: Fr. Ignatius.

"Ah, this Fr. Ignatius!" said the devil to himself. "How many schemes he has destroyed! He infuriates me! Therefore it is absolutely necessary that he hear nothing about this. I will whisper in his disciple's ear, persuading him that there is no reason to tell anything to the elder. To do this I must darken his soul, I must make him proud. How? Very easily—I will lavish praise on him. I will stir up the whole tree of his being, leaves, branches, trunk, and roots, with the wind of praise. I will remind him of the sacrifices he made to abandon the world, his parents and his studies; of his capability as a hermit, his cleverness, all his virtues, real and non-existent, his gifts and advantages. Maybe I can find some monk—one of my own—who will weave this crown of praise for him. All will be well!"

The enemy began to darken and cloud the monk's mind with the spirit of pride. Then, having prepared the ground, he went on with his plan.

It was late at night. Fr. Neophytus was sleeping and—who knows?—perhaps he even saw angelic dreams. But what was this? A gentle knock was heard on the door of his cell (the cell was on the upper floor) and a sweet voice said:

"Arise, my child. Go down to the church. My vigil light has gone out."

Immediately he leaped up and went anxiously down to the church, where the vigil lamp of the Theotokos had indeed gone out. Full of emotion, he lit it, prayed fervently, and returned to his cell.

"I have made progress," he thought. "I have risen high. The Mistress of Heaven and earth has visited me, and I heard her sweet angelic voice. I relit her extinguished lamp. How happy I feel!"

Several times he heard in his mind a gentle, quiet voice that advised him to tell his elder about this incident. But he repelled the thought.

"Why should I tell the elder? Is it a sin to be confessed? It's a holy incident, and the more I keep it to myself, the more its holiness will be preserved."

Thus he thought. With these thoughts, how could Christ knock on the door of his heart? The elder, however, was not asleep. He suspected something.

"Neophytus, my child, take care. You must tell me everything that happens in your spiritual life."

One day in confession he compelled him to relate the whole affair in detail. And he proved to him that the whole beautiful fabric had been woven on the devil's loom.

"What feelings prevailed in you when you lit the extinguished vigil lamp?" he asked him.

"Joy and thanksgiving that I was made worthy of such a blessing."

"Anything else?"

"Yes, and something else. I had a certain secret disturbance and uneasiness that I had not told you about it."

"That proves clearly the presence of the devil."

The elder spoke long to him about the snares of the enemy, and finishing, rebuked him fairly strongly:

"O deluded one! The devil deceived you. Does the Theotokos need either me or you? Does She need your assistance? Take care! If you hear a knock again, do not get up to light the lamp. I will be accountable."

Poor Fr. Neophytus! His wings were clipped. Never had he expected such an inglorious end to this exalted affair. Of course, later he was grateful to the elder who had rescued him from the snares of the enemy. Now, however, he was very sorrowful. He even had a doubt—could it be that the door would be knocked on again? But as soon as the designs of the devil confronted the light, they were scattered like smoke. Eggs that are not brooded cannot hatch, because the cool air reaches them.

In a similar incident related by Abba Cassian, Abba Serapion's elder said to him:

"O child, your confession saved you! As long as you did not speak, the devil wounded you. Now that you have spoken, however, you have massacred the demon. Now he has no more place in you, because his designs are revealed. O child, your confession delivered you!"

In order for the treacherous plans of the enemy to succeed, they need darkness. Woe to monks and to all Christians who conceal their states from their spiritual fathers. The prince of darkness will lead them to ruin and will rejoice over their perdition.

5. THE STRANGE ILLNESS

It is a sad thing that many Greeks outside their country fall victim through carelessness to anti-Christian ideas and heresies, losing the priceless treasure of the Orthodox faith. This happened to a man named Angelis Kiousa.

He had set out from the Lion of Thebes, his fatherland, for distant America, hoping for a good career. As he was clever and enterprising, he not only managed to succeed professionally but he even became very rich.

At the age of forty he wanted something novel to play with. Blinded by his wealth and darkened by arrogance, he became entangled in the nets of a satanic sect. His soul was so poisoned that he forswore Christianity in a solemn ceremony, and defiled the icons of Christ and the Theotokos. Others had performed this wicked deed, and nothing had happened to them.

But God, Who forbears and is silent, sometimes judges it right to break His silence. This happened in the case of Angelis—the scourge fell as he was leaving the room where the abominable deed was performed. God delivered him to the power of the devil. Outwardly it appeared that he had been stricken with sudden madness.

"Angelis, the wealthy one, is ill!" The rumor spread among the emigrant Greeks. "He doesn't know what he is saying or doing—he has a serious mental illness!"

His brothers now had the thankless responsibility of going around from doctor to doctor and from psychiatrist to psychiatrist. They were fortunate that they had so much money to spend. He was examined by the most eminent psychiatrists, given the best medicines, and nursed in the most modern sanatoriums, but there was no result. Several doctors said to themselves: "This is a strange illness! It doesn't seem normal. A peculiar case! What shall we do?"

His relatives began to understand that Angelis' illness lay outside the jurisdiction of medical science. They remembered the despised faith and brought him back to their fatherland, having recourse to the Church and the help of priests. Now in place of drugs he received the exorcism of St. Basil the Great. Their new course of action finally led the possessed man to the Holy Mountain.

"Shouldn't you take him to the Holy Mountain, so that some holy hieromonk can pray for him?" several people recommended.

This suggestion was immediately adopted, and Angelis with his brothers came to New Skete, where they had some friends.

Some time ago in New Skete we met the monk who had received them in his Kalyve, Fr. Eustratius the hagiographer. When we questioned him, he told us the story in detail. He also described the madness of the possessed man. He would carry four or five round balls like oranges and amuse himself by throwing them one by one into the air with great speed. He would catch them and throw them again, without any falling down. The most skillful jugglers would have envied him!

Various kinds of demons torment demoniacs. Some work at midday, others at night, others once a month.... Some are deaf or mute, others shameless babblers, etc. Angelis' demon was characterized as "harmful and distorting the mind" and "voluble." Under his influence the unfortunate man ceaselessly chattered and talked to himself, rambling on about all kinds of subjects. His tongue never stopped.

The Fathers of New Skete worked hard to drive it out, but were not successful. This demon was very difficult: "His neck was made of iron nerves." They bethought themselves to find some elder "mighty in battle." Such a one was Fr. Ignatius, who had healed many demoniacs.

Thus Angelis was led to Katounakia, where they met Fr. Ignatius and the battle was planned. Fr. Ignatius perceived that much labor would be needed to expel this spirit. His disciple of the same name would assist him in the struggle, in the Liturgies and exorcisms. For forty days they would fast, perform the Divine Liturgy daily, read the exorcisms, and beg God's mercy. Angelis, by Fr. Ignatius' command, had to go to confession every day and tell his most secret thoughts, and everything that the devil said to him.

For thirty-nine days they waged this hard battle, and on the fortieth day the sufferer breathed the air of freedom. The chains which had bound him for so many years were broken. His relief was indescribable. Rejoicing, he returned to his fatherland, and then to America, where, "clothed and in his right mind" he continued his life. And never did he forget the Holy Mountain and the venerable Elder Ignatius who had freed him from the devil's tyranny.

6. THE PROUD MONK WHO WAS POSSESSED

Elder Silouan of Mt. Athos (1866-1938), who by the grace of the Holy Spirit tasted the heavenly sweetness of humility, wrote: "O Christ-like humility! Sweet are your fruits, for they are not of this world.... O humble soul! You are like a blossoming garden, in the depth of which are wonderful abodes where the Lord loves to dwell."*

In the following account we will not praise humility directly, for we will not be telling the story of a humble monk. On the contrary, we will introduce the monk Hilarion, who was ruled by the spirit of pride. Nevertheless, the greatness of humility will be shown from the opposite side.

This incident happened in Katounakia in the year 1914, in Elder Macarius' Kalyve of the Nativity of Christ, a little below where Fr. Ignatius lived. In those days Elder Macarius' community was busy, for they were adding a second story to their Kalyve. The work was far advanced—they were building the roof.

"My children," said the elder, "glory to God, all goes well. Now the boards of the roof must be carried up. Be careful, the boards are heavy. Let's be patient and carry them up one by one. Don't hurry too much."

Everyone began carrying the boards. Fr. Hilarion, the youngest of the community, could not tolerate carrying them up one by one. Young and strong in the arms, he started taking three at a time.

"Fr. Hilarion," the other brothers said to him, "the boards are heavy. Don't take so many—you will hurt yourself."

He did not pay the slightest attention to their advice. "They should mind their own business," he said to himself. "I know how many I can carry."

---

*Archimandrite Sophronius, *Elder Silouan of Mt. Athos*, pp. 309-310. I can find no suitable words to praise this book, a height of theology, depth of mystical life, original in expression.... It is considered an excellent text of Orthodox spirituality.

The elder learned of his attitude and reproached him, but he paid no attention to his counsel, either. By his unprincipled behavior, ill-suited for a disciple, he angered his elder. It was a case of diabolical pride and disobedience.

According to monastic tradition, harsh scourges await the disciple who angers his elder. For Hilarion, the time of scourging was near. The proud monk, who always wanted to do his own will, climbed up to the roof of the Kalyve with the three boards on his back. As soon as he laid them down he received the blow—he was delivered to the power of satan and possessed by a demon. And what a dreadful, terrifying demon! His fury agitated the whole region. Abominable words came out of his mouth, and his actions horrified all who saw him.

"What happened? What is the matter?" asked the perplexed fathers from the surrounding Kalyves.

"Elder Macarius' Hilarion has been possessed! Hilarion is possessed! There is a savage demon inside him. God has punished him."

Fr. Ignatius, who was also their neighbor, was immediately informed of the event. Experienced as he was in these matters, he understood that a great struggle would be needed to expel this fierce demon. Immediately he commanded that several fathers and hieromonks assemble in the Kalyve of the Nativity, in order to combine their prayers and perform the Sacrament of Holy Unction for the sufferer.

Seven hieromonks took part in performing the Sacrament. This ceremony had something extraordinary about it. The atmosphere trembled with a special feeling. The sight would break your heart. In the middle of the church lay the demon-possessed Hilarion, tied to a board with many ropes. This unfortunate monk had not wanted to carry one board: he wanted three. Now he himself was carried on a board, bound. Several strong monks stood near him, because the demoniac had fearful strength and would break the ropes.

The prayers began to be read entreatingly, while every so often the sacredness of the Service drew screams and insults from the evil spirits.

"O Thou Who art without beginning, eternal, the Holy of Holies," Fr. Ignatius, who had preeminence in the ceremony, began to entreat with a voice trembling from emotion.

"Let this oil become the oil of gladness, the oil of sanctification, a royal garment, an armor of strength, the averting of all diabolical power...."

By the prayers and tears of the Fathers, the intercession of the priests, and the power of the Holy Sacrament, the miracle came to pass: the terrible occupant withdrew from Hilarion. The fearful experience was over, but a good lesson had been given to the proud monk, beneficial for many others also. Everyone had learned something.

Even Fr. Neophytus, the disciple of Fr. Ignatius, had profited by this experience. He was guarding the possessed monk before the Unction Service. Knowing that there must have been a definite reason for God to have sent him such a punishment, he asked:

"Evil demon, why did you enter Hilarion?"

"Come! You are going above yourself," answered the demon. "Do you think I would tell *you*?!"

"I command you in the name of the Holy Trinity to tell me the reason."

"Ha! How dare you put me on oath! Who are you? You're not even a priest! I entered into him because ... because he was proud."

"Again I command you in the name of the Holy Trinity—tell me what is a proud man."

Pressed by the command, against his will the demon made a remarkable confession.

"What is a proud man? This is what: one who in the twenty-four hours of the day never even once sets in his mind that he is a sinner, he is p-r-o-u-d." (The last words he shrieked in a high voice.)

Fr. Ignatius' Kalyve.

These words rang for a long time in the ears of Fr. Neophytus. "My God," he said from time to time, "save me from pride." He never forgot what the demon had taught him.

The Lord resists the proud. This God-inspired saying is repeated three times in the Holy Scriptures (Proverbs 3:34, James 4:6, and I Peter 5:5). The *Ladder* also emphasizes it: "Pride is the adversary of God" (Step 24). We have been told this many times, and it was confirmed by the suffering of the proud Hilarion, who had expected to receive glory by carrying up two extra boards, but had ended by being humiliated.

IV

The Light of Grace

1. A SWEET-SMELLING FLOWER

Those who are progressing in the spiritual life acquire all the virtues together. Nevertheless, sometimes we notice that certain virtues shine more brightly. In Fr. Ignatius one especially noticed the virtue of orderliness. In all his affairs, especially in his monastic obligations, he showed great regularity, exemplary correctness and order. He continued this until deep old age.

The command of Scripture, *Be attentive to thyself* (Deut. 15:9), he drew with bold letters on the banner of his spiritual combat. He was always sober, restrained in his speech, measured in his actions, upright in the inclination of his heart. His face showed his thoughtfulness, and one could see that he did not let his mind roam about in the four directions of the horizon. He was always vigilant and attentive, just as the sayings of the Elders instruct us: "A monk is obliged, like the Cherubim and Seraphim, to be all eye" (Abba Bessarion).

The virtue of abstinence also held a prominent place in his life. His spiritual grandfather, Elder Hadji George, used to repeat: *The struggler is temperate in all things* (I Cor. 9:25). For decades he followed faithfully the hard typicon of Hadji George. Only at the end of his life when his strength had diminished, out of obedience to his spiritual father he was obliged to eat seasoned food. But even here the spirit of abstinence prevailed: he never allowed himself to be carried away by the pleasures of the palate.

Once when he was ninety-eight years old, on a feast day Fr. Neophytus, an excellent cook, had prepared a delicious soup. At the table sat also the young Fr. Eustratius, the latest to join the community. At one point, astonished by some action of the elder, he asked:

"Grandfather, why are you putting vinegar in your food?"

"So that it will not be so tasty, my Eustratius. A monk should not eat delicious food."

He also had the virtue of simplicity to a high degree. The Fathers of the Holy Mountain told us much about this. He was simple like the thrice-blessed St. Paul the Simple, the "model of blessed simplicity," like Adam before the Fall, like guileless children. Cunning, suspicion, dissembling, flattery, or ulterior motives never clouded the heaven of his soul. If you said something to him, he would receive it as you said it, without adding or detracting anything, without suspecting or judging. Because there was no evil in him, he suspected none in others.

Simplicity gave beauty to his soul, since beauty in its highest manifestation goes together with simplicity. God, Whose beauty is indescribable, is preeminently "simple and uncompounded." He made all the fathers love him exceedingly. He behaved with them "simply, without hypocrisy, without duplicity or guile" (*Ladder*, Step 24), and he captured their souls.

However, the beauty of his soul came also from the virtue of "all-pure chastity," which deserves special notice here.

The Scriptures characterize a man who is consecrated to God and adorned with virginal purity as a "lily amidst thorns." This is because a lily is distinguished "by its purity, fragrance, sweetness and cheerfulness" as St. Methodius of Olympus explains. Purity is a spring flower in whose flower-cup incorruptibility blossoms. (*Banquet of the Ten Virgins*, 7:1 *)

---

*Hieromartyr Methodius, Bishop of Olympus of Lykia, was an eminent

IGNATIUS THE CONFESSOR

Fr. Ignatius was distinguished by the moral purity of his life, by the "purity, fragrance, sweetness, and cheerfulness" of his chastity. From young childhood he kept the candle unextinguished, the flower-cup white, the robe of purity unspotted. Untouched and white as snow on untrodden mountain-tops, he was worthy to wear the divinely-woven robe of the priesthood. His chastity gave him the priesthood, and his priesthood sanctified his chastity. On the day of his ordination the grace of the Holy Spirit was poured out on him abundantly, and it adorned his body with permanent and inalienable moral purity.

Let us be more explicit. Between the day of his ordination and his repose passed seventy years. In all this time he was untroubled by any carnal temptations. No dissonant note disturbed the melodic song of chastity. Even during sleep there was not the slightest disorder in his body, not the least carnal movement. The presence of the Holy Spirit accomplished this life-giving deadening of the flesh, and safeguarded the gift of "all-pure chastity." This enviable and admirable condition is due to grace. The great Orthodox Saint of the North, Seraphim of Sarov, named it holiness of the body.

Holiness of the body is followed by the gift of fragrance. Several times a sweet smell was noticed coming from the holy confessor. Elder Arsenius, co-ascetic of blessed Elder Joseph the Cave-dweller, reported the following to us:

"When we were young monks, we went with Fr. Joseph to Fr. Ignatius for spiritual conversation. He always gave us wise fatherly counsels. Among other things, I remember that he said to us: 'He who labors in his youth will have food in his old age. Now when you are young, you must pray, fast, perform ascetic labor, make prostra-

---

theologian, writer, and teacher of the early Church. His wonderful text, *The Banquet of the Ten Virgins*, extols the beauty of virginity. Ten virgins dine in a garden, in the shade of a willow, and extol in song successively the "beautifully shining star" of chastity. To lovers of the virginal life we warmly recommend this brilliant work. They will find it in the 18th volume of the Library of Greek Fathers (in Greek), published by "Apostoliki Diakonia."

Elder Arsenius, co-ascetic of Elder Joseph the Cave-Dweller, at the age of ninety-seven.

tions, so that you will have something to eat when you grow old.' His counsels were valuable to us. And something wonderful: Together with his words there came from his mouth a beautiful fragrance. When he talked, his mouth gave forth a sweet smell!"

This important information agrees with the testimonies of other aged monks who lived during the time of the holy confessor. Elder Chrysanthus from the Skete of St. Anne related to us:

"He was my confessor, and I visited him very regularly. Not only his words, but even his clothes and sweat spread fragrance."

At the end of his life, we will see that his bones also gave off fragrance. These are the fruits of chastity. The All-Holy Spirit gives

Athonite reflections.
Background: the Holy Mountain and Stavronikita Monastery. Photograph taken from Pantocrator Monastery, on the eastern side of the peninsula.

an abundance of gifts to the pure, because He is exceedingly pleased with them. "Just as incense delights the sense, even so the Holy Spirit delights in purity" (Ephraim the Syrian).

This should also be noted here: The greater the holiness of the body, the greater the gift of fragrance. To this exalted level of virginity belong also the bodies of the myrrh-gushing Saints. Myrrh-gushing presupposes shining chastity. Because of this, St. Gregory Palamas in his homily of praise calls St. Demetrius the Myrrh-gusher "virgin and all-chaste."

Blessed Fr. Ignatius, with your sweet-smelling chastity, O flowering lily of Athos, pray together with the myrrh-gushing Saints that even in our age, so difficult, troubled, and unclean, the sweet-smelling flowers of modesty, temperance, and purity may blossom forth. May his presence in our contemporary stench be an ornament aromatic with the myrrh of the Spirit, *clothed in fine linen, clean and white* (Apoc. 19:14) .

2. CLAIRVOYANCE

The mind of Fr. Ignatius shone with clarity. His ideas, thoughts, and observations were crystal-clear and fully enlightened. During serious discussions, confession, the revelation of thoughts, and so on, his words would astonish you. You would think that you were speaking with a prophet. We will be more explicit, relating several incidents of his clairvoyance.

* * * * * * * *

A certain elder from a Kalyve near Xenophontos Monastery took his disciple and set out for Katounakia, so that they could go to confession to Fr. Ignatius. The time came for the prayer of absolution. The confessor knew the elder, but not the disciple. Yet instead of asking him his name, he mentioned it on his own.

"Did you see what happened, Elder?" exclaimed the disciple as they were returning. "We hadn't told him my name, yet he knew it by himself. He must be a holy man; he must speak with God. God must tell him everything."

"He has the gift of clairvoyance, my child. God is ready to adorn us with extraordinary gifts when we love Him and keep His commandments."

* * * * * * * *

Two monastic aspirants from Athens came to a certain community in Katounakia. In a discussion about them, Fr. Ignatius told the elder of the community:

"You should not keep those two, Fr. Neophytus. They are not suited for monastic life, and will not make progress."

The elder did not pay due attention to Fr. Ignatius' words. He kept the two men and tonsured them monks, but later he repented bitterly. Every now and then they would cause commotions in the brotherhood. Finally they cast off the monastic schema and returned to the world. Sorrowfully, Elder Neophytus said to himself: "Fr. Ignatius knew what he was saying when he told me not to accept them."

* * * * * * * *

A monk from a neighboring Skete visited the confessor often, finding consolation in his admonitions. One day, however, Fr. Ignatius' words made him uneasy. From that time he began to feel anxiety, just as the Holy Virgin felt when the aged Symeon foretold the sword that would pierce her heart. What did the confessor tell him?

"For twenty-eight years you will live your monastic life peacefully. But after that, so many temptations will come to you that you will have to arm yourself with the patience of Job. To receive a crown, however, you must practice patience."

As was natural, the monk began to inquire about the future trials. He could not doubt the confessor's authority, because he knew that his words never missed the mark.

After twenty-eight years the prophecy began to be fulfilled. The hardships, suffering, and economic blind alleys caused by the sickness of his disciple sufficed to fulfill it. He had tuberculosis, which at that time could not be controlled. *Many are the afflictions of the righteous.* All of this Fr. Ignatius had foreseen, because the One Who allots afflictions, gives patience, and distributes crowns, had revealed it to him.

* * * * * * * *

As he often had before, the twenty-four-year-old Fr. Chrysanthus of St. Anne's Skete was walking along the narrow little path leading to the secluded Kalyve of Fr. Ignatius. Every time he would go to him, he would be weary from the fierce war that the enemy was waging against him at that time. And every time he left, his soul, consoled and strengthened by the man of God, was like a sea over-flowing with peace.

He walked on. "My spiritual father," he thought, "is a true man of God. One would think that the Holy Spirit speaks through his mouth." It was noon, exactly midday—not a time given to fear or suspicion. And then suddenly—a frightful noise, hissing, a terrible sight! He saw a hideous dragon, ready to rend him to pieces.

At this unexpected attack, the mystical prayer ever present in his heart greatly intensified. And at that moment the demonic vision, the "noon-day devil" that the Psalmist mentions, vanished.

However brave one might be, such an attack strains and agitates the soul. Shaken and praying, he came to Fr. Ignatius.

"Bless me, holy Father. Pray for me."

The confessor, as if he had been told everything in detail, said to him with fatherly love:

"Eh, my little Chrysanthus,"—so he used to call him in his great love—"do not lose heart, do not fear *them that kill the body, but have no power to kill the soul.*"

At these words Fr. Chrysanthus was astonished. The blind elder (this happened in 1922, when he had already lost his sight) had seen everything! The eyes of his soul were as keen as a prophet's. He knew what had happened before you told him, for the Holy Spirit Who delighted to dwell in his heart told him everything he needed to know.*

3. LIKE THE FACE OF AN ANGEL

St. Gregory Palamas, the hierophant of Orthodox mysticism, speaking "about light, and divine illumination, and holy felicity..." writes among other things:

---

*See Appendix 2 for another account of Elder Ignatius' clairvoyance.

… But even the body enjoys after some manner the actions of Grace that take place in the mind…. Even the body feels somewhat the indescribable mystery that is performed in the soul…. Thus the face of Moses shone. The inward brightness of the mind was poured out even to the body, and it shone so much that those who saw it with their bodily eyes could not endure that exceeding brightness. In the same way, the face of Stephen appeared "like the face of an angel," for inwardly the mind in an angelic manner comes to a mystical union with the otherworldly light and becomes angel-like (*In Defense of the Holy Hesychasts* 1:3:31).

Fr. Ignatius also belonged to the rank of those holy men who ascend like Moses to the "darkness above light" and are bathed by the brilliance of God. The uncreated light illuminated not only his inner man, but also his physical body, making his face shine "like the face of an angel."

We are indebted to the kindness of Hieromonk P. (he asked us not to reveal his name) for relating to us a wonderful incident from the life of the holy confessor. We met this hieromonk recently. Although elderly—over seventy years of age—his memory is fresh, and he remembers events from his early monastic life with remarkable precision.

"It was the day of St. Constantine," he began, "May 21, 1916. In Little St. Anne's Skete, Fr. Theodosius was serving a pannikhida for his elder, Fr. Stephen. All the hieromonks of the area were gathered in his Kalyve to concelebrate with him and pray together for the blessed one. At that time, I, a seventeen-year-old boy, had not yet been tonsured a monk. I was beardless, and I followed the Divine Liturgy from my *kavia*, through the cracks in the wall."

"Elder," we interrupted him, "what does the word *kavia* mean?"

"A *kavia* is a small cell. The older monks stretched a thick rope in the middle of the cell, and leaning on that they kept vigil, praying. In nautical language a thick rope is called a hawser [in Greek *kavos*], and therefore the cell was called a *kavia*.

"From my kavia, then, adjoining the small church, I enjoyed the compunctionate Liturgy celebrated by the hermit hieromonks. The Cherubic Hymn began, and Fr. Ignatius came out to cense. And what did I see! O Lord God, what a wonder I saw! A shining figure appeared to my eyes. His face was transfigured, illuminated, glorious with divine grace, shining like the face of an angel!"

"Did the other hieromonks who were serving look similar?"

"No, only Fr. Ignatius."

"And what did you feel, Elder, at this remarkable sight?"

"I felt within me great joy, exceptional delight. I had never before seen such a bright and glorious countenance."

Hearing Fr. P. tell us of this wonderful event, our faith was strengthened that Fr. Ignatius was indeed a living temple of holy light.

* * * * * * * *

Earlier we related how Fr. Ignatius helped Archimandrite Gabriel of Dionysiou on the eve of his tonsure, but we did not finish the story. Now is the proper time to do so.

We read how the novice compunctionately sang the Akathist to St. John Chrysostom. Finishing the Akathist to that luminary, the great Church Father, he devoutly made a prostration to his holy icon. Afterwards he turned to the elder to take his blessing. But what did he see? He was shaken, terrified, by the extraordinary brightness; he trembled before the glory of the Transfiguration. The face of Fr. Ignatius was illumined by the light of Tabor, shining like the face of a heavenly angel. Immediately he fell at his feet, at the feet of this earthly angel, and beseeched him with a trembling voice:

"Bless me, Father, bless me."

Laying his holy right hand on his head, he sealed it with the sign of the Cross, exclaiming:

"Blessed be Thy name, O Master of all!"

* * * * * * * *

We have related only two incidents of Fr. Ignatius' divine illumination. Who knows how many other times the face of the holy confessor shone with otherworldly glory? How many times, enclosed in his hermit cell, was he bathed by the waves of immaterial and uncreated light?

But who can see and describe these holy events? What eye can traverse "the darkness of hidden mystical silence" (Dionysius the Areopagite) and see the light-bearing lustre of Grace? The pearl is hidden in its shell, and the shell is sunk in the ocean. It pertains to *the life hidden in Christ,* according to the expression of Apostle Paul, the father of Christian mysticism. We receive the image of Fr. Ignatius as a ship continually sailing across the illuminated sea of immaterial light, its white sails fanned by the light-laden breezes of the Holy Spirit.

In the two incidents related above, we can see only partial gleams of the inward glory and brightness of this holy man, whose face appeared "like the face of an angel."

4. DURING DIVINE LITURGY

As a rule, silence reinforces the spiritual life. The greater the silence and seclusion, the more easily the soul is united with God. Rules, however, have exceptions, for *the Spirit bloweth where He listeth* (John 3:8). St. John of Kronstadt, a bright meteor of holiness in the Orthodoxy of the North, is a prominent example of an exception. In spite of his innumerable pastoral duties, he experienced so intensely within himself the presence of God that he surpassed even the most strict and secluded hermits.

This can be seen also in the life of Fr. Ignatius. He had many distractions: continual priestly duties, extensive work as a confessor, gatherings for worship in his Kalyve, etc. Despite all this, his spiritual level was so high that even the most isolated hesychasts of the Holy

Mountain wondered at him. The grace of the Holy Spirit replaced silence; "it made up the deficiency." The uprightness of his heart, his holy simplicity, his virginal purity, and his great love drew down abundant grace.

Nevertheless, he did not cease climbing to the heights, performing "ascents in his heart." The Apostolic admonitions *continue in prayer* (Col. 4:2) and *pray without ceasing* (I Thes. 5:17) set fire to his soul. His perseverance in prayer was marvelous. In his cell he had the standard type of bed. Instead of lying on it, he would support himself with ropes hanging from the clothing-hooks in his closet, in order to ward off sleep. Thus the closet became a holy place, where his soul found its Lord.

Another such holy place was a low chair. Sitting on this in the quiet hours of the night, he surrendered himself to intense self-concentration. By divine grace he brought down his mind to his heart, pronounced ceaselessly the name of the Lord, and obtained thus the unutterable blessings of mental prayer, culminating in visitations of the immaterial and otherworldly Light.

A place both holy and fearful, truly a *Beth-el* (Gen. 28:10-19), where like the Patriarch Jacob he encountered the unattainable and indescribable greatness of God, was the church during Divine Liturgy. In the innumerable Liturgies that he performed over the course of fifty-six years, he experienced inexpressible spiritual states, walking *on the wings of the* (liturgical) *winds* (Psalm 103:3). When he read the Gospel during Liturgy he brought all the churchgoers to compunction; indeed, it was more of a divine service than a reading. So intensely did he live through the events of the Gospel passage that he always burst into tears. When the reading told of the Passion of the Lord, it was only with divine help that he could finish it.

If this happened at the reading of the Gospel, what shall we say about the Cherubic Hymn? We saw a dim picture of his liturgical exaltation at this time in the preceding chapter, when we read how his face shone with angelic glory. And what of the fearful hour of the Sacrifice? He wept at the words of Christ—what would he feel at the torment of Golgotha, at the unbearable humiliation, grief, and suffering of the "Son of Man"?

However, he who experiences the suffering of Golgotha when performing the bloodless Sacrifice, will also taste the unutterable glory of the Resurrection. All the mystery of Christianity—a mystery of infinite humility and grief, and infinite exultation and glory—surrounds the Divine Liturgy. The celebrant who experiences these states trembles with the most powerful spiritual feelings.

When Fr. Ignatius liturgized, the atmosphere of the church was charged with these feelings. A hieromonk that we know who had seen him serve said to us:

"Fr. Ignatius served wonderfully, beautifully, with solemnity and magnificence. He had a beautiful voice, and all his movements were reverent. When he liturgized, spirituality emanated from him. No one could compare with him as a celebrant. No one was like him."

This simple phrase: "When he liturgized, spirituality emanated from him," if we carefully analyze it, tells us a great deal about his priestly virtues.

During feast-day Liturgies or other celebrations when many priests took part, such as the Unction Service, Fr. Ignatius, who being the eldest had the precedence, stood out. One could perceive in him a certain mystical priestly grace not seen in the other priests.

Even his physical appearance gave a special tone to his serving. He was of medium height, broadly built, ruddy, with a pure white beard, a round childlike face, and profuse eyebrows that slightly concealed his bright blue eyes. His voice, pure and beautiful, beautified and gave life to the higher meanings of the liturgical texts.

But the true reason for the splendor of his serving was his love for Christ. This made him tremble and dissolve into sobs from the time of the Gospel until the end of the Divine Liturgy. He loved Christ, because Christ first loved him. *We love Him, because He first loved us* (I John 4:19). This explains also that beloved expression of his that he addressed so often to his spiritual children: "My child, love Him Who has loved you."

5. TOWARDS THE LIGHT

One of the most beloved Gospel readings of Fr. Ignatius was the 14th Sunday of Luke (18:35-43). The intense yearning of the blind man of Jericho for the light, his imploring cries, "Jesus, son of David, have mercy on me," and "Lord, that I may receive my sight," always moved and inspired him. For the monk who cultivates mental prayer, a more beloved Gospel passage does not exist.

When Fr. Ignatius had passed his eighty-fifth year, he learned to know this aspect of blindness more intimately. His eyes were obscured by cataracts, and in the course of time he completely lost his sight.

Deprived of physical light, he did not cease distributing the immaterial light and illuminating the wayfarers who walked towards the city of never-fading light. The Lord gave him several more years of life, and the sheep of the Holy Mountain fold continued to have in him a "place of green pasture" and "water of rest."

Whoever sought an experienced father confessor was sent to Katounakia, to Fr. Ignatius the Blind, as he was called. They found in him an irreplaceable shepherd, an excellent physician, an unfailing guide, a bank with inestimable spiritual capital. They found a venerable little elder, blind, weakened and bent by years, who to the attentive would offer peace, consolation, and wise instruction. Until the end he kept his vigorous mental powers, and did not at all slacken in his work of guiding souls.

Usually he spent his time in his cell. It was difficult for him to go down to the church, and he went there only when there were Divine Liturgies. When occasionally he walked a little around the Kalyve, his loving and reverent disciples would watch him and remove the stones from his path so that he would not stumble.

Like all elderly people, he was troubled by bad health. He suffered from rheumatism, and many nights he would continually stroke his feet because of the pain. However, he endured this condition silently and uncomplainingly, never asking for medicine or special attention.

His spiritual height was also manifest in the matter of food. Whatever was brought to his cell he ate. If they were ever late, or even forgot him altogether, he said nothing. His mind was captive in the heavens, and did not worry about earthly things.

His greatest concern was the journey to eternity. He passed ninety years, ninety-five, and reached a hundred. One hundred years of earthly life, twenty in the world and eighty on Athos, were sufficient. The ship that had traversed the earthly seas for a whole century finally came to anchor in the heavenly harbor.

October of 1927 was the month of departure. Apparently the venerable elder had a presentiment of his end, and for fifteen days he gave himself up to a complete fast. He wanted to be as light as possible for his great journey.

On the twenty-fifth of October, a little while after the rising of the sun, a Russian hermit from Karoulia, Fr. Bartholomew, was vouchsafed to see how the saints die. He climbed up to the Kalyve of the Dormition, and was directed to the elder's cell.

"Good day, Grandfather. Bless me."

"Who are you?"

"I am Deacon Bartholomew."

"How are you, my child?"

"I am well, Grandfather."

"You are well. I am waiting for someone to come."

Whom was the grandfather awaiting? Whom other than the angel who would receive his soul? And the heavenly minister arrived, took the soul of the blind father confessor, and led it to the light of Heaven, "to a place of light and green pasture." The grandfather, as they characteristically tell us, "died like a little bird." Fr. Bartholomew never again saw such a peaceful death.

On the next day, St. Demetrius' feast day, under the grace of the Myrrh-gushing Saint, there was a public funeral. Never was such grief seen among the dwellers of the Holy Mountain as on that day. Fr. Gerasim of Little St. Anne's, the hymnographer, spoke to us much about the sorrow and unfillable void created by the repose of the elect father confessor.

After some years, his venerable relics were disinterred. All the fathers leapt from spiritual joy, because a wonderful fragrance poured from the bones of the blessed elder. In this way God confirmed and sealed the man's holiness.

* * * * * * * *

Ten years later I was on the Holy Mountain and was vouchsafed to meet Fr. Ignatius' disciples. The grace-filled figure of Fr. Ignatius, his second disciple, spoke to me vividly about the holiness of the elder. The excellence of the tree was revealed by its fruit.

I was not in time, however, to catch the unforgettable father confessor himself. But by his holy prayers may we see him in Heaven, liturgizing with divinely-woven priestly vestments in the "holy and heavenly and noetic sanctuary of God." Amen.

VIII

ELDER CODRATUS OF KARAKALLOU

Fr. Codratus was a true fisherman. With incomparable skill he managed to catch souls. For a net he had compunction. For a fishing pole the light of God. For bait he had love.
—Hieromonk Athanasius of Iveron

ABBOT CODRATUS OF KARAKALLOU

Author's Prologue to the Greek Edition

The present volume of *Contemporary Ascetics of Mount Athos* is dedicated to the dynamic personality of Hieromonk Codratus (1859-1940), who shone as Abbot of the Holy Monastery of Karakallou and as a confessor and spiritual director of many souls.

His many natural gifts, brilliant spirit, ascetic perseverance—his entire spiritual make-up—set him apart as a model spiritual leader. His skill in both administering the Monastery and shepherding souls, a rare combination, was the strongest characteristic of his personality. The twenty-six years of his abbacy (1914-1940), were a time of spiritual height for the Coenobium of Karakallou, despite the fact that tares hindering his good work were not lacking.

By his spiritual greatness Fr. Codratus gained recognition everywhere and created unforgettable impressions. In Kavsokalyvia there lived a unique character, an old sailor, Charalampus from Kastellorizo. He spent the last days of his life there. Photius Kontoglou, who was at that time studying the iconography of the catholicon of Kavsokalyvia, knew him and characterized him as "a genius of the sea, who lived on the steamships and who we know travelled the Yellow River of China." This sea-wolf was so impressed by the person of Fr. Codratus that he used to repeat: "Anyone who comes to the Holy Mountain and doesn't climb Athos or meet Fr. Codratus hasn't seen anything"—a phrase which became proverbial.

This is the great Athonite figure we will present to the reader. We must confess that the biographical elements we have gathered do not do justice to his spiritual greatness. Perhaps this can be remedied in a second edition. We owe warm thanks to Fr. James, a disciple of Fr. Codratus; to the Iveron Confessor Fr. Maximus; to Elder Eudocimus of Philotheou; to Archimandrite Andrew of St. Paul's; to the old monks of Karakallou whom we visited in the Monastery infirmary; and to all others who helped us in compiling this present volume. All these people spoke to us enthusiastically about the value of the man whose life we are describing, and about the flowering of Karakallou Monastery in his day.

By his prayers may this holy Coenobium recover its old prosperity, to the glory of God and the sanctification of souls.

Archimandrite Cherubim
Oropos, Attica
July 22, 1975

I

At the Place of Sanctification and Asceticism

1. THE HOLY MONASTERY OF KARAKALLOU

The Holy Monastery of Karakallou is one of the great Athonite monasteries, eleventh in the hierarchic rank, possessing a noteworthy history. It is located on the northeastern side of the Athonite peninsula, on a wooded, picturesque hillside overlooking the vast Aegean Sea, whose shore lies about a half-hours' journey away. A little above it rises the Monastery of St. Philotheus, and to the southeast, at a distance of four hours, the Great Lavra.

Examining the surroundings from the Karakallou guesthouse, the visitor will not fail to be impressed. "To the east extends the motionless Aegean, a vast peaceful sea, in which the depths are merged with the heavens. To the west wild ravines open up, descending from the heights of Athos and bringing us the song of the north in unceasing varied murmurings. The semantrons call us to the Liturgy at the first smile of dawn, when the light spreads over the rippling waters of the sea...." (N. Louvaris, *Athos, the Gate of Heaven*, pg. 49) These are the impressions brought away by anyone who finds himself at Karakallou Monastery on a summer morning.

The first pages of the Monastery's history are lost in the darkness of legend. The opinion that it was connected with the Roman emperor Aurelius Antoninus Caracalla (3rd century) is not accepted by modern historians. What is certain—as witnessed by the chrysobull of the Byzantine emperor Romanus IV Diogenes (1068-1071)—is that the Monastery existed before the 11th century.

Like all the other Athonite Monasteries, it has experienced many historical vicissitudes. With the fall of Byzantium it suffered a severe decline and was almost destroyed. Owing, however, to the concern of the Prince of Moldavia, John Peter Rareş (1527-1546), and his daughter Roxandra, the wife of a prince of Moldovlachia, it was restored and enriched.

Sts. Peter and Paul

Between the Monastery and the sea is a tall, majestic tower which was built in the 16th century with money from the ruler of Moldavia, Prince Rareş.

The life and development of the Monastery takes place under the supervision and protection of the leaders of the Apostles, Peter and Paul. The central church—the Catholicon—is dedicated to them, and on the day of their feast, June 29, there is a great celebration. Often words from the hymns to these two patron Saints come spontaneously from the lips of the Karakallou monks: "*What hymns of virtue shall we sing to Peter and Paul, who with wings of the wisdom of God....*"

The whole church is frescoed with wonderful 18th-century masterpieces of iconography. Highly valued is an icon which depicts in an austere Byzantine style the Apostles Peter and Paul embracing (a work of Constantine Palaiokapas). Also exceptional is the icon of the Twelve Apostles, a work of the renowned iconographer Hieromonk Dionysius of Fourna Agrafon.

Top: Karakallou Monastery, with the peak of Athos in the background.

Bottom: The Prince of Moldavia, Peter Rareş, with his wife Helen and his son, shown here presenting to Christ the monastery of Moldoviţa, which he founded.

In difficult situations and necessities the monks resort to the icon of the Mother of God *The Quickhearer,* which bears wonder-working grace. "No one fleeing to Her departs ashamed...."

The Beautiful Gate of the Catholicon—"created in 1562 by Theophanes"—is considered a work of particular artistic value.

In the Monastery library, besides the newer books, one finds also old codexes, both of paper and parchment, remarkable for both their quantity and their value.

Of the saints' relics, "more honorable than precious stones and more excellent than gold," which are preserved here, worthy of note is the skull of the Apostle Bartholomew, the skull of St. Christopher, portions of Great-Martyr Mercurius, etc. Special honor is given to the relics of the new Monk-martyr Gideon, who was a special nursling of the Monastery. A piece of the Honorable Cross is kept here in a silver chest. The helmet and sword of the Great-Martyr Mercurius are also preserved here.

In such an atmosphere, in the vivid presence of so many saints and holy figures, icons, relics, remembrances ... how can the life of holiness fail to develop?

But the grounds outside the Monastery are likewise suited to uplifting souls. The area between Lavra, Karakallou and Philotheou has always shown hospitality to holy souls, who in poor desert kalyves in the dense forest cultivate noetic prayer. In this place solitude assists prayer, and silence aids sobriety.

A certain devout priest from Larissa, who came as a pilgrim to the Holy Mountain in 1950, was astonished to see in this holy place outside the Monastery of Karakallou a monk who was praying in the air, a meter above the ground. (Archimandrite Chrysostom Moustaka, *The Holy Mountain of Athos*, Athens, 1957, pg. 40)

Among the elect Karakallou monks of later times are mentioned Paisius and Galaction. The first was renowned for his self-sacrificing love in the infirmary, and the second for his heroic asceticism. Here also lived Elder Andrew in continual compunction. His tears, which he acquired after a certain illness, accompanied him

Karakallou's relics being displayed for veneration by the sacristan.

constantly and sweetened his heart like a fountain of delight. He always held in his hand a handkerchief which day and night was soaked with the ever-flowing tears of his compunction.

In this exceptional environment—natural, architectural, and spiritual—lived the great athlete of the spirit whose life we are about to describe: the Abbot of the Holy Monastery of Karakallou, Fr. Codratus.

2. HIS ORIGIN AND MONASTIC CALLING

Fr. Codratus came from Vrioula of Asia Minor. This small town seems especially to have cultivated Christian, God-fearing families, for many fathers on the Holy Mountain have come from there.

As a layman he was named Cyriacus Vamvakas. His father was a timber merchant and consequently did much business with the captains who ferried wood to Asia Minor from the Holy Mountain. Little Cyriacus heard many tales and descriptions of the Garden of the Panagia, and his longing took wings. He too wanted to venerate that holy place, unique in the world, and to be made worthy to become a soldier of Christ and enlisted in His spiritual army. From a young age he was very strict and attentive to his life. It appears that his development was brilliant; the course of his life looked bright.

When he came to the mountain he was twenty years old, in the flower of youth. In every age, youths have their quests. They view the meaning of life, human existence, the future, and the struggles and vicissitudes of the world with different eyes. The young soul is easily enticed by the empty illusions of the world, but it also easily makes heroic decisions when it knows Christ. No other love on earth can exceed in depth and joy the divine love of a youthful soul for Jesus. It seems that some of these rays of divine love enlightened Cyriacus; a certain sweet arrow of divine love wounded his heart, exhausted by temptations, and he ran *like a deer thirsting for springs of water...*.

"When they learned at home that I had definitely gone to the Mountain, they lamented," Fr. Codratus later related. "My mother especially lamented. My father, however, was a more calm and even a more spiritual man."

"Why are you crying, my dear?" he said to her. "Has the boy gone to become a robber? No. Has he gone to become a murderer? No. Has he gone to become a scoundrel? No. Has he gone to become a thief? No. Has he gone to dissipate himself in low resorts and taverns? No. He has gone to become a monk, to give his youth to Christ and not to satan. You should rejoice, not weep!"

These words consoled her. They made her think more soberly, more wisely, in a more Christian manner, and to glorify the Lord that from now on she would have as one of her offspring a monk, a mediator for her salvation in this world and for her eternal glory in the other.

3. *BEHOLD HOW GOOD IT IS FOR BRETHREN TO DWELL TOGETHER*

We do not know what drew Fr. Codratus to the Coenobium of Karakallou after he had lived for a few years in New Skete.

At that time the Holy Monastery of Karakallou numbered more than sixty monks. "We have a small Monastery here," the fathers told him when he first came there, "but it is a Coenobium."

"As soon as I heard it was a coenobium I was especially glad," he said later. "A coenobium is what I had sought, and a coenobium I found. They told me the principles of the Monastery. I listened carefully to everything; everything made an impression on me."

Do we not see the same thing even today? Youths who have a noble heart and know to search for evangelical truth and the pure and unadulterated monastic life thirst for a coenobium. They detest the idiorrhythmic system, which brings a myriad of evils to the monastic life. The young monks who flock today to the coenobiums are a witness against the idiorrhythmic system.

Behold how good and how delightful it is for brethren to dwell together in unity. This is the hymn of the coenobium, which had also become the hymn of the young novice monk. His heart sang it with warm enthusiasm, because it embraced the coenobium "with a flame as great as Athos." Not only a common trapeza, a common treasury, common food, common typicon, but also one mind, one will, one sorrow, one joy, one life. Everything one in Christ.

From the first moment that Fr. Codratus entered the Monastery, he gave himself up wholly to the Abbot and the brethren. He labored in obedience tirelessly and creatively. All his obediences he fulfilled with orderliness and with a disposition to serve and contribute to the progress of his spiritual family.

For several years he served as steward at the Monastery Metochion at Cassandra. It is reported that his strictness and temperance did not diminish in the least while he was there. Sometimes Turkish visitors came to the Metochion. To them he would serve meat, but he would throw the leftovers away. At the Coenobium they ate no meat, and he wanted both himself and the other monks of the Metochion to keep the rule of the Coenobium.

For a long time he was also the cellarer of Karakallou, and he travelled regularly to Constantinople to buy wheat for the Monastery. It was after this obedience that he was later made Abbot.

He became Abbot in the year 1914. He was ordained by the Most Reverend Nilus, who had also been Fr. Codratus' teacher in Asia Minor. At his ordination His Reverence particularly praised him: "He was my student in school. I know his abilities and gifts well from the time he was still a child."

With his election to the abbacy, the lamp of virtue was placed *on a lampstand* and his light shone so that all *saw his good works and glorified the Father in heaven.*

4. "ALL FOR THE GLORY OF GOD"

The Lord distributes gifts to men. Every man has received from the hands of God special aptitudes. Nevertheless, some have not yet discovered His benefactions to them, and others are indifferent and do not cultivate His gifts at all.

The closer a soul comes to the Lord, the more it exercises its powers; as it comes ever nearer to Him, its gifts are developed and bear fruit.

Fr. Codratus, both as a simple monk and later as Abbot, dedicated everything to the service of God. "...All for the glory of God...." Certainly he was endowed by God with many natural and spiritual gifts.

As he was born and grew up in Asia Minor, he knew the Turkish language perfectly. He had studied the psychology, mentality, and character of its people. Thus, with the help of God, he managed to maneuver and in a marvelous way save Christians from certain death and other great punishments and condemnations. Because of this, the *kaimakamides** revered and esteemed him exceedingly. They marvelled at him and often called him "Afendi Codratus."

When the English and French came to the Holy Mountain, they exploited it heavily. Fr. Codratus' ingenuity, however, saved the Monastery from the plunder of its timber and possessions. Namely, on the day that the French officer climbed up to the Holy Monastery of Karakallou, he gave him a brilliant reception. He ordered all the monks to go outside and welcome him, to ring all the bells, to sing "Many Years" to the French officer in church, to set the trapeza, etc. The officer was enraptured by all this, and he gave the command to cut down the forests of other Monasteries, but to not trouble Karakallou at all.

Fr. Codratus knew how to wisely and correctly handle the serious concerns which occupied the Monastery, as well as the spiritual affairs of the brethren and the details of coenobitic life. He had placed his whole self and his talents of body and soul under the grace and illumination of God. Thus he had become a grace-bearing man with enlightened and pure thoughts.

---

*The *kaimakamides* were deputies or assistants of the civil or military commanders of the Turkish Empire.

5. A MODEL OF INDUSTRY

A characteristic of Athonite life is the labor at handiwork and self-sacrifice in obedience which every monk undertakes. Many ignorant men accuse monks of idleness and laziness. What a great falsehood and deception! Those who want to find out the truth should make a trip to the Holy Mountain. There they will see the monks continually engaged in work, in all kinds of handiwork and labor. Their main handiworks are icon-painting, wood-carving, sewing and knitting. They must often work uninterruptedly for many hours. One should also realize that their time is limited by long services and vigils in church. And besides this they have other routine chores: cooking, washing dishes, cleaning, gardening, hospitality to guests, transporting supplies to their Monastery or Kalyve, picking olives, etc.

When the wheat came to the harbor of the Monastery—thousands of pounds for the whole year—there would be the so-called "common labor." All together the fathers would go down to the harbor to transport it to the Monastery storehouse. First of all ran the Abbot, Fr. Codratus, eagerly descending the path with a sack hanging from his shoulder. He carried the sack with wheat on his back and worked together with the other brothers as a simple monk. If you didn't know him, you wouldn't know that he was the Abbot of Karakallou.

He set an example in common labors by carrying not only wheat, but also all the supplies and necessary materials which reached the harbor by boat.

Fr. Codratus was a typical working Athonite monk—willing, cheerful, perpetually moving, untiring, lively. Indeed! What impresses one on the Holy Mountain is how all work, even when hard and toilsome, is performed with eagerness and enthusiasm, not coercion and gloominess. Helping this is the realization that all handiwork and all obediences serve the glory of God and constitute prayer.

St. Basil the Great does not fail to emphasize the value of work for a monk. In the Long Rules, he notes among other things:

And as for the evil of idleness, of what use is it to speak of it, when the Apostle has clearly commanded that he who does not work should not eat? As each one has need of daily food, so also he has need of work according to his strength. For not in vain did Solomon write in approval: *The idle man ate no bread.* And again, the Apostle wrote of himself that he ate no one's bread for free, but that he worked with labor and toil night and day, even though, being a preacher of the Gospel, he had the right to live by the Gospel.

A monk on Mt. Athos hauling firewood.

* * * * * * * *

There was a certain renowned confessor in the Skete of Koutloumousiou to whom many fathers of the Holy Mountain came for confession or to receive counsel. Once there came to him an elder who had in his kalyve a disciple overcome by despondency. Dullness and melancholy often seized him, ate at him like a worm, and would frequently give place to despair. The danger was great, for if the disciple did not find a way to escape from the tentacles of despondency, he might succumb to the temptation of running away.

Therefore the elder of the wounded disciple went to the enlightened confessor. "My Father," he said to him, "tell me what to do with my monk. He is being lost. His mind has become darkened; he feels no interest in anything. He is in a black cloud, and his thoughts go around dangerously. He has everything good in our kalyve. He is not overburdened with physical work—all he has to do is read the services."

The old confessor listened to him attentively, thought for a little, and then, in a natural and unforced manner, told him:

"Marry him off!"

The elder was thunderstruck. "What's wrong with the confessor?" he thought. "Has he gone mad?"

"I tell you to marry him off," he repeated firmly.

"But, Father, what do you mean?" said the elder, his voice trembling.

"Marry him to work! Throw him into work! Do you understand? A monk must have work for a wife, in order to escape despondency and many other temptations." When the elder applied this command and gave his disciple work every day, he understood how right the confessor had been. His despondency subsided, interest returned, and joy shone again in the kalyve. Labor spread its blessing.

Fr. Codratus knew this story well, and he narrated it where and when necessary. But more importantly, he had experience of the basic principles of monasticism, which from its first beginnings has emphasized the great importance of hard work, especially for the skete-dweller and coenobite.

One time the abbot of the Holy Monastery of St. Paul went to visit Fr. Codratus:

"Where is the elder?" he asked a certain monk.

"He is down in the 'docheio'." (The 'docheio' is the storehouse of the Monastery where the wine, cheese, fish, etc. are kept.)

On that day they had been salting sardines for the whole year in a special storehouse. And of course, in this work as in all, the elder set the first example of service.

"Elder, *you* are here?" the abbot asked him, going down to the storehouse.

"What can I do, my brother?" answered Fr. Codratus. "Don't you know that the fish rots from the head down?"

As he said this he continued to place the sardines neatly in order, and to throw the coarse salt on each layer with his hands. His words had meaning. He wanted to say that the abbot is obliged to be an example of industriousness and service, to be aware of the deep responsibility of his position and to teach his disciples by his living example. It is the head which directs everything in the Monastery. If the head departs from the right way, then everything in the Monastery will decline towards corruption and decay.

Fr. Codratus knew that work humbles, smooths, and sanctifies the body and soul. When it is united with prayer, it becomes a hymn of praise to Him who *worketh until now,* in truth a continuation of divine worship, in harmonious union with the silent hymnody which all of creation offers up to the Lord of Glory.

II

A Model Abbot

1. THE GOOD SHEPHERD

Few are the abbots of the Holy Mountain like unto Fr. Codratus. This man had the grace of pastorship. One could even say that he was born to be a spiritual leader. From the time that he took the direction of the Monastery into his hands, he governed the brethren in a perfect manner and raised the Monastery to a true Coenobium with a high spiritual life.

"A true shepherd shows love; for through love was the Shepherd crucified" (*The Ladder*).

"The good shepherd lays down his life for the sheep," says the Lord, the first shepherd and Chief Shepherd of the Church. And Fr. Codratus was indeed this good shepherd, possessing an awareness of his pastoral duty, pain of heart and love for his spiritual children, sacrifice and self-denial for his sheep. His own needs and desires were marginal. He spent only enough time and care on himself to preserve his own life. From morning to evening, day and night, all his labor, zeal and practical love were turned to his flock.

His sleep was scanty. He saw his ascetic cell for only a few hours, and during these he would receive his spiritual children unannounced at any time they wished to discuss spiritual matters with him, resolve their problems, or ask for direction.

Abbot Codratus (with the cross and staff) and some of the Fathers of Karakallou Monastery.

Fr. Codratus clearly heard the voice of that worthy spiritual father, St. Simeon the New Theologian: "Nights and days equally, expend yourself in the care of the souls entrusted to you, that not one of them be captured by the wild beast or devoured by the bear of lust or consumed by the dragon of wrath or torn asunder by the vulture of high-minded thoughts ... but that you might bring your flock, safe and plentiful in children, to the Chief Shepherd, Christ God."

The elder knew the multifarious struggles which a monk undergoes. He knew the temptations, demons, and passions which battle night and day to hurl down and confuse a soul. The good herdsman knew that at times the demons strive from envy to create fantasies, dreams, and images with the aim of seducing the weary athlete of the spirit when he gives a little rest in sleep to the much-toiling flesh. Furthermore, he knew perfectly the weakness of human nature and its inclinations and passions, with its various changes. He wanted not only to be called, but to be, a spiritual father: a support, instiller of life, guide, consolation, hope, courage, and enthusiasm for his disciples. Happy are the disciples who have such a father, such an elder. Even if something injures them, there stands by them a doctor, friend, and good Samaritan to raise up their souls and render account for them.

"It is better," says St. John of the Ladder, "to separate yourself from God than from your elder." Because in the first instance the elder will be the help, the joining link which will reconcile you again with the Lord. But if you separate yourself in soul from the elder, then who will unite you with God when you fall?

Therefore the union of Fr. Codratus with his disciples was intensely evangelical and fatherly. He did not hold the position of abbot only formally and on paper. For (we must confess the truth) on the Holy Mountain the abbot tends to resemble an appointed superior clerk, who undersigns resolutions and documents and holds the abbatical staff without a pastoral vocation, mission, or responsibility.

Alas! This signifies a misfortune for the institution of monasticism, a blow from within, a derailment from the holy course which the experience of the Fathers, guided by the Holy Spirit, delineated.

Indeed, it is curious that the Holy Mountain, which preserves the holy traditions, customs, and habits of the ancient fathers with such exactness, is not more careful about this fundamental and basic question of the pastoral position of the abbot in the monastery. Besides this, in certain monasteries there prevails the custom of the brothers confessing to an outside confessor and not to their abbot, who is supposed to be a father, doctor, guide, noetic Moses, trainer in athletic combats, responsible for their souls from morning to evening. We hope and pray that the Lord will send the monasteries elect abbots possessing a holy awareness of their essential mission, for the glory of His name and the salvation of souls.

Fr. Codratus did not become Abbot because he thirsted for glory and honor. He became Abbot to be a minister and servant of the brothers, following in this point Christ Himself. "I am come among you as a servant," he could also say to his disciples.

"For the twenty-six years I was Abbot, my child, I never slept outside the Monastery, by the grace of God," he said. Truly. One time only he went out to a high mountain in order to examine the forest and trees and came back down immediately.

* * * * * * * *

In the hours of rest after the noon trapeza, Fr. Codratus did not retire to his cell. As a rule, he used to sit on a bench, which is found in the inner courtyard, outside the chapel of St. Gideon. There, leaning on his staff, he prayed mentally. At other times he would put on his eyeglasses and read some patristic book.

Many times, likewise, he sat in a chair at the threshold of the wooden staircase which leads to the yard of the Monastery, with his head leaning on his staff.

"What are you doing here, Elder?" they asked him.

"Well, I'm sleeping, my child."

"You're sleeping on a chair?"

"Eh! The shepherd must keep watch, my child. Even when he rests, sleep catches him on his staff."

The strong consciousness of his position as Abbot and protector of his rational sheep caused, even in sleep, *his heart to wake.*

2. DIVINE WORSHIP: HIS LIFE

"Just as the angels stand hymning the Creator, so we also must stand in psalmody" (St. Ephraim the Syrian).

Fr. Codratus wanted the brethren's attitude, attention, and psalmody in the Catholicon of his Monastery to be angelic. He desired all the brothers without exception, aside from the seriously ill, to attend the Divine Services and participate in the worship of God. He himself was devoted, soul and body, to prayer. He had "his eyes and soul always elevated in order to attend to psalmody and reading and to the power of the chanted and read words of the Holy Scriptures, that he might not be passed over by reason of laziness, but that his soul, nourished by all these things, might come to compunction and humility and the divine illumination of the Holy Spirit."

On the Holy Mountain a bell is rung in some coenobia at about 11:00 p.m. to rouse the monks for the midnight service, and in others it is rung a little later. The fathers do their "rule," i.e. their prostrations and Jesus Prayer, in the cell and then come to the Catholicon of the Monastery, where the Matins service begins.

The time of the midnight service is the most sacred of the day. Amidst the infinite peace of the night the entire Holy Mountain prays "for the peace of the whole world and the salvation of our souls." From one end to the other, it becomes a huge censer which sends up to the Lord of Hosts "like fragrant incense" its unceasing prayer.

> Ponder how, in the deep of night, men, beasts, and creatures are all asleep. There is deep silence, and only you keep vigil and converse freely with the common Lord of all. But sleep is sweet? But isn't prayer sweeter? (St. John Chrysostom)

"Nothing is sweeter than prayer" was Fr. Codratus' saying also. Therefore he lost no time, he did not calculate the toil in regard to feeding his flock with the words of divine worship, "sweeter than honey and the honeycomb."

During the reading of the first kathisma of the Psalter in the daily Matins, there is the custom on the Holy Mountain for each abbot to go around to the stalls of the monks, one by one, holding a lit candle in his hand. His aim is to see that all are in their places. Fr. Codratus had no fixed time for this review of his spiritual army. He inspected when he thought fit, and usually much earlier than the reading of the Psalter.

"One time I was a little late in going to church," Fr. Cyriacus told us. "I came at about the middle of the Midnight Service. At the end of the service the elder caught me and rebuked me:

"Why were you late, Father? Don't do it again. You come to the church before the Midnight Service begins. Now say one prayer-rope under the polyeleos [the large central chandelier in the church], and next time you will get a bigger penance. Medicines are bitter, but they are men's salvation."

At the First Hour—after the end of Matins—the elder always inserted a reading from the Catechesis of St. Theodore the Studite, that great teacher of coenobitic life. He wanted to strengthen the daily struggles of his disciples by the springs of the Saint's patristic wisdom.

The regular reading of patristic texts offers priceless assistance to a struggling monk, of which the wise shepherd was not ignorant.

Often he toured the cells of his disciples, going slowly from door to door. If he heard conversation inside, he called: "Prayer ropes, Fathers, prayer!" and went away.

By two words he restored the monks to their regular course, whose chief work, he believed, was unceasing prayer. He agonized over the spiritual state of his children as if he saw daily before him the Heavenly Judge demanding an account of their souls.

"One time there was coolness between me and a brother," Fr. James related to us. "We were the two readers in the church. 'Go and be canonarch,' the elder told me.

"'Elder, it's not my turn,' I replied.

"Then, without saying anything, he left his abbatical stall, put on a mantia, and was canonarch himself. His humility and the way he was instructing me by his example made me ashamed. I was confounded. I quickly went up to him and made a prostration.

"'Bless, Elder, forgive me,' I said to him.

"'God forgive you, my child. But I made you a monk to serve the church and the choir, not to sit in your stall.'"

One day Fr. Basil came back from his obedience tired, and the following morning did not manage to get up for service. The elder, as soon as he perceived this, ran and knocked at the door of his cell, as he did in every similar instance.

"By the prayers of our holy fathers.... Fr. Basil, the fathers are below reading the service, and you're still sleeping?"

He only left the cell when he had assured himself that the brother had risen and was getting ready. Always he urged and counselled the brothers with words as wise as those of St. Ephraim the Syrian:

> O Monk, do you not see that you are injuring yourself? Say in your thoughts: if it were a question of a gift of gold or some material things, wouldn't we hasten to respond before all? And if for carnal things you have such strong earnestness, how much more (should you have) for spiritual things?

All of the surviving fathers remember the terrible earthquake of 1932 which destroyed Ierissus—the neighboring city of the Holy Mountain—and which was strongly felt on the Holy Mountain and upset everyone. In the Monastery of Karakallou, as on the whole Holy Mountain, they were holding a vigil in church. It was the eve of the feast of the Venerable Cross, and they were singing the stichera of Vespers when the earthquake shocked everyone. At that moment Fr.

Codratus commanded that the service be halted and that they seize their prayer-ropes and begin praying: "Lord Jesus Christ, have mercy on us," without anyone leaving the church.

After they had prayed for a sufficient time with their prayer-ropes, he ordered that they continue Vespers according to the rule.

His faith in prayer, and especially mental prayer, was deep and unshakable. He wanted the saving and all-powerful name of Jesus never to be absent from the mouth and heart of his disciples. "By the name of Jesus flog your enemies" and "let the name of Jesus be attached to your breath." This was his password.

3. PASTORAL ART

It was unthinkable to Fr. Codratus for a monk to be absent from trapeza, which on the Holy Mountain is a second church. He demanded strict observance of this rule from everyone, except of course from those who were sick and had to be nursed in the Monastery infirmary.

His ingenuity, combined with his pastoral skill, always found a thousand and one ways to do good, to rectify an error, to rightly inspire courage, or to guide a soul.

"One time we were in trapeza," related a certain monk. "The reader, as usual, read a patristic text. At one spot Fr. Codratus stopped him.

"'Please, Father, read that passage again.'"

"He wanted to hear a certain point again which concerned the officers of the Monastery. The reader obeyed and repeated the passage with emphasis, while at the same time the elder cast a glance at the officers who sat across from him. The patristic answer spoke a great deal to them about certain differences they had had with their abbot. But they were told much more by his fatherly, and at the same time reproving glance, which pricked to the depth their monastic conscience."

Fatherly but also monastic was his treatment of the novices. With sincere love he strove to bring them wholly into the atmosphere of monastic life.

Novices resemble young shoots who are transplanted to the greenhouse of a monastery. "The best husbandman, when they see a small and weakly plant, water it liberally and expend much care towards its growth. On the other hand, when they see untimely growth in a plant, they cut off the superfluous leaves since they readily dry up" (St. Syncletica, BEPES, 35, p. 236).

Fr. Codratus was an experienced husbandman of the spirit. He knew by the illumination of God what kind of cultivation each soul needed in order to develop and bear fruit "a hundredfold." His main goal for all, and especially for the novices, was to turn their mind and heart towards the life-bearing Sun of righteousness, Christ the Savior, and to unite the young beings to His divine life, cutting off their self-will and pruning every other tie which might hinder this holy union. Given over to unceasing prayer and asceticism, his spiritual children would bear rich fruit. For Christ Himself said, *He that abideth in me, and I in him, the same bringeth forth much fruit: for without me ye can do nothing* (Jn 15:5).

Therefore the elder did not allow the novices to go out of the Monastery or to have relations and conversations with visitors. In this way he safeguarded the inner life, keeping it from the "evil license of tongue," from distraction, idle talk and criticism, and strengthened the spirit of silence and quieting peace of thoughts.

He himself cultivated silence and hesychia, and he also inspired others to it. Silence and hesychia are the natural atmosphere for every monastery which wants to be a true workshop for souls. For this reason, when a certain monk, Father I., visited Karakallou Monastery and shouted and laughed in the middle of the courtyard for a long time, Fr. Codratus, the vigilant guardian of silence, went out to the drying-yard and said to him from the railing:

"Father, we thank you for your visit to our Monastery. It has been long enough. Now go to the next monastery."

In a multitude of words there lacketh not sin (Prov 10:19), and "He who is not still cannot know God" (St. Nilus the Ascetic).

* * * * * * * *

Together with silence, hesychia, and prayer, which subdue the mind, Fr. Codratus also exercised the novices in temperance, which subdues the stomach.

One time the novices asked to clean his cell. When they had almost finished the cleaning, Fr. Codratus came up and said:

"Very good. So now, what would you like me to treat you with?"

"Turkish delight and cognac!" one of them—the most hot-blooded—hurried to say.

"Turkish delight, yes. But cognac, no!" he said, and explained to them the value of temperance in bridling the unmanageable impulses of youth.

When a certain brother happened to break one of the Monastery's utensils, Fr. Codratus commanded him to stand at the door of the trapeza, holding the pieces of the utensil, together with the server and the reader, who always remained kneeling there after the meal, asking forgiveness of those going out for any failings.

He paid meticulous care to the common goods of the Monastery, and he wanted to instill this care and reverence in all the brothers. One day he found a bean lying outside the kitchen, one of a batch the fathers had cleaned a little earlier. He bent down, picked it up, and brought it to the cook.

"Put this in, too. Don't disdain it. Economy and care for the common goods of the monastery."

The elder never lost an opportunity of giving instruction on the proper outward appearance of a coenobitic monk. Seeing a certain monk wearing a hard skoufia (considered more elegant and modern) he called to him from a distance.

"Eh, Father, what's that you're wearing? For a monk there is only one kind of skoufia: woolen!"

Fr. Codratus was no worshipper of forms. However, he was able to discern that along with the substance we also need the form, which is always helpful and protects from corrupting and dangerous influences.

To one monk who had committed a sin, Father B., he gave a penance to remain for some years at the gate of the Monastery and beg forgiveness of those coming in and going out. The *Ladder* mentions a similar instance. The wise shepherd knew how to use suitable medicines for each situation.

He wanted no newspapers in the Monastery. Newspapers bring distraction to a monk. They remove him from his chief goal, cause confusion, and bring the stormy winds of the world into the calm harbor of monastic life.

One time a monk found many watermelons at the Monastery metochion, carried them up on the donkey, and brought them into the Monastery without a blessing. A visitor had come that day. The elder called the monk who had brought the watermelons and told him: "My child, bring a watermelon to offer to our guest."

The monk, however, disobedient and insolent, went away muttering: "I don't have any watermelons for visitors. I only have them for the fathers."

Fr. Codratus had given him an opportunity to show obedience, for which he would have forgiven him his first fault. But by his pride he fell into a greater.

"So you have watermelons for the fathers?" Fr. Codratus replied.

And without wasting time, to give him a good lesson, he threw the watermelons down one by one and smashed them on the floor. In monasticism, disobedience is equivalent to the expulsion from the "Paradise of delight," to spiritual death, and therefore it is battled implacably.

He had a good monk called Fr. M., and desired to have him ordained a deacon. He proposed this to the Council* so they could

---

*The Council of Elders, headed by the Abbot, governs the monastery.

also give their approval, but with no result. They refused. "He has no voice," they said.

"Fathers," he replied "come, let us take the Rudder and look at the canons of the Church. Do they say anywhere that someone who doesn't have a good voice can't be ordained?"

Then the Council found another excuse: his land of origin. "We won't ordain him because he is from Morea (the Peloponnesus)."

They meant that in the Holy Monastery of Karakallou most of the fathers were from Asia Minor.

Truly, when God's illumination is lacking, human criteria become base and low. And when there is egotism in the soul, our reactions become foolish and harmful. Then we judge a man only by outward standards—his voice, stature, origin—and we do not see the grace of God which regenerates even the most hardened, unrefined heart, creating a "new man in Christ."

Fr. Codratus was vigilant day and night. He was all eyes and ears because he was all love—true love for his spiritual children. His love did not let him remain quiet, but made him attentive to everything: to work, prayer, and in general to everyone's spiritual progress.

One day he saw a monk, Fr. Peter, sitting idly at the gate of the Monastery after the midday trapeza. Fr. Peter was a gigantic man, and the administrator of the Monastery. The elder saw him at a distance and approached him with fatherly care.

"Fr. Peter, what are you doing here?"

"Well, Elder, I came to enjoy the fresh air a little."

"Go to your cell, Fr. Peter. What we need is the prayer-rope and study."

"May it be blessed, Elder," he said, and showed obedience.

Thus Fr. Codratus applied the method of St. Pachomius, whom the angel of the Lord commanded: 'Warm those near you in the fire which God will kindle in you.'

4. UNACQUISITIVE, ASCETIC, AND MERCIFUL

Happily for Karakallou Monastery, it was and remains a Coenobium. Fr. Codratus struggled with all his strength not merely to preserve the institution of coenobitism, but to elevate the coenobitic life to its ideal height, to its proper greatness. For this reason, in his time the Holy Monastery of Karakallou held a vanguard position within the great Athonite community in austerity, strictness, and in spiritual life generally.

The brethren are not allowed to acquire privately-owned objects or clothes, money, or property, without the abbot's will and judgment, for this is completely forbidden by our divine fathers and St. Basil the Great (St. Athanasius the Athonite).

Fr. Codratus especially strove to instill in his monks the principle of poverty—one of the three foundations of coenobitic life. He himself was poorer than anyone else in the Monastery. He almost always wore old clothing. His cell was bare and ascetic and contained nothing superfluous. In the evening he did not sleep in his bed. In a corner of his room he laid down a board, and around it, like walls, placed large peasant pillows. Thus his sleeping place resembled a grave. There he lay down.

O venerable struggler, Fr. Codratus! You *brought the body into subjection* and subdued the flesh, as a perfect soldier and athlete of Christ. You combined nonacquisitiveness with the remembrance of death, and poverty with the realization of the vanity of the world. You *gave no sleep to your eyelids nor rest to your temples* until you made yourself into a pure receptacle of grace.

The remembrance of death, his daily companion, made him willingly devote himself to sleeping on the ground, to vigil, fasting, hardship. Seeing his humble bed and lying down on it, surely brought into his mind his descent into the grave, the parting of the soul from the body, the fearful Tribunal and the defense he would give before it....

* * * * * * * *

In 1938, a monk from Kavsokalyvia, Fr. Seraphim, had troubles with his health—he suffered from a hernia. When a man carries sacks weighing a hundred pounds or more from the sea high up to one's Kalyve, and remains standing upright in church for hours on end, it is neither unusual nor improbable for him to suffer a hernia. One time he happened to pass through the Holy Monastery of Karakallou. He rejoiced greatly that he would see the renowned Fr. Codratus and receive his prayer and blessing.

The familiarity which the Abbot inspired in him gave him boldness to go further and describe the difflculties of his life, the illness which tormented him, and even to ask if he had a hernia truss. Fr. Codratus consoled and supported him and gave him a truss. Something else happened, however, which left Fr. Seraphim thunderstruck. The elder at one point arose, put his hands down by his abdomen, and made a motion over his body.

"See, my child," he said to him, "I have a hernia too, even in two places, on the right side and the left. I've had them for a long time. In spite of them I serve Divine Liturgy and attend the vigils. I practice patience for the love of Christ. We must all be patient."

After that the monk from Kavsokalyvia did not dare to complain about his illness.

The fact that he had hernias in two places meant that he had endured labor, hardship, toil, heavy burdens, upright standing. Truly the fathers never saw Fr. Codratus sitting in the abbatical stall. He was always upright, an unshakable pillar. Even after he suffered his hernias, everyone remained astonished by the greatness of his patience and longsuffering. That is to say, he subjected the weakness of the body to the greatness of the spirit.

One time he was asked: "Elder, what distinguishes a monk?"

"A monk is he," he answered, "who wants to sleep and does not sleep, who wants to eat and does not eat, who wants to drink and

Interior view of Karakallou Monastery.

does not drink. A monk is distinguished by 'continual forcing of nature.'"

His answer was the expression of his personal ascetic experience. For this reason all of the inhabitants of the Holy Mountain said that he was a great struggler, a perfect ascetic. His spirit ruled as a prince over all the manifestations of his life, without being overcome by the weaknesses and demands of the flesh.

Love, compassion, mercy, and attention to strangers were characteristic adornments of his soul. Up to today, Karakallou Monastery holds the virtue of hospitality as a precious paternal inheritance.

"If you gave him an apple," one of his surviving disciples told us, "he would cut it into four parts and share it."

And Fr. Arsenius from Bourazeri informed us:

"He was approachable, full of fatherly love and charity for the poor and the desert-dwellers. He allowed no one to leave the Monastery with empty hands. He treated everyone this way, both the greatest and the least. We went to Karakallou with Fr. Joseph the Cave-Dweller, barefoot, in ragged rassas, and he welcomed us with joy and love. We richly enjoyed the gifts of his hospitality."

The heart of Fr. Codratus, as of every genuine slave of God, was a life-giving sun which spread around it the warm and bright rays of kindness. How beneficial are such hearts amidst our harassed, confused society, pitiable in its apostasy!

III

An Exemplary Confessor

1. A SPIRITUAL PHYSICIAN

Fr. Codratus was one of those rare figures who combine administrative ability with great skill as a spiritual father. Those close to him marvelled at his illumined judgment and fatherly heart. He was always filled with pity for the broken and compassion for the repentant sinner.

"He was a true fisherman," Fr. Athanasius told us. "With incomparable skill he managed to catch souls."

"As strict as he was in observing the rule and typicon within the Monastery, he was just as gentle and sweet-spoken when his spiritual children confessed to him. His speech exhaled meekness and kindness, deep compunction and grace. He softened souls, crushed the fortresses of egotism, freed souls from the chains of passion. He emboldened the penitent to speak, to confess his sins, to open a heart closed by fear and shame. He consoled and gave hope, and above all he co-suffered with the penitent. The apostolic command *rejoice with those who rejoice and weep with those who weep* was the foundation of his pastoral care.

Fr. Codratus shed tears for the sins of others as though they were his own. He was a father. Frequently he prayed especially for the penitent, that God would grant him consolation, strength, resistance against falling again, or that He would strengthen him to do the penance he had given him. At other times, at the end of holy confession, he would say:

"Come, my child, now let's make several prostrations together to beseech Christ to preserve you."

"One time," Monk Athanasius of Iveron related to us, "I went to confession. My soul was so weary and dejected that you can't imagine. I confessed and he listened to me carefully. Suddenly he seized my hand and placed it on his neck, and bending down before me, said:

"'Here, my child, here cast all your sins. There! On my head!'

"Then, at that spontaneous act of his, I all at once received wings.... Something happened inside me. An otherworldly power and unrestrainable emotion uplifted my soul. It was the love of Fr. Codratus which had drawn down the grace of God and conveyed it also to my own being.

"This man attracted souls by his sweet manner. Spontaneously your thoughts and sins came out from within, and you displayed the wounds of your soul...."

He was a good shepherd, who at the hour of confession left everything in order to find the lost sheep and lead it to salvation.

Another of his spiritual children, Fr. James, who knew him well, related to us with obvious emotion:

"He almost always wept when he heard confessions, and he made the penitent contrite also.

"'Come, my child; come, monk, and tell me what you have done....'

"'Come, my little child, we'll make three prostrations together, that God may forgive you your sins.'"

The place where he heard confessions was the compunctionate chapel of St. Gideon.

His fame as a confessor spread everywhere. Besides his spiritual children from his Monastery, for many years the fathers of the

Holy Monastery of Philotheou, many fathers of the Iveron Monastery, of Lavra, and other monasteries went to him for confession.

A multitude of laymen from the world also came to the Holy Mountain to meet him, receive his blessing, and go to confession to him. The great number of letters which he received every day containing confessions of his spiritual children and requests for guidance he would put into sacks. After many years, one day he called the gardener and told him:

"Take these sacks, and, without looking at anything, burn them and bury them in a corner of the garden."

How many souls laid aside the heavy load of their sins in these letters and, unburdened, found the road to Paradise!

In his time, Metropolitan Chrysostomos of Pelagonia lived for a while in a large cell close to the sea, in an area called Mylopotamou, which is a little beyond Karakallou. He often visited Fr. Codratus together with the future Patriarch Athenagoras, then a deacon. When the latter went to America, he sent many Greek-Americans to the Holy Mountain to meet Fr. Codratus and confess to him.

* * * * * * * *

Fr. Codratus was like a hen who gathers her chickens under her wings with motherly love and yearning. More, he was like a nurse, as the Apostle Paul says: *But we were gentle among you, just as a nurse cherisheth her own children. So, affectionately longing for you, we were well pleased to impart to you not only the Gospel of God, but also our own lives, because you had become dear to us* (I Thes. 2:7-8).

Fr. Andrew, the Abbot of the Holy Monastery of St. Paul, knew Fr. Codratus as a spiritual father very well.

"One time," he related to us, "a great temptation came to me, of a sort to make me leave my Monastery. I went and stayed in a cell close to the Holy Monastery of Karakallou. In two or three days I went to find Fr. Codratus and go to confession. I opened my heart to him and told him everything. I was obviously agitated, however. He listened to me patiently, and at the end appeared to agree with me....

"'You did well, you were right. But come back in a week, my child, and we'll talk about it again.'

"I thanked him and left. His thoughts, however, were hidden from me, and I was curious to learn what he wanted me for in a week. I did visit him again, and after we had cordially conversed for a while, he finally said to me in a cheerful voice:

"'Will you be obedient to whatever I tell you?'

"'Elder, whatever you tell me I will do.'

"'You will do it? Then listen! We will put the bridle and rug on your donkey, and you will go back to your Monastery. That's excellent!'

"'But Elder,' I said to him astonished, 'before you said I was right. Now....'

"'Yes! But then you were angry. If I had told you then what I am telling you now, the wound would not have healed nor the temptation been dispersed.'

"I marvelled at his masterly handling of souls and glorified God that I had found such a spiritual father. I returned to the Monastery joyful and repentant."

One monk had the passion of secret eating. Once there came a certain visitor whom the elder knew suffered from the same passion, and he sent him to the monk for advice.

"Go to Fr. So-and-so. He has spiritual experience and will help you."

A two-fold good resulted. The monk was ashamed and realized his sin, and the visitor benefited from his counsels.

Together with the grace of discernment, the incomparable Fr. Codratus also had the gift of clairvoyance.

A certain disciple of the exceptional Elder Daniel of Katounakia was tormented by critical thoughts of his elder. He therefore left his community, being conquered by the devil. God, however, did not abandon him, but put into him the good thought of going to Fr. Codratus. He would be able to advise him and recommend some other virtuous elder to him. When Fr. Damascene—that was his name—had finished talking, the God-enlightened Fr. Codratus said to him:

"Why are you telling all this to me, Fr. Damascene? Listen. If you want real help, go to Katounakia and find a certain wise elder called Daniel. Whatever he tells you, that do."

Fr. Damascene was dumbfounded, having expected anything but that.

"Surely," he thought, "God enlightened the confessor to tell me to go back to my elder, since I hadn't told him what community I belonged to, or whom I had as elder."

In the year 1930, Metropolitan Irenaeus of Cassandra invited him to serve as confessor in his diocese. Marvellous and fruitful was the habit of certain bishops of summoning grace-bearing and ascetic Athonite hieromonks to conduct the mystery of Holy Confession in their dioceses.

In one village Fr. Codratus was attacked by certain men because he was not accustomed to yielding on questions of family morality. As a conscientious confessor he expounded the will of God clearly and boldly. He was discerning, being very lenient when lenience was called for, but also strict when that was required.

The men in that village, therefore, excluded him from everywhere and did not receive him. The mayor of the village commanded that no one take him into their home. Undaunted, Fr. Codratus exercised his God-enlightened ingenuity and decided to lock himself into the village church. He sent the mayor the following notice:

"Mr. Mayor, I didn't ask you for anything. A piece of bread and a few olives will suffice me so I will not die of hunger. You can't remove me from here. The church is my own."

Thus the souls thirsting for the mystery of divine confession could go to him in the church.

In the year 1936 there came a monastic aspirant who was undecided and of two minds about the monastic life. The elder used every means to help him, so as to disengage him from the world and establish him somewhere. He showed him love and kindness, but the man still could not detach himself from vanity. He even read worldly periodicals which he had brought into the monastery.

When he discovered this, Fr. Codratus called him and said to him:

"My child, you will not make a monk. You came to lead a monastic life, and you still read worldly magazines? Go therefore and make your life in the world. Go with God's blessing!"

In such situations there echoed in Fr. Codratus' mind the word of the Lord: *For which of you, intending to build a tower, does not sit down first and count the cost, whether he has enough to finish it...* (Luke 14:28).

2. IN THE CHAPEL OF ST. GIDEON

The chapel of the monk-martyr St. Gideon was Fr. Codratus' favorite, both because the heroic figure of the Saint was alive in it and because it had a deeply compunctionate atmosphere. In this quiet chapel, fragrant with incense and softly illumined by icon-lamps, he used to receive his spiritual children for confession.

He always delighted in telling his disciples about St. Gideon: "He was a hero. He denied Christ by his word, but he confessed Him by his blood."

When the younger ones who were not familiar with his life would ask him curiously: "Elder, why did you say that he denied Christ by his word, but confessed Him by his blood?" he would feelingly narrate the Saint's life.

"Here is why. When he was little, the Saint denied the Christian faith and under pressure from the Turks became a Moslem. Later, however, he understood his crime of betrayal. And after he confessed, he came to the Holy Mountain.

"For thirty-five years he was a model monk in the Holy Monastery of Karakallou. The longing for martyrdom burned in him, however. He wanted to wash away the shame of betrayal. He asked the blessing of the elder and the fathers, and after making a prostration went to Velestino, where he pretended to be mad in order to provoke the Turks into arresting him. After repeated provocations he was arrested. Brought before the judge, he confessed his faith with boldness, and underwent a frightful martyrdom. Namely, one by one they cut off the members of his body, his hands and feet.

"He endured his martyrdom not only with unimaginable patience, but also with unutterable joy.

"So I said to you: he denied Christ by his word, but confessed Him by his blood. So let us take care, my child, because a monk can confess Christ by his word, but deny him by his blood."

"But Christ doesn't ask for our blood today, Elder."

"On the contrary, He does ask for it. 'Give blood, and receive the spirit,' the Fathers say. A true monk sacrifices himself every day, cuts off his will, is obedient, is crucified to the passions and to the world. There is his martyrdom! The true monk is a martyr of Christ, and must confess Christ with both his mouth and his blood."

"And how, Elder, can a monk deny Christ with his blood?"

"How? When a monk confesses at his tonsure that he 'renounces the world and the things of the world according to the command of Christ,' that he will 'remain in the monastery and in asceticism until his last breath,' that he will 'preserve until death obedience to the abbot and all the brotherhood in Christ,' that he will endure 'every affliction and deprivation of the solitary life for the sake of the kingdom of heaven,' but does not keep the 'covenant' which he made with Christ the Master, then he denies Him. When a monk promises in the 'contract' which he makes with Christ that he will drive away every 'disobedience, contradiction, pride, disputation, jealousy, envy, wrath, shouting, blasphemy, secret eating, boldness, particular friendship, boasting, quarreling, grumbling, murmuring, tale-bearing ... by which things the wrath of God comes, and the destroyer of souls begins to take root in them' but does not fulfill his promise, nor repent over it, then he denies Christ....

"How terrible, my child! We set out to serve Christ, to become his soldiers, and if we don't take care, we can, in deed and life, be found to be his deniers.... But as for you, love Christ! Then the bloodless martyrdom of your monastic struggles will be accounted in the eyes of God as greater than anything else. And if you endure with joy and thanksgiving, your crown will be most radiant and enviable."

How many tears Fr. Codratus shed in this silent, beloved chapel! Behind its altar there is a small courtyard with one seat, from which one can see from afar the boundless sea, the Aegean, which lies outspread, wide and vast, as far as the eyes can see. As many times as he beheld this sea, he remembered the mystery of God's love and was deeply shaken. The mystery of eternal love, which resembles a sea without bounds, without end ... and yet one of its shores, one of its waves, caressed this chapel of St. Gideon every time it witnessed the confessions or Liturgies of a great heart, full of the love of God—Fr. Codratus.

3. HOW A DESPAIRING MAN WAS SAVED

During Fr. Codratus' abbacy a lay-pilgrim visited the Holy Mountain, wanting to confess his great sins. He went to Karyes, to Fr. Avercius the prayer-rope maker, and persistently asked for confession.

Fr. Avercius thought it good to send him to a confessor in the Holy Monastery of Koutloumousiou, which is near Karyes. He was a good confessor, but strict in following the canons, which he applied without leniency.

The man went to Koutloumousiou and confessed. He returned, however, a "broken reed," disheartened, full of sorrow and despondency.

"What happened? Did you go to confession?" Fr. Avercius asked him.

"Yes, Father, but...."

Fr. Avericius looked at him. He was grief-stricken, very pale, with a sorrow that was not according to God, but which the devil inspires in order to fatally ensnare souls.

"What's the matter? Tell me. What happened to you?" "Father, life is no longer worth living for me. It would be better for me to drown," he said with bitter pain.

"But why? Didn't you go to confession?"

"I went to confession, but the confessor told me that my sins are very heavy. I don't know. What can I say? He has brought me to despair."

When Fr. Avercius heard this and saw the spirit of sorrow and hopelessness craftily spreading its veil over the soul of this troubled man, he took a piece of paper and wrote a letter to the Reverend Metropolitan Hierotheus who was living in asceticism in Milopotamou. He would be able to help him, to find a way through for this soul.

He gave the letter into the pilgrim's hands, said some brotherly, encouraging words, and showed him the path that would lead him to the desert cell of His Eminence.

The bishop was in the garden when the pilgrim came. He wore a simple skoufia, and was hoeing.

"What do you want, my brother?" he said to the despairing man when he came up to him with the letter in his hand.

"I want to confess, Your Eminence."

"Listen, my child, I don't hear confessions. But I will send you to an elect confessor in Karakallou Monastery. His name is Fr. Codratus.

He took a pencil and paper, wrote a letter to Fr. Codratus, and sent the man to that experienced physician of souls.

The man climbed the steep foot-path which goes to the Monastery, and soon arrived. The fathers took care of him, as they did every visitor, with much love and joy. Afterwards they notified the elder.

"Let him come to the Abbot's office," he commanded.

There he welcomed him as if he had known him for years—with love, like a father. And the man hurried to cast off the weight that burdened him oppressively with a fear he had not known before, created perhaps by his first confession. He was like a hunted bird who has great wounds, but even greater terror. The devil had bound him—but he would not rejoice over him, for his soul was now in the hands of Christ, in the hands of Fr. Codratus, who applied his skill and power to break the bonds of sin and despair. He was in the hands of a physician who would perform the operation and treat the wounded man by the grace and illumination of the All-Holy Spirit.

The pilgrim beheld in the face of the confessor a man of God, and he leapt from joy.

"It is natural," writes St. John of the Ladder," for a sick man to rejoice when he sees the physician, even though, perhaps, he receives nothing from him. Therefore acquire, O wondrous man, (he says to the shepherd) plasters, potions, razors, eye-salves, sponges, instruments for bloodletting and cauterization, ointments, sleeping draughts, a knife, bandages. If we do not have these things, how can our science be manifested?" ("To the Shepherd")

Fr. Codratus was equipped with all the spiritual instruments that constitute the science of pastorship.

The sick pilgrim wanted the treatment to be short, but Fr. Codratus did not hurry. He sat down next to him and tried to create an atmosphere of intimacy, friendship, and trust with the penitent, despite his hurry to be instructed.

"I am a sinner, Father."

"Good. But I see you as an angel of God. Tell me, do you have children? When did you come to the Holy Mountain? What work do you do?"

They conversed for a while and then he put on his epitrachelion.

"Come, my child," he said to him. "You see this icon of Christ? Don't hide anything. The Lord knows everything, sees everything, hears everything. And I am a man of the same passions as you. So take courage."

Unforcedly and naturally all the bitterness and pain of the man's heart was discharged and poured out—with contrition, without doubt in the mercy of God which he saw living in the figure and epitrachelion of the old confessor. He confessed cleanly and repented sincerely. He wept. His soul, his speech and stance all expressed the Fiftieth Psalm of David, the psalm of repentance: *For I know my iniquity and my sin is ever before me.*

What else does the man-loving God ask of a man? Repentance. Return. This is the only road to Paradise, the road which was walked by the publican, harlot, and robber. This road the Lord opened also to this wounded soul by His wise, fatherly economy, through the sacred mystery of absolution.

This took place during Holy Week. When Fr. Codratus had listened to the penitent and as usual wept together with him, and when he had counseled him, he said to him, bending down to the wounded man with compassion:

"God sees your repentance and your tears, my child. Therefore listen. Today is Great Thursday, and all the fathers are fasting to receive Communion. You also stay here for these days. In the pure and holy surroundings of the Monastery you will see yourself better. You will pray together with us, you will fast, and you will receive Communion. I myself will serve Liturgy and give you Communion. 'Thy sins are forgiven thee. Sin no more.'"

The man's exultation at the end of his confession was indescribable. Everything around him shone with the light of peace and the forgiveness and mercy of God. He was saved. And the joy of Fr. Codratus, who had once more become a life-preserver to a man shipwrecked by life, was similar to the joy of Christ when He finds a "lost one," similar to the rejoicing which is in heaven *over one sinner who repenteth.*

4. A SPIRITUAL HERITAGE

The experience and counsels of every struggler in the monastic life, and much more of every guide of souls, constitute a treasure, a precious spiritual heritage for coming generations of monks.

Several fathers of the Holy Mountain remember with gratitude the wise and living sayings of Fr. Codratus. They had the kindness to hand on to us what their memory retained, so that we could record them here:

"My child, sacrifice yourself. Don't ever abandon the services and your rule. Fast on Monday, Wednesday, and Friday, for by fasting a man's heart is broken."

"Some want to tell us that the Holy Scriptures don't say anything about fasting. On the contrary! The first command about fasting and temperance was given in Paradise. Moses fasted to receive the tablets of the Law. And we also must fast, if we want the law of God to be revealed to us. The Prophet Elias fasted. The Lord Himself fasted for forty days in the desert."

"You must pray. The more one devotes oneself to prayer, to the 'Lord Jesus Christ, Son of God, have mercy on me,' the more one becomes attached to the heavenly and forsakes the earthly."

"Fathers, keep vigil. We monks imitate the angels, and the angels keep vigil and glorify God."

"Do your daily rule," he advised every monk. "Ascend every day like the point of a needle; but don't go downwards."

"Look after your obedience in the Kyriakon (the central church of a skete). And be the first in church. Don't accuse anyone. Do your work, without investigating how the other brothers behave."

"Fr. Maximus, whoever comes to the monastic life must have fire, enthusiasm, and zeal, in order to remain to the end."

This he said often in order to show two things: first, that at the beginning of the monastic life we need flaming love and heroic resolution; and second, that later, when the monk will be battled against painfully by the enemy, he will need to be supported in the first zeal and the first longing which God kindled in him.

"Maximus, Maximus, if a young man has temptations, he must cut them off from here." (And he pointed to his mouth, wanting to say that he must cut off food and practice temperance.) "A young man who has strength should do a thousand prostrations, if he can. When he grows old and cannot endure anymore, he will be nourished from the reserve of his youth."

"The prayer, the 'Lord Jesus Christ'! Say the prayer. It is the only medicine for a monk."

"As much as you humble yourself you will be exalted. If you are ordained or receive a rank, don't get proud. Our ability is not our own achievement, but a gift of God."

"Do you know how a monk should be? Like a dead man. Whether they insult him, whether they praise him, whether they strike him, he says nothing at all."

"Fathers"—he often said—"Obedience is great humility. He who is obedient enters Paradise; he who is disobedient is expelled from Paradise."

St. Simeon the New Theologian writes that he who has acquired "sufficient faith" in his spiritual father, seeing him feels that he sees Christ Himself, and following him believes that he follows Christ Himself. "Therefore what is greater or more beneficial in the present or in the future life than to be with Christ?" And when he hears the words of his spiritual father it is as though he heard Christ Himself. "And if he is also vouchsafed speech from him, he ever derives from it eternal life." And therefore, the words of our spiritual fathers have irreplaceable value. They are the echo of the voice of Christ.

IV

"Well Done, Good and Faithful Servant"

1. TRIALS

It is a part of God's plan that his elect be tried "as gold in the furnace."

A small affliction for God's sake is better than a great work performed without tribulation.... But thou, O struggler and imitator of the passion of Christ, do thou thyself struggle that thou mayest be counted worthy of tasting His glory. For if we indeed suffer together with Him, then are we glorified together with Him. Therefore the saints' love for Christ was proved in affliction, and not in relaxation (St. Isaac the Syrian).

With wonderful patience and longsuffering, Fr. Codratus endured two trials coming from certain disciples of his who, it appears, had not tasted either the essence of obedience or the grace of the coenobitic and angelic monastic life. Although the elder forgave them, they greatly disturbed the course of the Monastery, which had taken on a very good and blessed order. For the sake of history we must mention these trials briefly.

It will not astonish us that occasionally, when attentiveness and spiritual cultivation are lacking, human weaknesses and egotism survive in certain monks. Among other things, the devil wars against a monk powerfully and methodically. For a thousand laymen there is

Abbot Codratus (bottom row, third from left) with his community.

needed perhaps one demon; for one monk there are needed perhaps a thousand demons...!

Fr. Philip served for years as the representative of the Monastery at the Council of the Holy Mountain in Karyes. He was a man who influenced people and things, and so he once came to ask for money from the Monastery for certain matters. The elder refused for serious and well-founded reasons.

"Fr. Philip, you are a coenobitic monk. You are not permitted to ask for money," he said to him.

Fr. Philip, however, did not listen to anyone. He even managed to persuade the Holy Council, the police, and others to go to the Monastery and apply pressure and force on the Abbot.

Fr. Codratus then summoned the whole brotherhood and shut himself into the trapeza of the Monastery together with the brothers. He did not give in to pressure. The Holy Council went to the guest-quarters. After the members were entertained there, they sought the Abbot. The guest-master came to the trapeza, and the elder in a very natural manner commanded him to tell the members of the Holy Council who were waiting in the guest-house that the Abbot was with his flock, and that if they wished they should come down to the trapeza, where the whole brotherhood was to be found.

Naturally this did not happen, because if they had come to the trapeza they would have seen that all the brethren were united and gathered around the elder. And thus their attempt was fruitless and they departed unsuccessful and ashamed—and also wiser and repentant, for they understood how much they had been led astray by the rebellious Fr. Philip. Fr. Philip finally left the Monastery.

The second great trial was the take-over of the Monastery by the officers, who had agreed among themselves to remove Fr. Codratus from the abbacy. They therefore notified him one day, as he was returning from the harbor of the Monastery, that he was not to be abbot anymore.

"May it be blessed," he said calmly, and departed. He faced the trial with superiority and dispassion. He did not protest at all. He viewed the abbacy as a service which God had assigned him, and which He had taken from him according to His will.

He lived in silence for a little while in the Kathisma of the Monastery called Prophet Elias. There he remained with patience, glorifying God and finding opportunity to practice mental prayer. He would come to the Monastery and serve Liturgy in his turn. At that time there were only two priests, Fr. Maximus and Fr. Macarius.

In two months, however, the new abbot fell from his mule as he was going to the feast day of the Great Lavra, and became gravely ill and died.

Then Fr. Codratus was again summoned to the abbacy. The officers understood their fault and clearly saw the will of God. They asked forgiveness. The elder forgave them, and with the same humility with which he had accepted the termination of his abbacy he again resumed his duties.

Fr. Codratus had the fear of God. And much more, he had love; and he always believed that "all works together for good for those who love God."

2. SIGNS OF GRACE

Many wonderful things are circulated on the Holy Mountain about the life of Fr. Codratus, especially things related to its prayerful and liturgical aspect.

It appears that his metaphysical world was very intense and living—a fruit of his superhuman struggles to subdue matter to spirit and to free his inner man.

For example, wonderful things are reported to have happened when one time he went to serve Liturgy at a Kalyve and did not have a chanter. However, we did not manage to learn and ascertain what exactly happened, or how divine Grace manifested Itself.

To those who have cleansed their soul by the sanctifying power of prayer and asceticism, the Lord distributes the riches of the illuminating rays of the Holy Spirit.

"On souls undefiled and purified from every stain shines prophetic grace" (St. Basil the Great).

It appears that Fr. Codratus was also vouchsafed the special grace of foresight, as is shown by an occurrence that is well known and often spoken of on the Holy Mountain.

It happened during a vigil in Karakallou Monastery. The Abbot, Fr. Codratus, was sitting—one of the rare times he was sitting—in his stall, when sleep overtook him for a little while. Suddenly he flew upright, as if he saw something or someone had spoken to him.

"Fathers, your prayer-ropes! Our brothers are suffering in the sea! They are in danger of drowning!" "Lord Jesus Christ, Son of God, have mercy on Thy servants," he began to say, first of all.

Truly, at exactly that moment certain brothers who were travelling by boat to the Monastery Metochion at Cassandra were in danger. The boat, which was powered only by a sail, was almost unable to endure the great turbulence of the sea. When they arrived at the breakwater they were exhausted. Despite all of their efforts to tie up the boat (one brother was even in the sea up to his chest) they did not succeed.

The flaming prayer of Fr. Codratus and the fathers was answered; the brothers were strengthened and delivered from the danger. *The Lord will hearken unto me when I cry unto Him.*

The whole life of Fr. Codratus depended on prayer. He decided nothing, thought nothing, did nothing without prayer. Prayer was for him "a refuge of help, fountain of salvation, treasure-house of assurance, harbor of deliverance from great waves, a light for those in darkness, a support of the weak, a shelter in time of temptations, help at the height of illness, a shield of redemption in battle, and a dart hurled against the enemy" (St. Isaac the Syrian).

3. "I HAVE FINISHED MY COURSE"

Monks are true philosophers of life and death. Fr. Codratus was a genuine philosopher of the philosophy according to God. He did not cease even for one day to meditate on the mystery of life and death in the divine light of the Resurrection of the Lord.

"When he drew near his end, I visited him for the last time," Fr. Eudocimus of Philotheou Monastery related to us. "He could hardly move his tongue.

"'Welcome, Fr. Eudocimus. How are you? How are the fathers?'

"'By your prayers, Elder, well. And how is it with you?'

"'How is it with me, my child? The hour has come. 'Our years may be considered a spider's; for the span of our lives is seventy years, and if in the strong it is eighty years, yet most of them are in labor and pain.'

"Another day my elder, Fr. Dionysius, visited him. He went for advice on a pressing matter—namely, whether he should keep or send away one of his disciples who had a difficult and rough character.

"'Pray to the Sweet-kissing icon of the Mother of God,' he managed to say slowly and with difficulty. 'Pray, and keep him. Be patient with his imperfections, and God will save him.'"

* * * * * * * *

Fr. Codratus was a monk for fifty-eight years. For fifty-eight years he was a valiant athlete of the spirit in the great ever-living arena of the Holy Mountain. He came to the Mountain in 1879, was tonsured a monk in 1882, and finally reposed in the sleep of the just on January 31, 1940, after he had voluntarily resigned from the abbacy on the first of that month. It seems that he foreknew his end. He did not suffer from a particular illness; his death was caused by old age.

With his death a star of monasticism and of our Church faded from the Athonite heaven, but he left behind an ever-luminous trail of labors and asceticism.

The fifty-eight years of his monastic life were all given to God and his spiritual children, to prayer and the practice of virtue. Until his last moment, the ever-memorable one did not cease to counsel and guide his fathers and brothers on the path of the Lord. Until the last hour he worked with the talent that God had entrusted to him, with zeal, willingness, and a consciousness of his calling and responsibility, and as an honest worker of Christ.

Thus on the day that he closed his eyes and finished the course of his ascetic life, the work of fifty-eight years in the Monastery of Karakallou, he could say to the Lord:

Lord, thou gavest me five talents; behold, besides them I have gained five others.

And the Lord rightly answered him:

Well done, O good and faithful servant! As thou hast been faithful over a little, I will set thee over much; enter thou into the joy of thy Lord (Matt. 25:20-21).

An old engraving of Karakallou Monastery.

ELDER PHILARET OF CONSTAMONITOU

IX

ELDER PHILARET
OF CONSTAMONITOU

What your stature lacked in height
Exalting humbleness supplied.
Your intellect's simplicity
A treasure of good thoughts enriched...
O childlike Elder Philaret.
—Monk Mark of Constamonitou

I came not to be ministered unto, but to minister.
(*cf.* Matt. 20:28)

Author's Prologue to the Greek Edition

My soul has thirsted for Thee, and my flesh has longed for Thee, in a land barren and untrodden and unwatered (Ps. 62:1). The soul thirsts for God, and our people [the Greek people] thirsts for its Orthodoxy, which the holy monks of the East, the true philosophers, the initiates into the divine mysteries of the heavenly life in Christ, expressed "by deed and word."

This thirst of our Orthodox people has been manifested in recent years mainly by the avid study of patristic wisdom—but also by the lively enthusiasm with which the volumes of *Contemporary Ascetics of Mount Athos* have been received, one after another.

As is known, this series is only a sampling. The virtuous fathers, those "sweet-smelling flowers of Paradise" who spread abroad their overwhelming fragrance in the Garden of the Mother of God in the first half of the 20th century, constitute an innumerable multitude of unknown spiritual athletes. A selection of them was made based on the amount of biographical material available.

Our ever-memorable Athonite elder, Archimandrite Cherubim, inaugurated the series in the year 1968, giving it, before his repose in the Lord in 1979, its first eight books. After his death, many Christians urged and besought us not to abandon this spiritual offering, which has evoked such a great response among the wide strata of our own people, and also among our brothers in the faith in other lands, as is apparent from their past and present endeavors to translate it into their own languages.

Today, therefore, eight years after the publication of the eighth volume of *Contemporary Ascetics of Mount Athos*, we are found in the happy position of continuing this publishing effort, entrusting a brother of our Monastery, Fr. Ioannicius, with numbering among their "synod" yet another star of the Athonite heaven: Fr. Philaret of Constamonitou.

Fr. Philaret did not belong to the class of learned monks. We were told that he barely graduated from the third grade. He was, however, a graduate of the "university of the cell." In this university, by prayer and asceticism, by sobriety and the purification of his heart from passions, he mastered the sciences of "self-knowledge" and "God-knowledge." The lack of worldly wisdom and the acquisition of divine illumination enrolled the elder among the choir of blessed beings who have the Holy Spirit Himself as their guide and teacher—He Who "taught wisdom to the unlearned, made fishermen theologians...."

Another fruit of the Holy Spirit in the unforgettable elder was the exemplary meekness which distinguished him. The ever-memorable one was a "man of meek soul." The saying of Proverbs applied to him: *Every blessed soul is simple.*

The following venerable aged Fathers of the Holy Monastery of Constamonitou gave us material for his biography: Elders Modestus, Pachomius, Niphon, Philaret, Anthony, Euthemius, and Tryphon. We owe them warm thanks. We also thank the venerable abbot of the Monastery, Elder Agathon, who gave his blessing to Fr. Mark to deliver to us in writing and systematically many details of the truly *philaretos* (virtue-loving) life of Fr. Philaret.

May the prayers of the holy Elder shelter and support his sacred Coenobium, as well as all who will be inspired by his wonderful life to join in his spiritual combats.

Holy Monastery of the Paraclete, 1986

I

"O Lord, I Have Loved Thy Tabernacles...."

1. THE HOLY MONASTERY OF CONSTAMONITOU

One of the more quiet, hesychastic Athonite Monasteries is the Holy Monastery of Constamonitou. It is quiet because it is hidden like a mushroom in the forests and ravines of the southwestern side of the Holy Mountain, invisible to the curious eyes of tourists on the sea, leading in obscurity a hidden life, which provides the most desirable atmosphere for monks. It is hesychastic because of the venerable fathers and brothers who live there. Both the place and their manner of life make them genuine coenobitic hesychasts.

In the deep, endless silence of the forest, the many species of songbirds hold sway, especially in the springtime. Their unrivalled leader is the nightingale, who keeps tireless vigil day and night. During the hours of common worship the fathers sing with compunction, in the manner of the Holy Mountain, and then the Monastery resembles a many-voiced plaintive bird of the wilderness.

There are many theories about the founding of the Holy Monastery of Constamonitou. Its first builder remains unknown. One tradition names St. Constantine the Great as founder, and his son Constantius after him. Another mentions Macarius, bishop of Ierissos, who raised up the Monastery after the disaster wrought by Julian the Apostate. Macarius lived during the reign of Arcadius. He

Constamonitou Monastery

is depicted to the left of the Catholicon wearing a monastic mantia, and with the inscription "Macarius of Ierissos." Another tradition speaks about a certain hesychast who came from Castamona of Paphlagonia, and yet another says that the Monastery took its name from the chestnut forest which surrounds it (*castana* + *moni*).*

It is certain that the Monastery existed in the 11th century, because we have information that in the year 1107 the abbot was a certain Hilarion, a relative of Emperor Alexis I Comnenos.

At the end of the 13th century the holy Monastery was attacked by the Latinizing John XI Bekkos, Patriarch of Constantinople, and Emperor Michael Paleologus. They attempted to impose

---

* "chestnut" and "monastery" respectively—*trans. note.*

by force their anti-Orthodox views, which concurred with the idea of the primacy of the pope, and they struck first of all at our Acropolis of Orthodoxy, the Holy Mountain. Its monks, ever faithful (considered by some fanatical and unyielding), the defenders of the borders of the Truth, are dedicated soul and body to preserving the integrity and independence of the Faith. The Latinizers, therefore, sent wild beasts in the shape of men to the Holy Mountain, where they lit fires and burned monks, whom to this day the Church celebrates and honors as martyrs and confessors. The Monastery of Constamonitou was burned, but unlike the other monasteries the victims were not recorded.

In the year 1351 John V Paleologus delivered a chrysobull mentioning the Monastery's estates, while during the reign of Andronicus II Paleologus, the Queen of Serbia, Anna Philanthropini, gave to it the small Monastery of St. Anthony on Constamonitou's northwest side, and a precious wonderworking "Hodigitria" icon of the Theotokos.

A general renovation of the Monastery took place through the commander-in-chief of Serbia, Radits, who was tonsured a monk with the name Romanus. Radits-Romanus is considered a great benefactor of the Monastery, both for his gifts and for his care to establish firmly its coenobitic order.

In 1717 the Monastery suffered a great catastrophe from a new conflagration. It was in decline until 1799, when it was reestablished as a Coenobium through the solicitude of Patriarch Neophytus VII. The entire reformation of the Monastery took place in the second half of the 19th century by the initiative of the energetic Abbot Symeon, who came from Stageira. New buildings were constructed, and a new church (the catholicon) was erected from the foundations in the year 1867.

But let us return to the benefactor-general, the monk Radits-Romanus. The record of his gifts and offerings mentions, among other things, the following:

"I built a Monastery on the Holy Mountain in honor of the holy glorious Apostle, Protomartyr, and Archdeacon Stephen in a place called Constamoni. To wit, some (buildings) I renewed and raised up, and for others that were collapsed I built surrounding walls, and thus I consolidated the holy Monastery, for it was fallen down, ruined, and laid waste. I beseech the holy glorious Protomartyr Stephen to accept this as a great gift, as the two mites of the widow.... In this way I, with the advice of my spiritual father, the most reverend Metropolitan Mark of Achilsk, decreed that as it is a Coenobium all the brothers in common choose the abbot for the holy Monastery.... Moreover, if, according to my aim, I would happen to come to the Holy Mountain to become a monk and live the monastic life in my own Monastery or in another, (I decreed) that the holy Monastery be obliged to give me repose with all gladness, which is to be by the will of the abbot and the (monastery) council, and my expenses will (be covered by) the villages (72 in number) which I dedicate to the Monastery.... If, furthermore, my spiritual father, Metropolitan Mark of Achilsk comes to the Monastery, (I decreed) that he may be steward in the Monastery as long as he lives. Similarly, if any of my relatives wish to become monks, (I decreed) that the sacred Monastery be obliged to receive them and give them repose" (Th. I.E., Vol. 7, p. 1232).

This text by the commander-in-chief Radits, later Monk Romanus, is a witness to the undivided concern which the noblemen and dignitaries of that age had for the repair of the buildings, and the maintenance in general, of the holy monasteries. Indeed, many men holding positions of authority—ecclesiastical, political, social—such as Radits-Romanus, rightly desired to don the monastic garment and complete the remainder of their lives "in peace and repentance," as simple monks of the great and holy angelic schema.

Together with this text is distinguished the outstanding honor, reverence and love with which all the Orthodox have surrounded the Holy Mountain, independently of nationality, through the ages. Indeed, from ancient times until today the Holy Mountain has been and remains a center for all Orthodox people, unique in the world in the practice of monastic perfection, a link between all the Orthodox peoples, and an expression of the catholicity of our Church in the most noble aspect of Orthodox spirituality: in following the life of Christ-like ascetic experience, in the deification of man through pure prayer in the Holy Spirit within Orthodox Athonite monasticism. This also is a blessing of the Mother of God. Monks from all the lengths and breadths of the earth inhabit the Holy Mountain—from east and west, from north and south.

> *Lift up thine eyes about thee, O Sion, and see,*
> *For lo, thy children come to thee,*
> *From the west and from the north*
> *And from the sea and from the east,*
> *As to a beacon lighted by God,*
> *Blessing Christ in thee forever.*

This Paschal hymn applies also to the Sion which is called Athos. And within this frankincensed Sion lived "as a beacon lighted by God" Fr. Philaret (1890-1963), the Abbot of the Holy Monastery of Constamonitou, whose life we will trace out in the following pages.

2. MORAL PURITY

The Monastery register informs us:

Elder Philaret was born in the village of Phytia Verrias in Macedonia in the year 1890. His father was George Mastoras and his mother Catherine Stergiou. In baptism he was named Anthony. He entered the coenobitic life in our Holy Monastery in November of 1912, and was tonsured a monk of the great schema in April of the year 1921 and ordained a priest in October of 1924.

He was elected Abbot in March of 1949 and was installed on May 21 of the same year.

On January 28, 1963, the day of the Sunday of the Prodigal Son, and the commemoration of our holy and God-bearing Father Ephraim the Syrian, he reposed in the Lord during the time of Matins, and precisely during the reading of the third kathisma of the Psalter (Psalm 118), and at the verse *I have not forgotten Thy statutes,* etc.

As for his physical characteristics, the elder was short in stature (under 1.60 meters), with a round face, black eyes, and well-developed beard. He was sweet in appearance, meek and humble in manner, guileless and exceptionally simple, kindly, but of few words. To the gifts of his soul we must add his great obedience and patience, his continual forcing of himself in all the virtues, as well as mental prayer, abstinence in food, absence of contradiction, banishment of anger, lack of passionate interest in any unmonastic matter, his mystical spiritual life, wondrous poverty and irreproachable purity.

From his childhood years the elder received the "fiery darts of the enemy," but divine Grace preserved him as a pure vessel of election, and he himself struggled to not stain the garment of purity "shining bright as snow."

Once when he was still young he went for a walk with a youth greater in age and stature. Somewhere outside their village his friend, as he saw some oxen who were grazing further on, was seized by fleshly temptation and rushed against the young Anthony in order to gratify his shameful and despicable desire. Little Anthony then began to cry out for help, but the area was deserted. Immediately seeking divine reinforcement through prayer, and being small in body, like another David, with a strange and exceptional strength he pushed his large-bodied acquaintance far away, avoided the temptation like the fair Joseph, and ran away.

His great prudence and inner purity is shown by a second incident which he related in an edifying and humble manner to one of his disciples: "In America, where I went, I worked in a shoe-shining parlor. Many people passed through to have their shoes polished. A very beautiful young girl of a great family also came through. Since my co-workers were men who feared the temptation of the flesh, they sent me to serve her, because I did not feel any particular temptation. At the end she also gave me a good tip. God covered me; I felt no temptation."

If we think of the fact that he lived in America from the age of eighteen to twenty-two—that is, during the years when the greatest boiling of nature and rebellion of the flesh is felt—then we realize that Anthony must have had exceedingly abundant grace from God to remain pure and passionless. Even within the tumult of America with its many fascinations, divine help walled him round and preserved him unburnt and untouched "like the three children in the furnace."

> He who has conquered the flesh has conquered nature; and he who has conquered nature has without fail risen to the state above nature. And he who has attained this 'is made a little lower than the angels,' which is not to say that he is at all less than them (*The Ladder of Divine Ascent*, Step 15).

Anthony also, even before he became monk and hieromonk Philaret, was an earthly angel, "a little lower" than the heavenly angels, since he bore flesh. He was a fleshly angel.

Having such a foundation of a clean life and purified heart, in his youth he acquired capital of strength and resistance against the temptations of the future. At times when satan assaulted him with shameful thoughts—he had already become a monk—he was forced to increase his spiritual labors. Thus he rose every night earlier than the other brothers and prayed with burning tears before the icon of the Lady Theotokos (the Sweet-Kissing) which he had hanging in his cell. One night, as he was engaged in agonized and persistent prayer, the icon shone and filled his little cell with abundant light. At the same moment the shameful thoughts disappeared, and his heart was filled with an indescribable joy, peace and blessedness. "Who has conquered the body? He who has made the heart contrite. Who then has made the heart contrite? He who has denied himself...."

By such temptations, and with the passing of time, the battle-ready struggler obtained spiritual experience of the mental warfare of the demons and passions. At the same time he began to receive inward knowledge of the ways Divine Grace acts in the athletes of the spiritual life.

It was this experience which also bore fruit in the soul of the contemporaneous elder, Joseph the Cave-dweller, as written in the book *Eagerly He Ascended: An Expression of Monastic Experience*. The following is a quote from the 10th chapter, entitled "Grace Always Precedes Temptations as a Forewarning Preparation."

> He knew that grace always precedes temptations as a forewarning preparation. As soon as you perceive grace, gird yourself up and say: "Here comes the call to battle! Beware, attend, O clay, to where the wicked one will strike the battle. Many times it comes quickly, and many times after two or three days. In any event, it will come, and the earthworks must be firm. Confession every evening, obedience to the elder, humility and love towards all. By these means lighten the affliction....
>
> Grace is divided into three stages: purifying, enlightening, and perfecting. So also are deeds: natural, supernatural, contranatural. According to these three stages one ascends and descends. The great gifts one receives are also three: contemplation, love, dispassion.

3. HE SOUGHT TO SEE JESUS

Anthony, short in stature like Zacchaeus, great in seeking, high in spiritual ascents, a lover of divine treasures, had, as we said, gone to America at the age of eighteen. There he worked hard for one of his uncles, who was himself a struggler in spiritual life, a support and aid in the combats of his nephew. For the noble soul of Anthony, America was a huge mob, a mass-production crowd, prosperous in material goods and fleshly comfort, a worshipper of idols. All these things hindered the course and the longings of his youthful heart, which resembled a thirsting deer. He *sought to see Jesus* with an urgency like that of Zacchaeus, but he had to find a sycamore tree.

From there, high above the mob and the clamor, above the dizziness and the confusion, he would be able to see Jesus. And this sycamore tree would be the Holy Mountain.

Here is how Divine Providence arranged matters. When he was returning with his uncle from America to Greece, they passed through France. They spent the night at a hotel, and in the morning rose to board the oceanliner which would convey them to their fatherland. But, strangely, Anthony's uncle forgot his identification papers at the hotel. "You wait for me, and I will go to the hotel to fetch my identification," his uncle told him. But while he was yet returning, the ship with the young Anthony on board left without him—to the end, however, of leading the lover of God to his divine destiny.

By a happy coincidence, Anthony arrived in Thessalonica on the day of the surrender of the city to the Greeks, on the feast of St. Demetrius the Myrrh-gusher, in the year 1912. His heart was full of compunction and gratitude to the Saint who is pure and a friend of purity, and the protector of myrrh-gushing purity. He went and venerated his tomb, and in the evening the Saint returned the visit! He visited him in his sleep, and told him: "Do not go to the village. Go to the Holy Mountain and become a monk." And Anthony the child of obedience indeed travelled "with rejoicing feet" to the Garden of the Mother of God. Although there was no regular communication then, the difficulties of the road did not daunt him. He travelled by foot without stopping, and arrived auspiciously at the village of Gomati in Chalcidiki. From there he chartered a donkey with a driver, and set out with the intention of going to the Holy Monastery of the Great Lavra. They passed through Ouranopolis, and then, as they had planned to go through Karyes, they stopped at the Holy Monastery of Constamonitou.

The Holy Monastery of Constamonitou is dedicated to the holy Protomartyr and Archdeacon Stephen, as we mentioned above. According to tradition, his holy icon, which dates from the 8th century, came to the Mountain from Jerusalem in a miraculous manner during the iconoclastic period.

When Anthony venerated the icon of St. Stephen, when he saw the hesychastic surroundings of the Monastery, the love of the fathers, the coenobitic typicon—everything attracted him. *He sought to see Jesus,* and lo, the blessed hour was come. Here, on the Holy Mountain, in the Holy Monastery of Constamonitou, the meeting with Him, the acquaintance, the joyful life-long knowledge of the mystery of divine love, the revelation of God within him, would take place.

When one stands before St. Stephen at the right-hand icon-stand, before the Protomartyr whose *face was like the face of an angel,* there comes to mind the supreme hymn of praise of our Father among the saints Proclus, Patriarch of Constantinople:

O strange wonders of the Stranger King! Yesterday He was born, and today the martyr Stephen* brings to Him a crown:

Stephen, living crown!
Stephen, budding of many flowers for the faithful!
Stephen, most sweet-scented rose of love!
Stephen, most heavy-laden wheat-ear of grace!
Stephen, fruitful branch of the ever-living vine!
Stephen, honeyed grape-cluster of immortality!
Stephen, immovable pillar of confession!
Stephen, invincible soldier of piety!

Come, let us plait for Stephen a crown of a weave until now unachieved!

When he turned his gaze to the holy icon, Anthony felt that St. Stephen, the Saint "filled with the Holy Spirit and with power," was calling him to remain, that he might become to him the friend of the Bridegroom and conductor of the bride (Anthony's soul), and that he might give to the bride, to his virtue-loving soul, "a burning lamp of virtue."

---

*"Stephanos" is Greek for "crown"—*trans. note.*

PROTOMARTYR STEPHEN THE ARCHDEACON
*A drawn rendition of the wonderworking icon at Constamonitou,
from a Russian book of 1880.*

Resolving, therefore, to reside permanently in this Monastery, he called the driver of the donkey and informed him that he did not intend to travel any further. "I will stay here. St. Stephen has captured me," he told him. He was then twenty-two years old.

4. THREE WONDER-WORKING HOLY ICONS

The heretical Jehovah's Witnesses, like the Evangelical Protestants, accuse us Orthodox of being idolaters, because, they say, we worship the holy icons. The accusation is unjust and impious. Orthodox Christians, following the Holy Fathers, "render honorary veneration to the sacred and holy icons of our Lord, our Theotokos, and our saints. This honorary veneration "ascends to the prototype," according to the holy John Damascene. That is to say, when we reverently honor the sacred icon, the honor is not given to wood or paint, to the materials from which it is made. The honor is given and goes over to the person who is the prototype of the sacred image. The militant Jehovah's Witnesses and the water-tight rationalistic Protestants are not able to understand that warm Orthodox living experience before a sacred Byzantine icon. They are strangers to the spiritual feeling and theology of Orthodox iconography, alienated from the mystery of the Church.

For Orthodox Christians, and especially for the monks of the Holy Mountain, the sacred and holy icons are an inseparable part of divine worship. Upon our holy icons is depicted the course of our salvation, our sanctification, our deification. The nature of our Byzantine icons is liturgical and at the same time dogmatical; but before all it is a fruit of the mystical theology of the Eastern Orthodox Church. The Byzantine icon exists as a message and invitation of the world transfigured in Christ, of the deified face of man united to the Holy Trinity by means of the uncreated energies and uncreated light.

On the Holy Mountain, where every manifestation of worship and sanctifying work has the force and power of genuineness, where active worship is tightly woven together with contemplation, the monks honor most deeply, venerate with awe and kiss with fervent love the icons on the icon-stands in the holy churches, the portable icons and the frescoes. They light their lampadas during Matins, Vespers, and Compline, and during every prayer inside and outside the church, as well as in the chapels and the various small shrines. "Transfigured from glory to glory," they live, they dwell together, with the presence of the saints, with their holy relics and sacred icons.

Every monastery has its own icons with which its history is bound. In the Holy Monastery of Constamonitou, the three icons which stand out and convey sensibly the grace and blessing of God are: of St. Stephen, of the Mother of God *Hodigitria,* and of the Mother of God *Antiphonitria.*

About the sacred icon of St. Stephen, in whose honor the Monastery celebrates its feast day, we have the following information from the time of the reign of Constantine Monomachos (Manuscript No. 114, p. 133):

...Then also the holy icon of St. Stephen was brought from Jerusalem, which icon stands on the right side of the catholicon church, where it is seen and venerated by all. And for an unlying witness of truth, this icon is in the lower part a little burnt by the iconoclasts, since it was thrown into the fire and did not burn except only a part; and thus it appears until today.

In the same manuscript, on pages 133 and 134, we read also of the wondrous things performed by the holy icon of the Mother of God *Hodigitria*:

...Seeing these things, the elder and wondrous Father Agathon sorrowed greatly and wept with warm tears, and prayed with fasting before the holy icon of the Mother of God; and wearied from his much supplication, he fell asleep a little and, coming into ecstasy, saw revelations, and heard a voice from the holy icon of the Mother of God—O the wonder!— telling him not to grieve and worry over the scandals and temptations occurring, and that the Mountain would from that time be quieted from all the sufferings; and for a sign and assurance of what was said, behold, the large jar of the church was filled with oil. Similarly, the other vessels of the Monastery were also filled with the necessities of life.

When Elder Agathon awoke, from spiritual gladness together with marveling timidity he did not believe the word of the Mother of God that this vision was true. Therefore he sought for a light, and lighting a lamp went to the cask of the church to ascertain the truth; and seeing the true miracle, he was astonished and afraid, and in a loud voice proclaimed to all the brothers the great miracle of the Theotokos; and thus he related the things he had seen and heard from the Mother of God. Therefore from that time up to now a lampada is continuously lit before the holy icon of our Lady Theotokos in thanksgiving for the miracle.

For the immaterial being of Fr. Philaret, all the Monastery's holy icons constituted a foretaste of the space and time of eternity. But the wonderworking icons of the Protomartyr and Archdeacon and of the Mother of God *Hodigitria* were the living witnesses of the "joy-giving sorrow" by which eternity illuminated the elder's monastic spiritual experience. This was shown by the deep reverence, together with the joy, intimacy, and compunction with which he venerated these icons every day in all the services of the Monastery.

II

"O How I Have Loved Thy Law, O Lord"

1. MARTYRIC OBEDIENCE

Come hither, O struggler, come near me and stand ardent...
Thou dost excel all, as is written by God,
For thou dost walk the path of the First Martyr.
                (St. Theodore the Studite, "To a Disciple")

With these beautiful verses, the Saint also addresses, as it were, the struggler and athlete of blessed obedience, the novice Anthony. A disciple is considered a martyr of Christ; according to the Holy Fathers, he walks the path of the martyrs. Anthony performed not only a single, but a double and triple martyric obedience, for three reasons, as we will see.

It was the custom then to send novices to serve in the Monastery Metochia, which were scattered outside the Mountain. Our novice followed this rule; as soon as he entered the Monastery he was immediately sent to the Metochion of Tripotamos.

As he was given the obedience of cellarer, he had the duties of cooking for the steward, the assistant steward, and the workers; of setting the table, washing the dishes, sweeping, distributing food to the workers, taking care that food was not lacking from the cellar, and being completely obedient. Life in the metochia is very difficult for monks, and especially for novices. For one thing, they are deprived of their precious silence, and for another, many laymen—men, women, and children—work in the metochia. It is a life of continual struggle, amidst a furnace of temptations and scandals. This was the first cause which made the obedience of our novice martyric. But the fires of the devil and the burning of the flesh and the snares of the world did not prove sufficient to check the divine zeal of our beginning monk, or to harm the purity of the recruited soldier of Christ.

At the same time, the steward of the Metochion was a very hard man (eternal be his memory). He was known throughout all the Holy Mountain for his steel-like temper. Woe to anyone who happened to cross him in anything.... He was exacting and irritable in the extreme. With this man, Anthony's life was a true martyrdom. But he practiced patience and was longsuffering towards everyone. The steward, therefore, was the second cause of his martyrdom.

His third great trial was his illness: he suffered for a long time from a severe case of dysentery. Thus Anthony was purified "like gold in the furnace." And what other means of purification are more sure than obedience and humility and long-drawn-out illness?

For six months he was bedridden, suffering from pain, stench, exhaustion, a pre-tubercular condition, and, before all, from the steward's neglect and indifference.

But divine Grace sent him great consolation, strength of soul, and manifest intervention. In this trial of soul and body, the novice Anthony became the child of patience and could say to the Lord: *For the sake of the words of Thy lips I have kept the ways that are hard.*

One day, he saw as in a vision a young man who came in and stood opposite him, shining with an unutterable beauty. "Anthony, you are still in pain?! Your patience has pleased God," he said and became invisible. Who else? It was St. Stephen.

After this event he was examined by two or three doctors. Their diagnosis? Perfect health. The doctor of the Lavra, Monk Athanasius Kampanaos, wrote in a report to the Monastery: "For the first time in the annals I have seen such lungs, such a youthful organism, as if they belonged to a three-year-old child."

The steward was struck speechless by the miracle. He asked forgiveness for his behavior. "My child, I have grieved you beyond measure," he said again and again, repenting.

2. LITURGICAL ARDOR

Returning to the holy Monastery from the Metochion, the brave novice, after passing his exams as a novice and for the sake of his excellent conduct, was tonsured a monk in May of 1915 and named Philaret. They entrusted him with the blessed but fatiguing obedience of ecclesiarch. Nothing, however, was tiring for the abundant good-will, the full, enthusiastic eagerness, and the virtue-loving (*philareti*) heart of the rightly-named monk Philaret. He flew through the church like an angel of light, like a "ministering spirit sent to serve...."

The ecclesiarch is the monk who is occupied with many different duties in the church. He lights the lampadas, washes, polishes the brass candlestands, polyeleos, and candleholders; he sweeps and mops, prepares pure, clean candles, incense, wick-holders, wicks, wax lampadas; repairs the stalls, etc. All this he does outside the time of services. During the divine services he has other duties, with the result that he must be upright and moving continually, dressed in his special many-pleated mantia which symbolizes the wings of angels. Furthermore, he has the care of being attentive, of not making noise, and of being uncritically obedient to the abbot and the serving priest.

The blessed Philaret proved to be a model of a diligent and tireless ecclesiarch. During a divine service, after he had arranged everything "decently and in order," he confined himself to his stall, head bent, submerged in the sweet prayer of one who loves Jesus. Music he never managed to learn, and when he did sing, his voice was usually hoarse. But what significance had this shortcoming? Poor-voiced he was, but of exalted mind; uneducated, but initiated into "the divine and ineffable choir of the bodiless ones."

In April of 1921 he was ordained a deacon. In this first rank of the priesthood he felt a special relationship with the Protomartyr and Archdeacon Stephen, the guardian and protector of his holy Coenobium. Three years later, in October of 1924, he was ordained a priest. From the day of his ordination until the day of his repose the elder served Liturgy daily, without interruption. Every day his soul thirsted, yearned, pined for the Divine Liturgy. Few would be the occasions, chiefly for health reasons, when he would not perform the Mystery of mysteries, the Divine Eucharist. He lived to liturgize, and he liturgized to live. For without the Divine Liturgy he felt dead, bereft of Christ, Who is the life and the resurrection, the light and the repose.

At that time there were two other hieromonks beside the Abbot, but the one, Fr. Agapius, was very sickly, while the other did not greatly desire to serve every day. For this reason Fr. Philaret undertook the permanent duty of performing daily Liturgy. Even when the other hieromonk decided to serve, the elder went and liturgized at one of the eight quiet, compunctionate chapels of the Monastery. Four of these are inside the walls: 1) of the Theotokos, which has a beautifully carved wooden iconostasis and houses the wonderworking icon of the Panagia *Portaitissa*, which worked many miracles in Russia; 2) of St. Constantine; 3) of All Saints; 4) of St. Nicholas. Outside the walls are four other chapels: 1) the chapel of the Archangels in the cemetery; 2) of the Holy Trinity; 3) of the "Panagouda" or "Panagitsa," a loving diminutive appellation of the Mother of God, located in the ravine; and 4) of St. Anthony at the site of the old Monastery. Each one is beautiful and adorned with its own grace.

Fr. Philaret liturgized unceasingly even when his health was shaken and he suffered hernias on both sides of his body. The hernias were symptoms of the many hours he spent standing upright and laboring every day. To give him rest, the fathers suggested paying an outside priest to serve every day, because later Fr. Philaret had, besides the daily serving, the duties of Abbot and Confessor of a

Interior of the chapel housing Constamonitou's wonderworking *Portaitissa* icon of the Mother of God.

multitude of monks, pilgrims, and workers. To this proposal the blessed and humble elder answered: "My fathers, you labor more than I do. I don't know any other work; I only serve Liturgy. Let me labor together with you in this way. If my strength fails, then I will tell you to bring an outside hieromonk."

By his ceaseless liturgizing he showed not only brotherly love and willingness of soul; he showed the liturgical flame, the zeal of the Mystical Supper, desire for the endless and eternal Pascha, love for the presence of the Master, the entrance of his burning heart "into the splendor of the saints."

If we think to open this heart, we will see that it burned with a liturgical fire. He had once confided to Fr. Pachomius that when he served Liturgy he felt a leaping in his soul, a transformation, a revelation of another world.

The unceasing singing of the sacred doxology of the Trisagion by the holy angels is generally symbolic of the equal-in-honor co-dwelling, mingling and symphony of the powers of heaven and earth, which will be realized in the future life, since by the resurrection men will receive their deathless bodies. The body will no longer burden the soul by its corruption, nor itself be burdened by it. By its passing to incorruption it will receive power and capability to endure the coming of God (St. Maximus, *Mystagogia*).

This spiritual sense of incorruption, of the equal-in-honor co-dwelling with the angels, of the coming of God, was present in the deepest content of the elder's every Divine Liturgy.

When Fr. Philaret liturgized he was all light, all joy, all peace; thoughtful, serious, wet with tears. He also often wept for the carelessness of his co-celebrants.

In 1929, Fr. Philaret was a young hieromonk when that terrible fire broke out in the forest of the Holy Monastery of Vatopedi by the negligence of the "coal-dealer" workers. The fire spread and began to advance towards Constamonitou Monastery. The fathers of the Monastery set off to help put out the blaze. In front went Fr. Philaret, holding in his hands the icon of the Theotokos and encouraging the fathers, saying characteristically with a deep faith: "Little fathers, the fire will be out before we arrive. Don't worry." And for the whole length of the road he sang from memory the Supplicatory Canon to the Mother of God. When the fathers and brothers reached the boundary of the two monasteries, the fire had gone out by itself, after previously completely burning the grounds of Vatopedi Monastery. The all-devouring blaze did not dare to touch even ten centimeters of Constamonitou property, even though the boundary was nothing but a foot-path between one and two spans wide. Everyone attributed the miracle to the prayers of the young Fr. Philaret and the intervention of the Lady Theotokos.

The zeal of the ardent priest to liturgize, to liturgize unceasingly, is shown by the following event. On the night of January 17, the feast of St. Anthony the Great, he set out after Matins to serve Liturgy in the chapel dedicated to the Saint. This chapel is 500 meters above the Monastery. He took with him two prosphora, a water-vial, and an oil lantern. He had gone some distance from the

Monastery into the wild Athonite nature, made yet wilder by the moonless night, when he stumbled at a difficult passage, fell, and broke the water-vial. Attributing the event to the envy of the devil, he went back, took another water-vial, and joyfully set out again to celebrate Liturgy. But at the same spot he stumbled again, fell, and broke the second water-vial. Then, becoming angry with a holy anger against satan, he said: "Tempter, this evening I will serve Liturgy at St. Anthony's, no matter what you do or what obstacles you put before me!" He returned, took another water-vial, and finally reached his destination, praying.

During most of his Divine Liturgies he was bathed in tears—tears of compunction, joy, and love. His compunction culminated at the Consecration.

One year he was saying the dismissal prayer of the Ninth Hour at the leave-taking of Pascha. For all the saints, Pascha is the most moving time of the year. At the dismissal, therefore—the moment when they would take away the icon of the Resurrection—he was shaken, he shed tears, he all but burst out in sobs because he was losing the Resurrection.... To his easily moved and sensitive soul it appeared as if the Risen Lord was ascending, was leaving them.

When serving, he wanted his mind to remain undistracted during the fearful hour of the Liturgy. Attention and prayer were his whole life. For this reason he placed a curtain at the opening of the sanctuary to the side-altar, so that those coming in and going out would not disturb his devotion to the Divine Liturgy.

"Fr. David, next time please don't pass through here," he said to one monk who repeatedly passed through the Holy Altar.

In the reading of the Gospel he surpassed the best theologians. "I liked to listen to him very much," Fr. Niphon says up to now. Remember that he was almost uneducated.

After every Divine Liturgy he immediately shut himself in his cell. There he would pray on his knees to the Mother of God, or study the Gospels, the *Evergetinos,* and St. Ephraim—his most beloved texts. As much as possible he wished to preserve the divine illumination and activity of the Sacrament for the duration of the day.

At the end of one vigil, as he was returning together with Fr. Pachomius to their adjoining cells, he turned and said to him:

"Right now I could serve yet another long vigil.... This night a multitude was about me...."

"What? What?" Fr. Pachomius asked in perplexity.

"Angels of heaven!" answered the devout priest.

Fr. Pachomius visited the Monastery with his father in 1931, at the age of fifteen, during the second week of the fast. During Compline they stood in the back of the church. When the fathers came out, he saw Fr. Philaret, then a simple priest, for the first time. He saw him as an angelic figure, with a face entirely different from the countenance of the other fathers, shining like the moon.

Fr. Onouphrius the confessor also confided that he once saw him during a Divine Liturgy elevated two spans above the ground at the Great Entrance.

III

"For I Am Thy Slave... "

1. *LET HE THAT IS CHIEF BE AS HE THAT DOTH SERVE*

In the year 1949 Fr. Philaret was elected Abbot almost unanimously, that he might be placed as *a lamp upon a lampstand* and illumine *all that are in the house.* In this honorable position and responsible rank the elder preserved the greatest humility and increased his patience and forbearance. He knew his flock, his reasonable sheep, which of his disciples could withstand rebuke and which could not. He knew the characters of each one, their gifts and faults. Mostly by persuasion, and less by the rod, he sought to raise up the negligent or inattentive to the monastic order and angelic discipline.

Fr. Philaret was the good shepherd who "could seek and heal the lost reasonable sheep by his guilelessness, zeal, and prayer." He was the pilot "who had obtained from God and his labors spiritual power, and could pull up the ship even from the abyss, and save it." He was the physician "who had acquired immunity from disease of body and soul." He was the teacher "who had received from God a spiritual book, namely by the activity of divine illumination, and had no need of other books" (St. John of the Ladder, "Word to the Shepherd").

Rarely did he rebuke anyone for his faults. Rather, he utilized much guilelessness and meekness, so that he himself might not be be tempted by the demon of anger and censuring. When one novice monk was talking idly with older fathers, he summoned him in a clever manner and advised him to desist from this idle association and conversation; however, he did not scold him on the spot and publicly.

He often said: "After the three-layered foundation of the monastic life, namely, obedience, chastity, and poverty, *a monk's two eyes are his daily services and his rule.*" The "services" are the prayers said together with the brothers every day in church according to the monastic typicon, and the "rule" is the personal, private prayer and prostrations which each monk fulfills in his cell. "If you don't have one of these two," Fr. Philaret would say, "then you are one-eyed. And if both are lacking, then you are sunk in darkness and spiritually blind."

The elder wanted his children to have spiritual sight, eyes healthy and clear, minds illumined by the light of prayer and compunction. For this reason he attended his flock sleeplessly. The blessed one had a custom of lighting a candle after the Six Psalms and walking around within the church to see which of the fathers were absent. When he ascertained someone's absence he would send a novice to call him to Matins, or, more usually, he would himself go to his cell and ask him: "Brother, what's the matter? Aren't you going to come to the service?" He did not forsake this habit even in his old age, despite the pain caused him by his double hernia. He thought himself jointly responsible if the absentee did not come to Matins through negligence or the influence of sleep. But he was also moved by his love for his brethren to see if perhaps the missing brother was sick and needed immediate assistance.

As Abbot he did the most menial chores, ministering according to the example of our Master and Teacher Jesus, "taking the form of a servant." One would meet the elder, one time kneading the prosphora himself, another time at the oven, another time in the sewing room. He was the first in the "common labors," the labors done with the participation and help of all the brethren. The holy

Abbot did not fear that he might "soil his hands" with these lower tasks. Rather, he knew to sanctify his hands by humble labor, to anoint them with the myrrh of humility and toil, and thus to offer them in the service of the divine and sacred Mysteries.

The rank of Abbot was unable to change the character of Fr. Philaret, which was leavened with humility and simplicity. Once or twice he even wanted to resign from the abbacy, but the brothers would not let him. "Ach, how I was cheated, the foolish one," he would say, "when I undertook to be Abbot. When I was a simple priest serving every day, I did one Liturgy and flew to the heavens. And now poisons from here, poisons from there, and many days I repent that I served."

Every month the elder blessed holy water and sprinkled the Monastery's vineyards and gardens regularly, and at extra times when a disease struck the plants.

He would take the holy relics from the Monastery to the Metochion of Parthenonas in Chalcidiki, where there were flocks, olives, and pine trees, and sprinkle them with holy water after reading the necessary prayers. Almost always Divine Grace answered the heartfelt supplications of the blessed elder.

One year, on the feast of St. John Chrysostom (November 13), he took out the relics of the Saint and placed them on the Holy Table the evening before the vigil. A fragrance filled the whole Catholicon. When they entered, the fathers were perplexed and amazed: "What is this? What is this fragrance?" they asked one another.

For the Athonite monastic conscience, the holy relics are the greatest spiritual treasure of the Holy Mountain, together with the sacred wonder-working icons. Through the holy relics the fathers experience the glory of the Church Triumphant amidst the Militant. Heaven and earth, the heavenly and the earthly, are united. Indeed, what words can describe the greatness of the Lord Who is manifested also in the grace-bearing relics of the saints? "Great art Thou, O Lord, and no word suffices to hymn Thy wonders."

This spirit of glorification filled also the heart of Fr. Philaret before the divine energy and grace of the holy relics.

2. THE KINGDOM OF GOD IS TAKEN BY VIOLENCE

...and the violent take it by force. Fr. Philaret had well digested this truth, spoken by the unlying mouth of our Lord. He was a "violent" monk. "A true monk is he who continually forces his nature and uninterruptedly guards his senses" (*The Ladder of Divine Ascent*, Step One).

This violence against himself consisted of exile, poverty, fasting and temperance, silence, the inuring of his body to hardships.

Never did he neglect his monastic duties. Every year he did the established "trimero" (a fast from all food and water for three days at the beginning of Great Lent). Once he even said at the end of one "trimero": "I have the strength to continue fasting yet another three days."

From the hour that he entered the Holy Mountain, the arena of the athletes of Christ, and grasped the plow of the monastic order, "he did not turn back." He did not pity himself. For the love of Christ he exiled himself from all his relatives and friends. They once summoned him to come to their village. His mother wrote him letters with tears and sighs, asking him to go to give her the Spotless Mysteries before her death. He, taking counsel in everything from his confessor, did not even want to hear of going away from the Mountain. He also had a brother according to the flesh named Thomas, who would come to the Mountain two or three times a year. He also said to him: "Won't you come to the village just once, to serve Liturgy for us? You disown us too completely." His aim was to keep him as priest in the village. If this had been God's will, his spiritual father would have told him, and not his worldly brother. Thomas, however, received an answer from the Protomartyr and guardian of the holy Monastery, whom Fr. Philaret had as a friend and helper.

It was night. Thomas was sleeping in the Monastery. Suddenly St. Stephen appeared in his sleep, strict and implacable.

"Ungrateful one," he said to Thomas, "Isn't it enough for you that you have come to see your brother, but you even want to take him to the village?"

Thomas arose terrified. The Saint's appearance made a fearful impression. How could he again dare to think of such a scheme?

The ever-memorable elder was diligent in his spiritual duties. Therefore, when admonishing his children he would say: "Fathers and brothers, let us do our spiritual duties, and Divine Providence will take care of all our material needs. The compassionately-loving Lord will not abandon us when we renounce the world and the things of the world for His love. He will feed us. Doesn't it say, 'Seek ye first the kingdom of God, and all these things will be added unto you?'"

And he was not only diligent, but also exact. His exactness in his monastic life was exemplary. Every night he arose at midnight to do his rule. *At midnight I will arise...*—this verse of David echoed arousingly within him.

His cell was plain, ascetic, coenobitic. There was in it neither sugar, nor coffee, nor other foods, as other brothers had by concession. A low stool, which he used for mental prayer, was transformed into a "heavenly ladder by which God descended, a bridge" leading the lover of virtue and silence "to heaven."

When he was enthroned as Abbot, the enthroning fathers wanted to see his cell. As soon as they entered it they were struck speechless. They faced four bare walls. His bed was a few planks, and his mattress a goat-hair blanket, made from those hard sacks in which olives are crushed. There was a pillow filled with dried weeds, and a blanket for covering. He himself would often humbly take a broom and sweep, or light the lampadas, or do other menial tasks.

He shunned idle talk, worldly or political subjects. Neither did he wish to see a newspaper. He was self-effacing, never bold in speech. When he talked with you, being bashful, he always lowered his eyes to the earth. He did not wish to gaze at men, but at God. He was temperate in all things, "a never-lapsing guardian of the senses." His modesty and bashfulness inspired a boundless reverence.

When the winter is severe, the snow takes fifteen to twenty days to melt at Constamonitou Monastery. All the fathers had stoves in their cells. The elder did not have a stove. Fr. Niphon, who took care of the heating, would say to him with reverence and love:

"My father, we must put a stove in your room, too."

"Let it be, Elder Niphon. We'll do it later."

This he said with the aim of letting the cold season pass little by little, always delaying putting heating in his cell. Two or three years before his death he finally received the stove.

If you opened his door, never, never would you find him doing any other work in his cell except praying on his knees.

Such a struggler was the blessed one. In fasting as well he was always a model.

"Elder, I'm not afraid of work, as long as I eat well," he was once told by Fr. Euthemius, who had been a peasant and shepherd in the world, and who was always given heavy tasks.

"The body, my child," he answered, "doesn't fear work; it fears fasting."

When he was over seventy years old, the ever-memorable one went by foot to Karyes, which is a three-hours' journey from Constamonitou. He went together with one brother, and took the mule, but did not mount it. Tireless on the road, he jumped over the branches of the shrubs like a light-hearted child.

Did he act thus from love and sympathy for the mule, or from being inured to hardships and suffering? Evidently for both reasons. He saw the mule and philosophized: This also is God's creation, made to serve and minister to man, that great miracle and at the same time, dead corpse. In the soul of a monk, with time the feeling is born and consolidated: *I came not to be ministered unto, but to minister,* to "minister" even to the dumb animals by enduring hardship and toil for their sakes.

3. THE GIFT OF CLAIRVOYANCE

In monasteries Mondays are set aside as fast days, besides Wednesdays and Fridays. One Monday, therefore, when the Monastery guestmaster happened to be absent, the young assistant guestmaster, Fr. Ch., fell into the temptation of secret eating. Without a blessing he boiled vegetables and fried potatoes in the special kitchen of the guesthouse. He was ready to begin the meal when he heard the footsteps of the Abbot outside, and he hurried to hide the food in a cupboard. The door opened, and in came Fr. Philaret.

"My child," he said to him, "bring the potatoes and vegetables you prepared, so we can eat together."

The assistant guestmaster was struck speechless! How did the Abbot know what he had cooked? At first he wanted to deny it; but the elder said to him kindly:

"I won't give you a penance for what you did. Bring the food so we can eat."

One can guess at the repentance of Fr. Ch., and also marvel at the clairvoyance, lenience, and pastoral skill of the wise Abbot.

The hero of this incident was the assistant guestmaster; the following will present the guestmaster himself.

The guestmaster had a good habit: On his nameday he would invite the fathers to the guest-house and treat them to coffee and a sweet. One year, however, he closed the guesthouse and shut himself in his cell. This did not pass unobserved by the Abbot, Fr. Philaret. He went to the guest-master's cell and said to him with a cheerful look:

"Why didn't you offer treats to the brothers? To avoid the labor, or for some other reason?"

"To avoid the labor," the guestmaster answered contritely.

"Ah, my child, you have really missed the mark. Today you will have to endure much harder work."

Saying this, he departed.

And indeed, a little later a brother informed the guestmaster:

"Go immediately and prepare the guest-quarters. Governor Goulas of Polygyros is coming with the doctor and three clerks, and they need special care."

Later the Abbot met him:

"Remember what I told you, my child?"

"I certainly remember, Elder. I endured four-fold labor," answered the guestmaster.

Another incident shows Fr. Philaret's deep humility and simplicity, as well as his clairvoyance.

In 1959, Fr. Zacharias of the Holy Monastery of Grigoriou invited his friend Fr. Pachomius to participate in the celebration of the feast of St. Nicholas.

A week in advance, Fr. Pachomius asked a blessing from the Abbot to go to the celebration. On the eve of the feast the Abbot came to the guesthouse and said to him with simplicity:

"Will you take me to the celebration, too?"

"Before God, Elder! It would be a great honor to accompany you," Fr. Pachomius answered eagerly.

As he had no money, Fr. Philaret humbly asked for fifty drachmas from the treasurer for the motorboat fare. However, since the Athonite etiquette provides that the Abbot should be accompanied by one of the officers of the Monastery, he was careful that no one should see them together. He wanted to avoid rivalry and scandal. However, he said to Fr. Pachomius:

"You will have a temptation, but don't be afraid. It will pass."

When they reached Daphne, the temptation which was to trouble them came. A certain merchant shouted to Fr. Pachomius:

"You're wanted on the telephone!"

One of the more difficult officers of the Monastery, at that time the representative in Karyes, was waiting indignantly on the other end of the line. He immediately burst out at Fr. Pachomius:

"Aren't you ashamed? Who gave you the right to accompany the Abbot? Don't you know that only officers accompany him?"

Fortunately, the brethren of Grigoriou soon consoled him. It was noon when they arrived at the Holy Monastery of Grigoriou, but one hieromonk, seeing them in time, ran to the harbor, welcomed them, took their bag on his back, and protested to Fr. Philaret:

"Why didn't you tell us you were coming, Elder, so we could welcome you properly?"

In the Abbot's quarters, Abbot Bessarion (now reposed) rose and embraced him:

"What joy your visit to our Monastery gives us!" he said with feeling.

He ceded to him the abbatial room and the first place in the feast day vigil, in which, let it be noted, twenty priests concelebrated.

Fr. Philaret's gift of clairvoyance had manifested itself while he was still a simple priest, when he had foreseen the death of his sister. He had gone to Fr. Symeon, then the Abbot, and said to him:

"Elder, my sister will die tonight."

"How do you know?" the Abbot asked him, surprised. "I know," the modest hieromonk answered humbly.

In a few days a sorrowful letter came to the Monastery, exactly confirming Fr. Philaret's prophecy.

Those who knew the elder well began to count seriously on this extraordinary gift. At least, so it appears from the following incident.

A young monk of Constamonitou had an uncle, the monk Ioasaph (first cousin of his father), who lived in the cell of Ravdouchou in Karyes. This uncle repeatedly came to the Monastery and besought his nephew to come and stay with him in Karyes, in order to help him build his cell.

The young Constamonitou monk hesitated, but finally he gave in to the persistent supplications. Therefore he agreed that the uncle would come to the celebration of Sts. Constantine and Helen, and that they would leave secretly during the vigil. And although until then the nephew had had the saving monastic custom of confessing all his thoughts to Fr. Philaret (even before he became Abbot), this frightful thought he avoided mentioning.

The eve of the feast came, and the Monastery prepared for the feast day vigil. The uncle also set out from Karyes on a mule which was noted for its docility. This afternoon, however, the mule was unexpectedly wayward and threw him down. Fr. Ioasaph arrived at the Monastery with wounds on his face. His nephew cleaned away the blood, but the marks remained.

In the middle of Matins, after the Polyeleos, Fr. Philaret discreetly approached the wounded visitor and said to him:

"Elder, can I say something to you out in the narthex?"

"Gladly," answered Fr. Ioasaph.

The two went out.

"Why did you come to our Monastery?" he asked him.

"Aren't you celebrating a vigil? I came for that."

"Unfortunately, you did not come for that. You came to take the young monk. Pay close attention! If you come a second time and persist in your intention, the mule will kill you."

Fr. Ioasaph was speechless. As soon as he met his nephew and found a suitable opportunity he told him the prophecy. Then the nephew said to him:

"If Fr. Philaret prophesied this to you, uncle, you mustn't dare to set foot here again to take me away."

4. THE ELDER'S DEVOTION TO THE THEOTOKOS

O all-praised Mother who didst bear the Word, holiest of all the Saints, accept this our offering, and deliver us from all offense, and redeem from future torment those who cry in unison to thee: Alleluia.

How many times in his life, how many times in the fifty-one years of his monasticism did he say this hymn, together with the whole Akathist to the Mother of God! His soul perceived the "All-praised Mother truly bearing the Word most holy" and took refuge in Her divine motherly love with hope, faith, and a devotion which strongly characterizes the lives of all saints.

He said the Akathist many times a day. Always after the Divine Liturgy he hurried to his cell, lit a lampada before the "Sweet-kissing" icon of the Lady Theotokos, and with love and piety began the hymn:

"An Archangel was sent from Heaven to say to the Mother of God: Rejoice!"

He also advised his disciples to pray often with the Akathist to the Theotokos. With the simplicity which distinguished him, he would say, as if to scold them: "Why don't you love the Panagia?" For a penance he would tell all who confessed to him, both laymen and monks, to say the Akathist at least once, with a lampada lit before Her icon.

Oh, the love for the Panagia which pulls us out of the hell of egotism, despair, and the passions, and leads us to the paradise of humility!

Once a Bulgarian monk named Fr. Ignatius came to Fr. Philaret. After they had conversed for a while, the elder, as always, asked him with his sweet voice:

"Do you read the *Hairetismoi** every day?"

"Yes, I read them. Not the whole Akathist, only the Hairetismoi," answered the Bulgarian monk, who had not understood exactly what the elder had said.

"Show me what you read," said the elder, to be sure.

Monk Ignatius took out a gold-bound little book in the Bulgarian language, opened it, and showed him. Indeed, he showed him the beginning, namely "An archangel was sent from Heaven...." But to be even more sure, Fr. Philaret turned one or two pages to the place where it is written: "The shepherds heard...."

"What's written here?" he asked him.

And the Bulgarian monk, who knew little Greek, answered him with his thick accent:

---

*In Greece the Akathist Hymn is usually referred to as the *Hairetismoi* ("Salutations")—*trans. note.*

"Here it says, 'The herders got wind...'"

Smiling like a child, the elder said:

"Good, good, you understand what the Hairetismoi are. Always say them. Don't ever omit them."

Together with the Akathist, he fervently loved to read and recommend the Theotokarion, a book with special canons and hymns to the Mother of God for every day. In his Monastery it was in the Typicon, but he himself read it wherever he went or happened to be.

This devotion to the Mother of God changed Fr. Philaret into a fragrant lily in the ever-green garden of the Panagia. Daily he was nourished in his cell *like a sparrow alone upon the house-top* by his spiritual nurse and mother. And his soul "as a servant ... as a handmaid ... at the hands of her mistress" asked the spiritual milk of the grace of the All-Immaculate One, repeating again and again his beloved Theotokarion:

> *As a servant raiseth his outward eyes*
> *To the hands of his own master, O All-Praised One,*
> *So I too lift up both outward and inward eyes*
> *To thee, my Mistress, my Lady and my Life,*
> *As thou hast pity on me.*

If the Panagia is for all monks a mother and nurse and guardian, the Ever-virgin Protectress and Leader of virgins, she is so even more for the monks of the Holy Mountain. In the minds of the fathers of Mount Athos, she is obligated to be so by the promises she gave to St. Peter the Athonite about the whole Mountain and those who dwell there. They consider her as much their own as the mother and mistress of a house is to her children.

For this reason, all the festivals of the Mother of God are accompanied by vigils, while the feast of the Dormition is celebrated with particular splendor, and inspires such enthusiasm as to be a second Pascha. Souls leap with joy, the angel-like ascetics of Athos

The Mother of God *Glykophilousa* ("Sweet-Kissing")

exult, and like sweet-singing nightingales hymn the greatness of the All-Blameless Bride, the Sweet Spring-time, and Her most sweet Child.

IV

"The Exposition of Thy Words Enlightens and Instructs Infants"

1. BLESSED ARE THE MEEK, FOR THEY SHALL INHERIT THE EARTH

If we were to try to paint the spiritual figure of Fr. Philaret, the strongest and most characteristic color giving him the "first-created beauty" would be the color of meekness. He was meek, guileless, forgetful of wrongs, and never angry; his soul was merciful, long-suffering, and full of pity, a true dwelling of God. For in truth, "where there is quietness and meekness and humility, there God dwells" (John the Prophet, *Book of Barsanuphius and John*, p. 225).

An icon of meekness, bright and living, was the blessed elder, and that is why he received such a wealth of grace and wisdom. "None of the virtues," writes Evagrius, "so gives birth to wisdom as does meekness." This saying is most true. Almost uneducated (a graduate of the third grade), Fr. Philaret, by reason of this evangelical, Christ-imitating virtue of meekness, acquired such wisdom that many who knew him said that it seemed as if the Holy Spirit, and not he himself, spoke through his mouth. He spoke simply, without adornment, but wisely. We can observe this God-taught wisdom and God-given grace in many saints of our Church, as a fruit of their great humility—for example, in Moses, David, and Abba Bes, by whose meekness, reports Palladius, even wild beasts were tamed:

> Then we saw in the Thebaid another old man, called Abba Bes, who surpassed everyone in meekness. The brothers who lived round about him assured us that he had never sworn an oath, had never told a lie, had never been angry with anyone, and had never scolded anyone. For he lived a life of the utmost stillness and his manner was serene, since he had attained the angelic state. He was extremely humble and held himself of no account. We pressed him strongly to speak a word of encouragement to us, but he only consented to say a little about meekness, and was reluctant to do even that.
>
> Once when a hippopotamus was ravaging the neighboring countryside, the farmers called on this Father to help them. He stood at the place and waited, and when he saw the beast, which was of enormous size, he commanded it in a gentle voice, saying: 'In the name of Jesus Christ I order you not to ravage the countryside anymore.' The hippopotamus, as if driven away by an angel, vanished completely from that district. On another occasion he got rid of a crocodile in the same way (*The Lives of the Desert Fathers*, VI, tr. by Benedicta Ward SLG).

A certain person told Elder Philaret about a vision he had read about in the life of a saint—namely, that when a Divine Liturgy is finished the angels take the prosphoras and carry them up to the throne of God. Once the Divine Liturgy at the Holy Sepulchre finished later than those at other churches, and the other angels had to wait for it to finish in order to follow behind its angels in elevating their prosphoras. Therefore from then on the zealous and most simple Elder Philaret wanted his own Divine Liturgy to finish before the others on the Holy Mountain, lest by chance he might delay the holy angels (such was his simplicity). Therefore he appointed only a little time to rest after Matins, in order to begin Divine Liturgy all the earlier. In the interval between the services he never slept, for fear that he be tempted during sleep, while the whole time he worried that the angels might be waiting to raise his prosphoras to the throne of God. Therefore he almost always rang the warning bell prematurely and knocked on the door of the ecclesiarch, telling him to prepare the church, light the lampadas, etc.

This habit offended the fathers, and especially the ecclesiarch, who is also responsible for ringing the bells. But everyone was patient with this pious weakness of his.

At one vigil the ecclesiarch, Fr. Gennadius, asked Fr. Philaret:

"Elder, how many hours will we have between Matins and Divine Liturgy?"

The answer was "two hours"; but since it was certain that the elder, according to his custom, would strike the wake-up bell earlier, he could not endure it. This time he went and locked the door of the church.

All had retired and were quiet in their cells. The elder stayed awake. Every once in a while he looked at his watch. Finally, when it reached one after midnight, he went and rang the bell. Afterwards he knocked on the door of the ecclesiarch's room and timidly and shyly called to him to get up. (As this brother was a little hot-tempered, he avoided irritating him—for one thing, that the brother might not be incriminated, and for another, that he himself might not be reproached by his conscience as undiscerning.)

"Fr. Gennadius, eh, Fr. Gennadius!"

"Bless! Who is it? What's the matter?" he answered from within, half-asleep.

"It's me, the elder. Well, aren't you coming down to light the lampadas?"

"Very well, very well, I'm coming," he said, and continued sleeping!

Fr. Philaret, therefore, descended the stairs, went to the door of the church, took another key and tried to open it. In vain; the door didn't open. Again he climbed the stairs and knocked on the cell of Fr. Gennadius—but to no effect. He went down and waited outside the church: silence everywhere, no response. Meanwhile his simple and ingenuous heart was anxious. He thought he would be late in serving Liturgy, and what would become of his prosphoras which the angels were to take? Again he tried to open the door. Nothing.

At that moment Elder Niphon, one of the older fathers, pious and ascetic, of the same age as Elder Philaret, came down the stairs.

"Eh, Fr. Niphon, can you open the door for me?" he said beseechingly, like a small child asking a great favor.

"Well, my Elder, what hour is this that you are ringing the bell?"

The elder began to justify himself charmingly, and finally said:

"And that blessed Fr. Gennadius has locked me out!"

Elder Niphon of Constamonitou

Then Fr. Niphon, with a serious face but a laughing heart, answered him:

"It's good that he did. You do this to us every time."

Elder Philaret was sitting outside in the freezing winter night, therefore, recollected, unspeaking, and praying, when Fr. Gennadius arrived, frantic, and began a series of complaints. The elder, feeling that he had acted badly in breaking his word about when the vigil would resume, humbly bowed his head and said: "Bless me, bless me." And with a meekness that would soften even the most stony heart, he made a prostration to his disciple in order to serve Liturgy.

The "Bless!" and "May it be blessed!" which are difficult words for some monks, were natural and easy for Fr. Philaret. They were his "personal trademarks" not only as a disciple, but also as Abbot, although he avoided faults as much as possible. He said it to the good-intentioned in order to rouse them to an easier acceptance of their faults, and to the bad-intentioned in order to calm them with his own patience and meekness.

Learn of Me, for I am meek and humble of heart, and ye shall find rest unto your souls. These words of the Lord directed his every thought and word and action.

And he always conquered with his gentle manner. This monk Gennadius had a hard character, difficult to govern, but by the elder's kindness and exalting humility he became with time obedient, a true lamb. As we read in the patristic narratives, meekness subdues even fierce wild beasts; much more can it tame fierce humans.

There was also another monk, more disobedient than Fr. Gennadius. It will not harm the conscience of the reader, we think, to report his unbecoming and insolent behavior, knowing indeed that in the community of monks, as in a garden, thorns will suddenly spring up. On the contrary, we will thus manifest the virtue of Elder Philaret.

This wretched and impudent monk had for a time the obedience of ecclesiarch, and he very often disobeyed the Abbot and the officers.

One day in church the elder said to him:

"My child, fix the *dracontion* [a thick candle] of St. Stephen, because it will be ruined."

The monk turned, stared at him with a rude look, and remained motionless in his stall. After a while, however, to avoid a new request from the elder, he got up and went into the altar.

The elder, feeling sorry for the *dracontion*, arose from his stall and himself went and cleaned and trimmed the wick. At exactly that moment the nominal disciple came out of the altar and said to him angrily:

"What do you mean by meddling in someone else's work? Are you an abbot or a torment?"

"Now, my child, just so the *dracontion* wouldn't be ruined," the elder said, and then, grieved as a man, he quietly bent his head and returned to his stall, softly whispering a complaint:

"Ach, ach, then they tell you it's good we're guiding young monks."

As soon as Vespers ended, the warning bell for trapeza (the refectory meal) sounded. One of his disciples came and called him: "Elder, come to trapeza," but the elder remained motionless in his place with bowed head. Another came and said the same thing; the elder didn't move. He came near and saw that the elder was half-unconscious. He had suffered a hemiplegia. The fathers lifted him up, took him to the old-age infirmary, and gave him first aid. Later he recovered sufficiently to continue his duties.

Satan's greatest warfare against a disciple aims at disturbing his harmonious relationship with his elder. The great glory of Sinai, St. John of the Ladder, tells us:

> "Do not think strange what I am about to say, for I have Moses to support me. It is better to sin against God than against our father; for when we anger God, our director can reconcile us; but when he is incensed against us, we no longer have anyone to make propitiation for us (*The Ladder of Divine Ascent*, Step 4).

The saying of the Apostle: *Let every wrath and shouting and anger and blasphemy cease from you, with every evil* (Eph. 4:31), found incarnation in the elder. Peaceful and quiet was his company, like a harbor without waves, without the least storm or turbulence. Never did he murmur or complain. He was an inexhaustible reservoir of patience and forbearance. During the sessions of the Monastery which he held with the officers, he would sit humbly, listening.

"Elder," they would ask him, "what do you say about this matter?"

"What can I say, Fathers? Let it be as you say."

At other times, at the end of the meeting he would say:

"I will speak now also, Fathers and Brothers:

Preparing, O man, to eat the body of the Master, first be reconciled with those who have grieved you; and then dare to consume the mystical food...."

This was the living experience of the good Abbot Philaret. His soul could not be at peace if there was any difference between him and a brother. Once he interrupted the Proskomedia before Divine Liturgy and said to the monk Philaret:

"My child, go and tell Fr. Paisius (his disciple) to come, so we can make prostrations. There has come a coolness between us, and I can't continue."

As soon as Fr. Paisius appeared, the elder and disciple made prostrations at the same time, asking forgiveness. He could make prostrations even to novices, if he felt he had troubled them in any way.

Such was the unclouded, childlike heart of Fr. Philaret.

St. Isaac the Syrian had captured his heart by his words about meekness and peace:

> If thou lovest meekness, remain in peace. And if thou art vouchsafed peace, thou wilt rejoice at every hour. Seek wisdom and not money. Clothe thyself in humility and not in royal sumptuous garments. Acquire peace and not the kingdom.... He who is not peaceful is not humble. And a peaceful man cannot be otherwise than always joyful. In all the paths which men pursue in this world, they do not find peace, until they draw near to the hope of God... (Homily 58).

2. THE ELDER'S SIMPLICITY AND INNOCENCE

It would be a great omission from this portrayal of the blessed Elder Philaret not to devote a chapter to his simplicity, which became proverbial among those who knew him. He was another Paul the Simple, guileless and unsophisticated.

ELDER PHILARET OF CONSTAMONITOU

At that time there were banknotes for ten drachmas and a hundred drachmas, but their size was in inverse relation to their worth: the 10-drachma bill was larger than the 100-drachma bill. The simple, unavaricious and unacquisitive Fr. Philaret, who rarely used money, thought that the 10-drachma bill, as being the larger, was worth much more than the 100-drachma bill. One time his disciple, Fr. P., asked a blessing to go to Karyes to have his tooth fixed. The elder used to put whatever money his spiritual children in the world sent him for forty-day Liturgies or as alms into his prayer book, until he handed it over to the steward.

"He took out the prayer book and gave me a 100-drachma bill," related Fr. P. Afterwards he thought and said: 'Take this better one—maybe the money won't be enough.' And taking back the 100-drachma bill, he offered me a 10-drachma bill! Simplicity, passionlessness, detachment."

Three years before his death, the brethren insisted that he go to Thessalonica to be operated on for the hernias from which he had suffered for many years. After much pressure, he finally yielded. Before departing, he served a moleben to St. Stephen, kissed his right hand, and made a prostration to all the brethren. He had not gone out into the world for fifty years! Everything seemed strange to him. When he saw the automobiles on the roads, he said to his companions:

"Fathers, I didn't know there are carriages without horses."

He remembered the old carriages pulled by horses.

When he first entered the hospital and saw the nursing sisters dressed in white, he glorified God.

"God has sent angels to serve me," he said, and he hid his head under his sheets from shame.

Living on the Holy Mountain he didn't remember what women are like. He thought of them as St. Marina, St. Barbara, etc.

There lived in Constamonitou Monastery also another monk unrivalled in simplicity—Fr. Agapius, previously a herdsman with flocks of sheep and goats. Fr. Philaret the Simple himself told a merry story about him:

When Fr. Agapius was fulfilling his monastic novitiate in the Metochion of Tripotamos, the steward told him one day:

"Apostolos (his worldly name), put out some boiled eggs to eat with the food, but leave them soft."

"May it be blessed, Elder," said Apostolos, and ran to fulfill the command.

After a while, Apostolos removed an egg from the boiling water, squeezed it here, squeezed it there, and put it back in. A little later he came back, took out another egg and tested it—still no good. He did the same a third time, and realized with surprise that the eggs, for all the boiling, were not softening! He called the steward, Elder Germanus, and said to him with obvious grievance:

"Elder, these blessed eggs aren't good for boiling! I've been boiling them ever so long, but they're not getting soft."

Then Elder Germanus, unable to restrain his laughter, told him:

"Leave them in a little longer, Apostolos, and they'll get soft."

And Apostolos answered seriously:

"May it be blessed, Elder."

V

"Thy Judgments Have I Not Forgotten"

1. A DISCERNING CONFESSOR

You will be unable to come to discernment if you do not labor at its cultivation. See first to silence. (Abba Isaiah)

The elder's hesychastic life in the Coenobium (as far as such was possible), prayer, and purification of the heart gave him "mental light and discernment of spiritual matters." The many monks and lay Christians who confessed to Fr. Philaret experienced both the measureless love and the enlightened discernment of the spiritual father.

Mr. Constantine Constantopoulos was the distinguished civil governor of the Holy Mountain for twelve years (1951-1963). He took care to visit the Holy Monastery of Constamonitou often and to confess to Fr. Philaret. When he was asked why he did this, he answered:

"I respect the Abbot most deeply. I marvel at his discernment and wisdom, and at the endless number of biblical sayings he uses, though he is almost uneducated."

His fame as a confessor spread far. He received letters with written confessions even from Australia.

The elder co-suffered with his penitents. Almost always he sprinkled his epitrachelion of forgiveness and compassion with his tears, and mingled the prayers of absolution with compunction overflowing from the "super-abundant" grace.

One time a hierodeacon from a monastery outside the Holy Mountain came to confess to the elder.

"When I began to confess," he told us, "the elder wept. I was also moved with him. I felt a compunction I had never known before.

"Afterwards the elder said to me: 'Stay on the Mountain, my child, and don't go back to the world, where there are so many temptations. Among other things, your finances won't go well. You have 35,000 drachmas in your pocket.' (I had exactly what he said!)"

The hierodeacon finally remained on the Mountain, became a schema-monk, and today is still alive.

He gave another penitent, a layman, advice on how to handle certain concrete future temptations. Indeed, he had foreseen all his difficulties. After Fr. Philaret's repose, this Christian layman asked the Monastery for a relic of the elder.

During his period of convalescence in the hospital in Thessalonica, pious laymen formed a long line to receive the blessing and counsel of the simple man of God. Many souls he gave rest in the "harbor for those sailing on the sea of life"; many souls he gave peace as a "peacemaking son of God." Many married couples he helped to resolve quarrels and disperse the temptations of the devil.... The mere presence of the God-bearing Father brought brilliant results. One thinks of the true saying of the holy Elder, St. Seraphim of Sarov, and sees it fulfilled in the peaceful Fr. Philaret: "Acquire the peace of God, and thousands of souls around you will be saved."

In the year 1948 he rescued the son of an inhabitant of Ierissus from the dangers of the civil war by his prayers and advice.

Let us note a few of the biblical and patristic admonitions which he used to give to his spiritual children:

"Let us take care not to leave the fields of our souls uncultivated. If they remain uncultivated, it will be difficult to clean and till them later."

"Pursue righteousness and holiness, without which no one will see the Lord."

"God does not enter into a foolish heart; and if He enters in, He quickly goes out."

"A mind that has left the contemplation of God becomes either like a demon or a beast."

Next to Constamonitou Monastery is the Holy Monastery of Zographou, inhabited by Bulgarian Orthodox monks. They esteemed the elder highly and came to him to confess and receive spiritual direction. And with his large heart he always received them as an affectionate father and loving brother.

"When I was still a young monk," Fr. P. related, "I found myself having to go to the world. 'Don't be afraid,' the elder told me, 'I will pray for you.' During my stay in the world I endured terrible attacks—the burning arrows of the evil one for thirteen days, from a provocative woman who suggested sin to me. But something astonishing happened in me. You could say I wasn't myself. You could say I was without feeling—a stone! The prayers of Fr. Philaret were so powerful that the attacks of the young woman didn't trouble me at all...."

The voice of St. John of the Ladder echoed loudly in the ears of the good governor of souls:

> If you have received eyes to foresee the surge of the troubled sea, foretell it clearly to the ship's company, lest you prove to be the cause of shipwreck, since with complete confidence all have entrusted you with the pilotship ("Word to the Shepherd").

2. THE MERCIFUL FATHER PHILARET

We will mention certain incidents which illustrate the genuine love, philanthropy, charity, and compassion of the elder whose life we are describing.

A mechanic of the Greek Telephone Company named Constantine Adamis, of Thessalonica, who had worked on the Holy Mountain, related: "When I was working in the Monastery for six months or a year, he would call me to the Abbot's office and give me money, putting it in my pocket. He didn't want me to tell anyone."

Whatever he had and didn't have he gave away. He was a "cheerful giver." He always wore an old skoufia, because he gave away any new ones he received to the other fathers. New towels, handkerchiefs—he gave them all away.

The workers had much to say about his merciful heart. One old man who was a worker at the Monastery for years, Costas Korakis from Ouranopolis, did not forget the elder's flowing kindness. He said with gratitude:

"Fr. Philaret was a holy man. A man like that is not easily found. I was a driver; I would cut wood from the forest of the Monastery and transport it to the harbor with mules. One time, I remember, when I was exhausted from the work, I gulped my food in the trapeza because I was hungry. The elder saw me with his loving eyes. Since he understood that I was not yet satisfied, he got up by himself, while the other fathers were eating and the reader was reading, and brought me his own food...."

"It is more blessed to give than to receive." To give, to scatter love to everyone, monks, workers, pilgrims—this was his own joy and blessedness.

Fr. Pachomius, who ended up being the guestmaster for twenty years, had become tired after the first five and asked Fr. Philaret to change his obedience. But the elder had told him:

"If you practice patience, my child, you will entertain angels."

And he related to him a certain wondrous personal incident inexplicable to many:

For one period, Fr. Philaret happened to be guestmaster. One time, therefore, he was preparing the trapeza. The doors were all locked. Suddenly he saw a beautiful youth enter and say:

"Bless! I am very hungry."

Surprised, Fr. Philaret answered automatically, with his characteristic hospitable courtesy and friendliness:

"Welcome! Sit down! What is your name?"

"Michael," said the youth.

And before he had time to prepare food for him and have him sit at the table, the youth suddenly disappeared!... He had the conviction that it was an angel of the Lord. He remembered with special feeling and warmth of heart the hospitality of Abraham, who had entertained the Holy Trinity Himself in the form of three angels.

His love was not limited only to rational beings, but extended also to animals and nature. This sympathy toward unreasoning nature is a characteristic element in the grace-filled lives of the deified saints. One day there was a great tumult outside the elder's cell. Two swallows had begun a fierce duel. The elder was troubled. Going outside, he saw a painful sight—the stronger swallow was striking the other one with his bill and literally plucking it. Not wasting time, the elder chased it away and affectionately took the beaten bird in his hands and saved it. He took care of it, with the result that the swallow lived.

Just as the lion of St. Gerasim of the Jordan followed the Saint everywhere, showing his gratitude and devotion, so also did the swallow. He flew before the elder, beat his wings, played his games, and sang. One day Fr. Philaret had gone out a little, either to glorify God, "wondrous in His works," in the rare natural beauty of the Holy Mountain, or to pray in silence. The swallow, his faithful friend and companion, flew near him. Lying down on a threshing-floor a little distance from the Monastery, he fell asleep without knowing it. But suddenly the swallow began to fly frantically above the sleeping elder's head, making noise as if he wanted to waken him and indicate some danger. And in fact, when the elder awoke, what did he see? A little distance away was a large snake.... His companion had in his turn shown mercy to the merciful elder.

3. "A CHRISTIAN ENDING TO OUR LIVES"

The elder received the first blow to his health in church on that day of the unprincipled behavior of his stiff-necked disciple. In three months he recovered; but ever after his health was unstable, while before then he had never been sick, even with a headache.

The second blow came three years later, when he became bedridden with hemiplegia. The fathers summoned two doctors to examine him. They told them: "If he doesn't come around in three days, the end will come."

And truly, on January 22, 1963, the venerable and loving elder, Fr. Philaret, delivered his pure soul into the hands of his beloved Lord and God, our Savior. He fell in battle, standing on the spiritual ramparts of pastorship, love, patience, and asceticism. *The souls of the righteous are in the hand of God, and the hand of the tormenter shall not touch them. He that believeth on Me, even if he dieth, shall live.* The Lord came to earth to abolish by His Resurrection the "dominion of death," to crush its power and disperse its fear. The souls of the virtuous and the virtue-loving are in the hand of God.

During the night of the elder's holy repose, his already reposed mother appeared to her daughter-in-law in sleep and said to her: "For fifty-one years I have been waiting for him to come, and tonight at midnight you will send him to me." Let it be noted that he had never left the Holy Mountain, except for one time when, after much pressure, he had gone away for medical reasons, out of obedience.

The venerable Abbot of the Holy Monastery of Dionysiou, Fr. Gabriel, protested when they did not notify him in time to come to his funeral. When he visited the Monastery, he knelt at the elder's grave, sang the Trisagion Hymn, and took a little earth in a clean handkerchief as a keepsake.

His spiritual children, as well as the new brothers of Constamonitou Monastery, preserve and continue the ascetic Athonite tradition, by the holy prayers and intercessions before the Lord of the ever-memorable Elder Philaret, and they hold his luminous person in great reverence and esteem.

One example of this respect is the following metered encomium to the blessed elder by the monk Mark:

What your stature lacked in height,
Exalting humbleness supplied.
Your intellect's simplicity
A treasure of good thoughts enriched.
Your voice, a little harsh in sound,
Ceaseless prayer beautified.
Your awkward words' unskillfulness
Your eager brotherly love perfected.
But more than all, your love for Christ,
And your heart's bright purity
Harmoniously interlaced
Your adamantine character,
O childlike Elder Philaret.

Today, fifteen years after the transfer of his relics, one of his spiritual children preserves some bones which have an amber color and emit a delicate, sweet, heavenly fragrance. His skull has the figure of a cross in the frontal bones. These signs are confirmations of his virtue-loving life and God-pleasing struggles.

Perhaps, in the last moments of his life, the illumined mind of Fr. Philaret was accompanied by the verses of Psalm 118, which is read in every monastery during the midnight service. Wonderful thoughts are contained in it—compunction, devotion, love, and divine longing for the "testimonies," the "judgments" of the Lord, the *words sweeter than honey and more precious than gold*....

In the monastic silence of the catholicon, the fathers were reading the third stasis of Psalm 118—verses well fitting in the mouth of the ever-memorable elder during his last moments:

Look upon me and have mercy on me
According to the judgments of those who love Thy name.
Thy zeal has consumed me
Because mine enemies have forgotten Thy word.
Thy word is tried by fire,
And Thy servant has loved it.
I am young and accounted as nothing,
Yet Thy judgments have I not forgotten.

At this point, Fr. Philaret, who perpetually kept the memory of the judgments of the Lord, gave up the spirit.

Contemporary men think they will become happier if they struggle for the predominance of the rights of man. Fr. Philaret, in contrast with the worldly way of thinking, became blessed because he set aside the "ego" and conquered self-love, which is the cause of most evils. He struggled never to forget the judgments* of God. Thus he was able to repeat: "Thy judgments, O Lord, have I not forgotten."

---

*Or "rights"—*trans. note.*

X

Elder Gerasim Menagias

On Athos there are scientists who have humbled themselves until they have become purer than the hermit, and more flaming than he in their faith.

> —Zacharias Papadoniou, author and sceptic, in reference to Elder Gerasim.

Repentance before the Tomb of Christ.

I

From Birth to Rebirth

1. "MY OWN TREASURE"

"I do not want the riches of the earth any more. Thou art and wilt be *my own treasure* in this life and in eternity. To Thee I dedicate all my heart and will. Before they were insubmissive to Thee, but now I dedicate them to Thee entirely. Grant me to know what Thou seekest from me; I am ready to fulfill it through Thy grace. Set in order everything about me. With complete self-renunciation I welcome in advance whatever Thy goodness dost will to send me. O my God, infinitely beloved! Thou hast loved me to the point of dying for me. I love Thee from my heart. I love Thee more than my own self, and I commit my soul into Thy hands. From today I renounce all the labor and love of the world. I abandon my work and surrender myself to Thee. O my Creator, through Thy holy Passion receive me and keep me faithful until my death. From now on, O my Jesus, I do not want to live any more but for Thee. I do not want to seek anything but Thy will. Help me by Thy grace. And thou, All-Holy Theotokos, my hope, do not refuse me thy protection, I pray."

Such a prayer, the sacrifice and incense of the heart, signified return. It is the prayer of a prodigal restored to life, who, thirsting for life, cries out to the Father: "Father, I have sinned against heaven and before Thee.... Make me as one of Thy hired servants."

Elder Gerasim indeed walked in the footsteps of the prodigal son of the Gospel parable. He had expended all the life of his soul in prodigality, until "there was a great famine in that land." That land was Europe, where he had been studying for many years: Europe, starved of spiritual life and satiated with greed and immorality.

At some point, however, he regained sobriety and awoke to his grievous plight. "Oh, how many good things I the wretched one have deprived myself of! Oh, what a kingdom I the miserable one have fallen from!" he groaned painfully from the depths of his soul. Therefore he arose and began the path of return. He fell at the feet of the Father and said, "I do not want the riches of the earth any more.... From this day I renounce all the labor and love of the world. I abandon my work and surrender myself to Thee." By this prayer he struck the three first passions that generate the remaining five: love of money, love of pleasure, and love of glory, the "chieftains" of the other evils, as the Holy Fathers call them.

Undoubtedly he had experienced the bitter servitude of these three masters while still a smart young man living in Europe, in that "far country" where a great spiritual famine coexisted with a surplus of the material goods of technological civilization. But Truth came and Grace shone forth even on this much-suffering and tormented man. The heart that was formerly insubmissive and prodigal submitted to the bridle of the enlightened "sovereign mind."

"Thou art and wilt be my own treasure," he cried out to the Father. It was a cry that marked the end of the old life and the beginning of a "new creation" within him; a prayer that could be considered the first troth prior to the great vow of the tonsure, the first promise before the covenant of the great schema: the prayer of Spiridon Menagias, subsequently Monk Gerasim.

2. HIS BIRTH AND UPBRINGING

Fr. Gerasim, in the world named Spiridon Menagias, was born in 1881 in Corfu into one of the more prominent and wealthy families on the island. His father, Panagis Menagias, worked as a wheat merchant in Romania. When he was still a young child they moved from Corfu, the island of St. Spiridon, to Cephalonia, the island of St. Gerasim. After a short time the family forsook Cephalonia and set up residence in Athens. There he completed his intermediate education together with his brother Gerasim and his sister Kali. At the high school one of his instructors was the eminent Greek author Alexander Moraitides.

Moraitides, together with the glory of modern Greek literature, Alexander Papadiamantis, were called the "twins," or, according to Xenopoulos, the "double stars of Skiathos." Both of them were journalists and folklorists, inspired by the immortal Byzantine spirit, by the Greek Orthodox tradition, which is the nature and heart of our people, even though many have tried and still try to forget it.

Moraitides writes somewhere: "When we were children (he and Papadiamantis), we would accompany by night Papadiamantis' father, a priest, when he went to the country churches to serve Liturgy. Oh, those years were beautiful! We walked along distant roads in the light of the moon, and sang to the quick melody, 'Let every breath praise the Lord.'"

This pure Greek and Orthodox Christian, about whom Tellos Agras writes that he is distinguished by "purity, pliancy, elegance, and grace," this Olympian of the spirit, Spiridon Menagias had for a teacher. Surely some roots of his training were planted by his own hand in Spiridon's adolescent soul. It is indeed a privilege to find a teacher that is another mother, who will give birth to and suffer pain for the student, his true offspring, of his own "blood," his own spirit. If literature respects itself, if it respects man, who is the "word" and icon of Divinity, then it honors its mission and is an honorable educator of youth, society, and mankind. If it serves the spirit and the word-man, it is truly literature.*

Spiridon received this background of Greek Orthodox training during his high school years, but when he travelled to Europe for

---

*Literature: in Greek, *logotechnia*, or "word-art"—*trans. note.*

studies it was trampled under by the sacrilegious feet of the materialistic 19th century.

3. AN ADVOCATE OF MATERIALISM

After Spiridon finished high school, he left for Zurich to study chemistry. He was indeed gifted, his dreams grandiose, and the vehemence of youth sharpened yet more his passion for science. His six years of study in Europe were six years of a worldly life of wastefulness and prosperity. The student Spiridon Menagias, the wealthy child of Athens, "lived his life," danced, entertained, lived the dissipated life of the student world. His byword: "Soul, thou hast many goods ... eat, drink and be merry." And he was not only an adherent of practical materialism, but also a defender of theoretical materialism. He read Haeckel, devoured every writing that preached his ideas, and in general made a gospel of every materialistic book, agreeing with its fallacies and delusions....

We are in an age when the violent wave of atheism has swept over everything in Europe. The universities especially struggle powerfully on behalf of materialism and Darwinism. "When I was a student," Fr. Gerasim would later tell the fathers of the Holy Mountain, "they made us write that man is descended from the monkey. If we didn't write that, they wouldn't give us a passing grade!" "Oh, Fr. Gerasim," some simple ascetic would say to him, "what they teach at the universities! Have we ever seen a cypress give birth to a walnut, or a pine tree sprout from an almond? The first is one kind, and the second another. And why don't men come from monkeys now?"

This was the "scientific" climate of Zurich when Spiridon was studying there. Slowly—but ever surely—these materialistic theories have come to our fatherland also, and their teachings are heard in our schools and in many contemporary books. Therefore we shall speak briefly about this pseudoscience and its unsound structure.

Two Western scientists of the last century, Darwin and Haeckel, formulated the well-known theory of the evolution of simpler life forms to the more complex. Haeckel, a German zoologist and materialist (when Menagias came to Zurich he was still alive) and his many followers asserted that the world is the result of blind chance, that man is descended from animals, that everything, including matter itself, came into being spontaneously, and that God the Creator does not exist. *The fool has said in his heart: There is no God* (Ps. 13: 1).

In order to prove the common ancestry of various species, and especially the descent of man from animals, Haeckel introduced the so-called "biogenetic law of recapitulation," and did not hesitate to falsify certain photographs of embryos in his writings. This dishonest action was revealed by a professor of anatomy and zoology, and was pilloried as "a sin against scientific truth."*

To give the reader the contemporary view of serious science on this subject, we will mention the conference at the Museum of Natural History of Chicago held in October of 1980 (*Sunday Times*, March 8, 1981), in which 160 paleontologists, anatomists, geneticists, biologists, etc., participated, who confirmed that "no intermediate links have been found.... The supposedly iron law of Darwin, that every new species represents a continuation of the preceding, appears to have been shattered...."**

Know that the Lord is our God; it is He that has made us, and not we ourselves; we are His people and sheep of His pasture, sounds the harmonious and deathless prophetic voice of David (Ps. 99:3).

In a conference of the British Union for the Advancement of Science (August, 1980), Professor J. Purant maintained that "Darwinian evolution has turned into a modern myth, to the detriment of science and social life."

We rejoice over this admission. For indeed, the theories and deductions of atheistic scientists have direct repercussions in human relations, and create an atheistic social life.

---

*Apostolos Frankos, *From the Monkey?* Athens, 1985, pp. 125-127.
**Darwin and the Truth*, pub. by "Zoe," Athens, 1983, pp. 24-25.

But who, in the end, is morally guilty of this atheism in scientists? Perhaps it is Western Protestant theology, divorced from miracle and mystery? Perhaps it is Protestant rationalism, which remains on the surface of the great anthropological questions, and does not show man as a divine image, able to share in the divine glory, according to the teaching and experience of our holy and Godbearing Fathers of Orthodoxy?

4. IN THE NETS OF SPIRITUALISM

After the abyss of atheism, the young student Menagias, lively and restless by nature, was entangled in the nets of spiritualism. So he went from one fall to another, from materialism to spiritualism. Spiritualism is a demonic enterprise well camouflaged. It appears to offer contact with the spirits of the dead, which in reality are demons, who have the power to change and transform themselves. Spiritualism is equivalent to demonism. In our times there are thousands of victims of these demon actors. The evil spirits play, acting out the roles of various humans, and at the same time making toys of those dabbling in their works.

Menagias, the future Fr. Gerasim, was not possessed, but he did become entangled in spiritualism. So have many others also, among them the venerable Elder Theodosius of St. Paul's Monastery when he lived in the world, as he himself confessed.

Since there is terrible ignorance on the subject of spiritualism and its relative, magic, and many are deceived by them, we recommend that our readers read what St. Nicodemus of the Holy Mountain has written on the subject. We also include here one of the ancient stories that portrays the demonic deception clearly.

In Constantinople there lived a certain pious youth, who was the secretary of a great magician. The youth did not know that his master was a magician. One day after sunset the magician mounted his horse and ordered the youth to follow him. They went out through the city walls and walked without stopping until they arrived at a flat plain. In the meantime it had grown darker. In the plain they saw a large palace. The magician descended from his horse, and immediately several servants came from the palace and took hold of it, and he entered in. The youth followed him. They walked forward until they came to a large hall. There he saw a great lord sitting on a magnificent throne, with many spear-bearing servants. At the Lord's command they brought another throne for the magician to sit on. The youth stood behind his master's throne. Then he who looked like a lord began to question the magician about how things were with him. The magician replied that he thanked him greatly for the benefactions he had given him, and he glorified him. As soon as he heard this, the youth understood that the lord was Satan, that his servants were demons, and that his master was a magician.

After the conversation, Satan asked:

"Who is that youth standing behind you?"

"He also is your slave," answered the magician.

Then Satan asked the youth himself, saying:

"Are you my slave, boy?"

And that blessed youth, making the sign of the Venerable Cross, answered with courage and boldness:

"I am the slave of the Father, the Son, and the Holy Spirit."

And at these words, the palace, the thrones, Satan, his servants, and his own master immediately became invisible, because his friends the demons snatched him away and cast him down into the fire of hell. And the youth found himself alone on the flat plain...."

Menagias' involvement in the practice of spiritualism was by the economy of God, because, as he himself related later, it convinced him that the world of spirits and the devil exists. This fact shook him. It was the occasion of his return. Thus, a little after his involvement in spiritualism, he bought his first Holy Bible. In the depths of his heart, under the ashes of denial, he saw the spark of faith burning secretly. But many years were needed before it would blaze into flame.

Glory to the All-Compassionate Lord, Who had mercy on this restless and heavy-laden soul and delivered it from the nooses of materialism and spiritualism, the two fabrications of the man-hating demons.

5. REBIRTH

Having a deeply patriotic nature, Spiridon could not be at peace when he learned about the events of the Macedonian struggle and the guerilla war led by the heroic Paul Melas. In 1905 he left Zurich and, unknown to all, came to Thessalonica to enlist in the army of Paul Melas as a volunteer soldier for the much-suffering Macedonia. His flight from Zurich and voluntary enlistment did not remain hidden. His mother was informed of it, and, being worried, came from Athens to Thessalonica to see him. She found him in a cellar, where the Greek consul Kontogouris had temporarily hidden him.

After the happy outcome of the Macedonian struggle, he returned to Zurich and graduated from the University in the first place. He also received a degree in chemistry. After a little while he went to Egypt, where he was appointed as water inspector. A little later he resigned from this position and, coming to Athens, was appointed to the Department of Provisions.

He lived together with his family on Stadiou Street, and was intensely occupied with his scientific research and studies. The war year of 1917 arrived. The blockade caused a shortage of gasoline. Menagias' clever scientific mind led him, after much research, to invent a synthetic petroleum, but since the cost was prohibitive it could not be developed. In one of his experiments he caused a conflagration in which he received such serious burns that he had to be hospitalized.

In 1919 he was deeply impressed by the divine preaching of Fr. Dionysius Farazoulis in Athens. He was drawn closer to the Church. But his soul, that deer of the mountains, thirsted for richer springs, and he was not slow in discovering the fountainhead of

Orthodoxy, the Holy Mountain. In the year 1920 he visited the Garden of the Mother of God for the first time.

At that time, unfortunately, many monasteries there were idiorrhythmic. Glory to the All-Good God, in recent years most of them have become coenobia where blessed obedience and heaven-soaring poverty reign, where common trapezas are set, and where the words "mine" and "yours" are forgotten. After visiting several monasteries, Menagias set out for home a little disappointed, not having received a good impression of the Holy Mountain.

In the harbor of Daphne, however, he met the elect of God, the diamond of the desert, Elder Abimelech, the hermit of Little St. Anne's Skete. He had heard about this man, but until that moment had not met him. And behold, by God's providence they met in Daphne. Elder Abimelech was an unforgettable elder, always praying with bowed head. He listened with special interest and love to the young pilgrim, and after sufficient spiritual conversation advised him:

"My child, you should go to the desert. There live the unseen hermits and hesychasts, given wholly to prayer and silence. There you will see virtue...."

This meeting and talk with the venerable Elder Abimelech was the cause of Menagias' final decision: to go to the desert, and even to the great hesychast of Katounakia, Elder Callinicus.

6. PILGRIMAGE TO THE HOLY LAND

There are two places on the earth which rightly bear the name of "holy." The grace of the Three-Sunned Divinity, which sanctifies the whole of the animate and inanimate creation, has sanctified also these two spots on our planet: the Holy Land and the Holy Mountain. The Holy Land was hallowed by the earthly presence of the Son and Word of God, and the Holy Mountain by the living "visitation" and protection of our Immaculate, All-Blessed Lady, the Theotokos and Ever-Virgin Mary, and by the multitude of "Athonite fathers shining in asceticism and holiness."

Before Spiridon Menagias enlisted in the angelic regiment of the Athonite monks, therefore, he fulfilled his holy dream: to venerate the Holy Land "in which stood the immaculate feet of the Lord," where "was accomplished the great mystery of the Incarnation and godliness," where "God appeared in the flesh, was justified by the Spirit, was seen by the Angels,... ascended in glory." The experience of a pilgrim to the Holy Land is one of strengthened faith and love, a radiant rebaptism in the great font of the evangelical events and divine teachings of our Redeemer. After his soul-saving searching of the Holy Scriptures, the young Spiridon yearned to see also with his own eyes the sacred places of pilgrimage, to approach even with his bodily senses the inconceivable mystery of the earthly presence of the Lord. He longed to acquire this sanctifying "vision" of the Holy Land, a vision which does not remain only in the outward eyes, but is transformed to an inner mental vision and contemplation....

He venerated the holy cave of the Nativity in Bethlehem, which witnessed the infinite poverty of the pre-eternal God "rich in mercy," compunctionately singing the troparion of the Nativity:

*Thy Nativity, O Christ our God,
has shone upon the world
(and upon me who was in darkness)
with the light of knowledge....*

He went to Nazareth, the village of the silence of our Lord the God-Man. He went to the Jordan River, to the waters of the sanctified stream where "the worship of the Trinity was made manifest." At the life-giving well of the sacred Gospel, his soul, like a second Samaritan Woman, worshipped the holy place of the historical biblical dialogue. He saw Tiberias, Cana, Capernaum, the Mount of the Beatitudes, the Dead Sea. He went to Bethany and to Gethsemane, to the earthly compass of the agony of the God-man, and to the most sacred tomb of the Theotokos. He visited the Upper Room, where the holy Washing of the Feet and the Last Supper took place, and where the Master gave the Testament to the disciples.

The Church of the Nativity in Bethlehem.

The Church of the Holy Sepulchre.

In the chapel of the Crucifixion and the Holy Sepulchre Spiridon felt the whole greatness of God's humility and love: *For God so loved the world, that he gave his only begotten Son, that whosoever believeth in him should not perish, but have everlasting life* (John 3: 16). "My God, remember not the sins of my youth and ignorance. But remember me when Thou comest in Thy Kingdom," he whispered quietly on his knees, feeling like the robber, the publican, the lost sheep. And tears—burning, sweet, expiatory tears—rained on the holy place....

A special impression was made on him by those bastions of Orthodoxy, the monasteries of the Holy Land: the Monasteries of St. Sabbas, of St. Theodosius the Coenobiarch, of St. George the Chozebite with its numberless ascetic caves and holy hermitages, of the Mountain of the Forty Days. This mountain and desert laid within him the foundation of his future monastic life upon the example of Christ, by the contemplation of the asceticism, the struggle of fasting and vigil, of the God-man, the first hermit....

After his pilgrimage to the Holy Land, the desire to follow Jesus, to become a participant and communicant of His Passion and Resurrection, blazed up much more strongly within him. An irresistable power now led his steps to the other sanctified place, the Holy Mountain.

II

"Life is Blessed for Those Who Dwell in the Wilderness, For They Fly Upon the Wings of Divine Love."

1. IN THE DESERT OF KATOUNAKIA

Coming to the Holy Mountain for a second time, he had recourse, on the above-mentioned recommendation of Elder Abimelech, to the sober hesychast of Katounakia, Elder Callinicus, the high-soaring eagle of mental prayer and contemplation.

Elder Callinicus received Spiridon, who was then thirty-nine years old, with joy. The hermit's Kalyve is located about in the middle of the other desert kalyves, between two rocky slopes which form the ravine of Katounakia. It is a poor, humble Kalyve, dedicated to St. Gerasim of Cephalonia. The compunction of Spiridon increased day by day as he came to the humble chapel of the Saint of Cephalonia, the fearful persecutor of demons. It culminated when, on the blessed day of his tonsure, Elder Callinicus gave him the name of St. Gerasim.

On the eve of the tonsure, the evil spirits gathered *en masse*. As he later told Elder Theodosius of St. Paul's Monastery, they beat him so badly that they left him senseless. His deliverance from spiritualism and decision to become a monk had greatly aggravated Satan's envy. From then on, his life was never free from the harassment of the dark demons. But he practiced great patience. He reported his temptations to his spiritual guide, and the latter would sometimes, as a wise doctor, give him suitable medicines, and at other times, as an experienced warrior, teach him the science of battle. In this way he escaped from all the snares of the enemy.

* * * * * * * *

They say on the Holy Mountain that obedience works miracles. And the Athonite children of obedience have much to say about its wonderworking power.

Fr. Gerasim entered into the mystery of this great virtue very early, as we see from the following wondrous event, which happened in the first years of his monastic life, under the spiritual direction of Elder Callinicus.

One time the elder sent Fr. Gerasim to the Great Lavra, which is about three or four hours away from Katounakia. It was winter and snow had fallen, but the matter was urgent and the elder insisted that he go. Fr. Gerasim showed obedience: he made a prostration, took the elder's blessing, and set out. When he had gone a little past Kerasia, a terrible snowstorm burst out. Soon he was enveloped in a veil of dense snowflakes; he almost couldn't see where he was. Meanwhile, snow covered over the footpath; he lost the trail and stopped, contemplating his danger. He began to pray fervently to the Lord and the Panagia, asking for some kind of divine intervention and aid:

The Lord will hearken unto me when I cry unto Him (Ps. 4:3). *In Thee, O Lord, have I hoped, let me not be put to shame in the age to come; in Thy righteousness deliver me, and rescue me. Bow down Thine ear unto me, make haste to rescue me, be Thou unto me a God to defend me and a house of refuge to save me...* (Ps. 30:1-3).

And behold! Not many minutes passed before the Lord answered. There appeared before him a beautiful little child of eight or ten years.

"Bless, Elder!"

"God bless."

"Where are you going in this weather, Elder? The snow will bury you. In such a snowstorm you will be lost in the forest."

"What can I do, my child? My elder sent me to the Lavra. There is an absolute need for me to go."

"Come, then, I will help you get your bearings."

He led him to a certain spot and said to him:

"Take the lower road, and later you will come out on the footpath going to the Lavra."

Fr. Gerasim rejoiced, but when he had taken a few steps he came to his senses. "How can it be that such a young child is here in the snow?" he wondered. He went back immediately, but saw nothing, not even a footprint in the snow. The child had vanished. It was an angel of the Lord.

He shall give His angels charge over thee, to keep thee in all thy ways (Ps. 90:11). Thus with tender feeling he glorified the name of the All-Good Lord, who uses many means to show His Providence for His servants, for those who unhesitatingly obey His will.

According to St. John of the Ladder, "Obedience is unscrutinized action." But this work of a disciple, namely absolute faith in his elder, manifests his unshakable faith in the All-Good Providence of Him Who by His nod alone directs the whole universe, and who bids spiritual fathers: *He that heareth you heareth me; and he that despiseth you despiseth me* (Luke 10:16).

Fr. Gerasim worshipped his elder. He considered him the "mouth of Christ." "His death has left an unfillable void," he would write later, on September 5, 1930, "and especially for me.... In sorrows and temptations, my Elder was my only consolation after God.... But his blessing, which he gave us until his last breath, gave me courage and consolation for my future life...."

The hard ascetic life in Katounakia, and above all its difficult climate, soon undermined Fr. Gerasim's precarious health. A pre-tubercular condition appeared. Elder Callinicus blessed him to go for a while to Bulgareli in Arta, until his health would improve and he would regain his physical strength.

In Bulgareli Fr. Gerasim became a "great light" by his virtue and conduct. Up to today the Christians of that region remember his spiritual stature—his sweet-spoken mouth, kindly manners, simplicity, and the example he left them during his sojourn in their land.

2. IN ST. BASIL'S "GOAT-HUTS"

In 1925 Fr. Gerasim returned to Katounakia, to the Kalyve of his repentance. Seeing that the health of his disciple was getting worse, however, the discerning Elder Callinicus, after much prayer, summoned him and said:

"My child, your weak health won't allow you to stay here in Katounakia, where the climate doesn't suit you. The Skete of St. Basil has a drier climate, better for your health. From there you can come to me regularly so I can attend to your spiritual state."

Thus, with the blessing of Elder Callinicus and the armor of mental prayer, Fr. Gerasim *fled afar off and dwelt in the desert* (Ps. 54:8), in the desert bearing the name of the great ascetic hierarch Basil the Heaven-Revealer.

This is the smallest, least conspicuous, and most ascetic Skete of the Holy Mountain. Unless you are well directed, you won't easily find it. Hidden in the deep wilderness, it can be seen from almost nowhere. It is located about 2400 feet above the sea, near the region of Kerasia. The Skete's natural advantage is, as we have said, the lack of dampness, the dry climate; its spiritual advantage, "silence which purifies the mind of the soul." It is a completely desert place, located on a steep mountainside under Kerasia's Mount Carmel, a cone-shaped hill crowned by a chapel to the Prophet Elias.

There is a tradition in St. Basil's Desert that it was inhabited by ascetics from Caesarea of Cappadocia, and that they therefore named the Skete and Catholicon after the Heaven-Revealer. Up to the time of Fr. Gerasim, the hermits' kalyves were "goat-huts"— namely, made of dry stones, with low-ceilinged rooms like caves. They are roofed with rusty sheet-iron. There are no floors but the

Top: The wooden cross marking the boundary of St. Basil's Skete

Left: A large Kalyve of St. Basil's Skete.

natural earth and stone. The drinking water comes from the cisterns, where is stored whatever water the roofs can collect during rains.

The view from the Skete: enormous rocks, steep craggy ravines that run violently to the sea.

It is believed that St. Gregory Palamas, the preacher of Grace and Uncreated Light, the "adornment of monks," lived in asceticism for a while in this desert.

In this wild magnificence the famous Russian ascetic Paisius Velichkovsky lived for two years, translating the *Philokalia of the Holy Ascetic Fathers* into Russian.* It may be that in all Athos there is no more hesychastic place than this Skete.

Here lived fathers who were great strugglers, performing eminent ascetic combats and leading a deep spiritual life. Such were Barnabas, the sober teacher of mental prayer, and the Romanians Martinian, Jonas, and Theophylactus. Most of them practiced the handiwork of woodcarving, making combs, spoons, and paperknives. Elder Martinian always lived on the alms of the other brethren. When they gave him a "blessing," that is, a little food, he had an established expression of gratitude:

"Oh! Teos schoresh. What's your name? What are your father's and mother's names?" (He asked their names in order to pray for them and commemorate them.)

Elder Jonas was a scholar, a graduate of the Polytechnic, and was occupied with notable works of translation in the hesychastic and spiritually vigilant atmosphere of St. Basil's Desert. He translated books by St. Nicodemus of the Holy Mountain and other patristic works into the Romanian language.

---

*Elder Paisius discovered here a large collection of the Patristic books (enumerated in his famous autobiographical letter to Elder Sophronius; see *Blessed Paisius Velichkovsky*, Schemamonk Metrophanes, St. Herman of Alaska Brotherhood, pp. 83, 85) and engaged calligraphers in this Skete to copy out these books. This work took at least two years, continuing up to the time of his departure from Mount Athos. In the meantime he maintained continual contact with the monks from the Skete who had come from Asia Minor. These manuscripts later served as a major source for his Slavonic *Philokalia*.

Elder Theophylactus was a holy figure in the choir of the Skete's heavenly citizens. It is told about him that once he went out from his little Kalyve and saw a deer with a broken foot. He drew near it, and with his compassionate voice spoke to it as to a man:

"Sit down, and I will bind up your broken little foot so it will get well."

The deer obeyed him and sat quietly. The elder, with his "love and merciful disposition of heart for all creation," took two reeds for a splint and a strip of cloth for a bandage, and like a good orthopedic doctor bound up the poor creature's broken member. Afterwards he petted it compassionately and said to it:

"Go now, my dear, with the blessing of the Panagia, and come back in thirty or forty days so I can loosen it for you." Indeed, when the stipulated time had passed, the deer came back to the elder's Kalyve. He loosened the orthopedic bandage. The foot had healed completely.

The repose of this sanctified man was holy. In his last moments his face shone like a bright moon, like the face of an angel.

In this blessed Skete Elder Joseph the Cave-Dweller, the hesychast, also lived for many years. For a period of time he had created what might be called an experimental community, composed of Fr. Gerasim Menagias, the Lavra doctor Spiridon-Athanasius Kampanaos, and the pharmacist Athanasius Balsamakis. They all practiced the strictest asceticism. He usually gave them one tin of moistened rusks for the whole day, and they followed a program of prayer which he had set up: all the services were said with a prayer-rope and the cultivation of "silence with understanding."

Fr. Gerasim lived in St. Basil's desert for about fifteen years.

In the hermitages and caves surrounding the Skete lived noteworthy hermits of the time, adorned with various spiritual gifts, like Elder Cherubim, Hieromonk Ephraim, and Hieromonk Gerasim. Elder Cherubim had attained the measure of perfect non-acquisitiveness. One year when he was snowed in, after fasting for a week he was visited by an angel of the Lord in the form of a monk who

ELDER JOSEPH THE CAVE-DWELLER

brought him food. Hieromonk Ephraim was a cave-dweller. Hieromonk Gerasim combined wonderful theoretical instruction on the Philokalia with a philokalic inner life.

3. ASCETIC STRUGGLES

If you had visited St. Basil's Skete at that time, you would have vindicated the blessed life of the hermit fathers. You would have seen holy figures pale from fasting and vigil, illuminated by many years of laborious prayer. Walking along the little roads of the Skete, you would have heard resound the sweet Name of our Lord with longing and expectancy: "Lord Jesus Christ, Son of God, have mercy on me."

In this spiritual meadow resided Fr. Gerasim. The Jesus Prayer was his daily food. He experienced the "comprehensive virtue" of prayer as the virtue which sanctifies every work, bodily and spiritual. But the struggle of prayer was hard. He had to battle, face to face, with the "ruler of this world."

> Let him never cease, even for a moment," writes St. Hesychius the Presbyter (*Philokalia*, Vol. I), "from prayer and watchfulness and the contradiction of evil thoughts and prayer to Jesus Christ our God. For better help than Jesus we will not find in all our life. He alone, the Lord, knows as God the wiles and tricks and intrigues of the devil. Let the soul, therefore, have all its trust in Christ. Let it beseech Him and not lose heart at all. For it does not do battle alone, but together with the fearful King Jesus Christ, the Creator of all beings, bodiless and embodied.

An indispensable prerequisite for the practice of prayer is fasting. For this reason the hermits nourished themselves with simple natural foods—with rusks, greens, vegetables, and a few legumes.

There in his barren and poor Kalyve of St. Basil's Skete, made of earth and stones, Fr. Gerasim, the distinguished young man of Athens, the aristocrat, the great name of Menagias, was like the desert-loving turtledove of the Psalmist who found a nest to lay her young. In this "nest" his body, wasted by many illnesses, was strengthened, and his spirit received wings *like a dove.* (Ps. 83:4).

He was irreconcilable to the "beloved enemy," the flesh. And anyway, the environment did not give him much opportunity for reconciliation.

When he lived in Katounakia, Elder Callinicus used to make some concessions for him in the matter of food. When he came to this desert, however, things became more difficult. Elder Joseph, the elder of the small community, as we mentioned before, made him eat beans for many days.

"Elder, I will die, I can't eat beans constantly," Fr. Gerasim complained.

"To die is why we came here. Don't be a coward," was the answer.

"And behold! Not only did I suffer nothing, but I even became well. It is another power which acts in these circumstances, the power of obedience, higher than the power of logic," Fr. Gerasim said, relating the miraculous results which the prayer and blessing of the elders have.

Later, as Fr. Bartholomew, who lived with him for a time, related, he was unshakable in fasting. He would pass the whole week on only a little simple food.

Fasting and intense prayer very shortly led him to the "pastures" of compunction. His tears became his daily food. *My tears have been my bread by day and by night,* he sang together with the great prophet of repentance and "joy-creating sorrow," David (Ps. 41:4). With how many tears did he not water that ascetic earth, ploughed by repentance, for the period of denial, the lost years....

"All my life I have shamefully and prodigally wasted, O Lover of man.... But now as I return, O Savior, receive me as the prodigal...."

"With a compassionate eye, O Lord, behold my humility and save me," resounded the compunctionate hymns of joy-creating sorrow from the stone hut of Fr. Gerasim.

Many winter nights, as he kept vigil in his cell with the prayer-rope, his neighbors outside heard his loud and poignant sighings. On summer nights he prayed on a rock, one of the many the desert offered him, under the stars of heaven or in the moonlight.

However, the divine love of Fr. Gerasim for the longed-for and all-venerable face of the Lord Jesus culminated, by means of the mystery of unceasing prayer, in the great Mystery by which we become "communicants of the divine nature. " In one of his writings about the Divine Eucharist, passages of which we will quote at the end of the book, he calls the Divine Eucharist "a mystery of the love of Christ and storehouse of all divine treasures."

Meanwhile, as much as the struggling hermit fought the "opposing ranks" of the devil by prayer, Holy Communion, and study, so much did satan rage against him. He strove, therefore, to keep the "eye of the heart" vigilant. Once when he was returning from Athens to the Holy Mountain, he said: "I go to subjugate the rebellious mind." In these few words are comprehended the whole noble battle for perfection, the war against the passions and the demons, the holy life of monks: to bring the mind into subjection, to acquire the "mind of Christ," to attain to purity, enlightenment, deification.

He often told Elder Theodosius of St. Paul's Monastery about the various harassments of the evil spirits, who did not cease disturbing him day or night. One of their tricks was to make him study the writings of Origen, which, as is known, contain heretical doctrines, and to all but cast him into delusion.

"I'm confused, Fr. Damascene, I'm confused," he confided one day to his beloved co-ascetic. "Origen says that hell will have an end, it won't be eternal!"

"But didn't I tell you not to read him at all?" the other scolded him in return.

"He had a continual struggle," the same Fr. Damascene told us, "because he was not able to abandon the dream of knowledge and of the vainglory which knowledge brings, to deny himself. He found simple, uneducated ascetics and he marvelled at them, how they spoke with wisdom and simplicity about matters which he could not understand by science.

"One time several fathers were talking about whether there is life on other stars. Fr. Gerasim was also present. Then an uneducated ascetic spoke up and said:

"'Fathers, do you know what's the matter with us men? A master sent his workers to dig in his vineyard; and when they went out to work, they began to discuss if their master had other vineyards, where and how many. That's what we do, too. What does it matter to us if the Master has other worlds on other stars? We must till our vineyard here on earth....'

"What an impression that simple ascetic made on Fr. Gerasim! Nevertheless, he contemplated the greatness of God from another point of view. He often said to me:

"'My brother, these astronomers and great physicists who observe the wisdom of God in nature glorify the Lord for His greatness and believe in Him very much. But the divine wisdom exists not only in the infinite universe, the macrocosm, but also in the unseen microcosm with its ceaseless motion of microbes and living organisms, which only the microscope perceives. *Magnified are Thy works, O Lord....*'

"When a thunderbolt struck in the rainy season, he said to me:

"'You should know, my brother, what mathematical wisdom is concealed in this jagged line in the sky.... *The heavens declare the glory of God, and the firmament tells of the work of His hands.*'"

He confronted the difficulties and problems of daily life with simplicity and deep faith. One time they had no yeast to make bread with. Then Fr. Gerasim took the prayer-rope of St. Nectarius, which he kept as a precious heirloom, made the sign of the Cross over the dough together with Fr. Bartholomew, and made prosphora for Divine Liturgy. His reverence for St. Nectarius, our newly-revealed Saint, was characteristic of him. In a letter to his friend and spiritual brother, F.S., he wrote: "...I also received the parcel with the holy oil and several pieces of the garment (archiepiscopal sakkos) of St. Nectarius, which I delivered over, after keeping one for myself, to the suffering brothers, for which I thank you endlessly. As I was waiting to receive the photograph you wrote to me about also, I put off writing to you from day to day.... I very much want to know when it has been decided to transfer his holy relics, and therefore I fervently beg you to keep it in your mind to write me in time to inform me."

Those fathers who knew Fr. Gerasim have told us about the meekness, forgetfulness of wrongs, honesty, and lack of judgment that adorned his character. He judged no one, but treated even those who accused him with patience and humility.

Very often Fr. Bartholomew would shout at him unjustly, "You have a devil, Gerasim!" But he would not get upset, but would only humbly bow down and make a prostration.

Because of his great simplicity and guilelessness, he received the English spy Balfour during the time of the German occupation. Seeing the spy praying and making prostrations, he was enthusiastic, being deceived into thinking that he had come to live as an Orthodox monk. "He even has the priesthood," he said. "Where does he have it? In a cocoon?" the fathers answered. Nevertheless, Balfour did his work....

Always sickly, Fr. Gerasim besought God that some person would come to him for consolation and company. And indeed, our Panagia sent him Fr. Andrew, afterwards Abbot of the Monastery of St. Paul. Being of a hesychastic nature, Fr. Andrew also lived in the desert, so he came and lived for a period of time with Fr. Gerasim as his disciple. Fr. Gerasim was consoled and glorified God. "Brother helped by brother is as a strong city." So it was with those two fathers. Each one helped the other, in both physical and spiritual things.

"One day, after the daily service," related Fr. Andrew, "I went to do my rule and be quiet. Suddenly I heard knocks on my door. I thought Elder Gerasim was calling me. I went out and looked around, but no one was there. I went to his cell and saw him sitting where I had left him.

"'Elder,' I said loudly (the blessed one was a little hard of hearing), 'what were those knocks on my door?'

"'Don't be disturbed,' he told me. 'Next time when you hear knocking, don't open. When I knock at your door I will call to you, "Through the prayers of our holy fathers... It's the elder, open!"'

"Another time the ever-memorable one sent me to the Lavra. Approaching Coldwater, I saw chestnuts from the forest strewn on the path. The thought came to me to fill my sack—I had with me a large sack with a capacity of 50 okas [about 140 pounds]—and to return to our Kalyve at St. Basil's and then set out again for the Lavra. So I did. After I had come back from the Lavra and boiled the chestnuts, Elder Gerasim called me and said to me:

"'Beautiful chestnuts, my father. Get a plate and take the blessing to our neighbor ... another plate to the next, then the next—to all the fathers....'

"And we also kept a few chestnuts. The blessed one had a merciful heart. He loved the elders, the ascetics, with abundant love. He did the same thing when we had received two sacks of flour and baked some beautiful bread in our oven. He sent me to give a hot loaf to each kalyve in the skete."

The blessed one *hath dispersed, he hath given to the poor* (Ps. 111:9), while he himself lived in great voluntary poverty and deprivation, to the extent that in his letters to Elder Theodosius of St. Paul's Monastery he would ask for alms of clothing or shoes.

Perfect unacquisitivenss frees a monk from material things and their cares, and makes him "a palm tree tall and fruitful. "

III

"On the Lampstand"

1. ON THE RAMPARTS OF CHARITY

When war was declared in 1940 and the Germans occupied Greece, Fr. Gerasim had to serve as interpreter in Karyes and at the guardhouse which the conquerors had set up at the end of the Athonite peninsula, next to the Romanian Skete of the Honorable Forerunner. His perfect knowledge of the German language and his gifted, virtuous character brought great service to the Holy Mountain in that time of crisis and during the whole period of the German occupation. With the blessing of the Holy Governing Council he even translated a letter to Hitler himself, in which the fathers begged him not to harm the Holy Mountain, emphasizing the uniqueness of the ancient Athonite monastic life and the "peaceful life of prayer and fasting" of the ascetics. It was perhaps the only instance that the cruel and inhuman Hitler relented.

Fr. Gerasim was placed in the position of interpreter by Divine Providence because he loved the Garden of our Panagia exceedingly. His chief concern in this time of trial was the safety of the Holy Mountain. As for his views on the Germans: *Flash forth lightnings, O Lord, and scatter them...* (Ps. 17:15).

Writing to Elder Theodosius of St. Paul's Monastery on November 26, 1940, he called the Italians cowardly and unmanly, and in another letter he expressed pain for the victims of unfortunate Cephalonia.

One of the most distressing consequences of the German occupation was the shortage of food. Certain elders of the Holy Mountain—poor, destitute ascetics, who had never stored up supplies of flour, but always lived in voluntary deprivation, with a few rusks, carefree as the *fowls of the air* (Matt. 6:26)—lacked even daily bread. About these poor creatures of God, spiritual *birds of the desert* (Ps. 101:7), he wrote to Fr. Theodosius.

Fr. Theodosius had been appointed as an administrator of the Department of Provisions in Karyes, which gave help to the destitute and the suffering. As the thought had come to him that he was being distracted by many cares and worries, Fr. Gerasim sent him a wonderful letter on November 5, 1946:

> I received your friendly letter of the first of the month, which pleased me very much, seeing in it your fervent desire to give help, as much as it depends on you, to the poor brethren, fathers of the Holy Mountain, who have already begun to feel the lack of bread.... Believe me, my brother, this sign in your heart is from our Protrectress and Mother, the Lady Theotokos, the nourisher of our existence up to today. As for what you write me, that it would have been better for you never to have left off weeping for your sins than to have undertaken such cares for the assistance of others, I remind you, as surely you know yourself, that there is no more suitable medicine for the remission of our sins than almsgiving.
>
> St. John Chrysostom teaches us, saying: "Even if you have many sins, almsgiving is a defender ... for he who bears in his hands (this) special promissory note will claim a debt from the Master." And again: "Give to the poor, and even if you are silent, a myriad of mouths will defend you." And again: "Almsgiving is the redemption of the soul...."

Full of love, mercy, and good fruits, Fr. Gerasim mentioned in his letters all who were poverty-stricken and needy: the Romanian fathers of the Skete of the Honorable Forerunner, the ascetics of Vigla, of Kavsokalyvia. Often he signed with a characteristic signature: "Gerasim, false monk."*

In the Monastery of the Great Lavra Fr. Gerasim left very good impressions. The ever-memorable Abbot of the Lavra, Archimandrite Athanasius, told us:

"Fr. Gerasim was a man of self-denial. At that time the desert was hard, not like today when it has many consolations. His was an unselfish, noble, gentle character."

Fr. Philip of the Lavra added: "He came regularly to visit us. He was a man who was conscious of his mission. He saved my elder, Ambrose, intervening with the Germans and saying to them: 'Such a man of God you are accusing of sabotage?' He also saved ten other fathers whom the Germans had accused."

During the period of the occupation he travelled between St. Basil's Skete and the Lavra because of his duties as interpreter, until after a few years he settled in the cell of St. Athanasius' cave, which the Monastery of the Great Lavra ceded to him. There he lived in silence, doing his lifelong "rule": enduring unmurmuringly the pains and afflictions of his many illnesses, which grew continually worse.

This cave received the name of St. Athanasius the Athonite because the Saint often went there to pray and be silent. It has two small churches and one room. The spiritual presence of the builder of the Great Lavra, the teacher and instructor, the glory of Athos, the protector and loving Father of all Athonite monks, strengthened the new inhabitant in his hard, superhuman struggles.

In this cave Fr. Theocletus of Dionisiou visited him one day. It was winter, but the day was sunny. He found him outside, warming himself. Among other things, Fr. Gerasim told him of a wonder-

---

*i.e., *Gerasimos monachos amonachos,* "monachos" having the double meaning of "monk" and "geniune," and "a" being a negative prefix—*trans. note.*

The chapel of St. Athanasius' Cave.

ful event: "It had snowed a lot, my brother, and I was sitting inside the cave. Suddenly I heard a little bird chirping outside without stopping, crying with a strange and inexplicable persistence, which made me go outside. At the exact moment that I was looking to see why the bird of the air was so agitated, there fell a large rock which had come loose from the ceiling of the cave, and which, had I been there, would have crushed me. Glory to God and the Panagia for their shelter and protection."

2. WITH THE BREASTPLATE OF PATIENCE

Only one who has visited the Holy Mountain and has studied St. Isaac the Syrian might be able to understand the greatness of the virtue of patience. When the Fathers of the Holy Mountain tonsure a monk, they give him the laconic but richly meaningful blessing: "Good patience!" When they converse, they adorn their simple speech with the byword, "Patience, practice patience." When drinking water they cross themselves and again say their beloved blessing. And when they load the mules, those likable and indispensable beasts, the means of transport and communication, they exhort them to patience, saying, for example, "Practice patience, Kitso," "Be patient, Arapi!" St. Isaac the Syrian writes:

> Every adversity and affliction, if not accompanied by patience, produces double torment; for a man's patience casts off his distress, while faint-heartedness is the mother of anguish. Patience is the mother of consolations and is a certain strength which is usually born of largeness of heart. It is hard for a man to find this strength in his tribulations without a gift from God, received through his ardent pursuit of prayer and the outpouring of his tears (Homily 46, Greek Theotokis text).

Everything on the Holy Mountain reminds one of patience: the hours-long services, the endless vigils, the obediences, the handiwork, the warfare of the demons, the trials from men, the cross of obedience, the cross of sickness. Everything contributes to the growth of this precious virtue.

Patience on the cross of sickness was the daily bread of Fr. Gerasim. The blessed one practiced the patience of Job, patience that was Christ-imitating. *Forget not the patience of Thy paupers to the end.* (Ps. 9:33). What was even more worthy of wonder, he combined patience with glorification of the Lord's goodness. Considering sickness a benefaction, he thanked God for it. "Glory to Him," he writes in one of his letters, "Who cares even for the ants."

Let us see how he himself describes these experiences in his letters to Fr. Theodosius.

> ...In six or seven days I will stop the grape therapy, and so with the help of God I hope to recover my lost strength and to resume regularly the activity of the heart. For I suffer from it, having heart trouble, which I have much more now. (Letter of August 15, 1947)

...Therefore, all the sicknesses which have visited me since the last winter come from the murderous and treacherous dampness of the cave, which imperceptibly has penetrated my ill body, and today I suffer mainly from my heart and from bronchitis, which I caught during the time of the Spanish flu, which has healed.... But since God has allowed this for my sins, may His Holy Name be blessed... (Letter of October 26, 1947).

Writing to a young theologian about the meaning of temptations in our lives, he says with fatherly feeling:

Being All-Good, God lets temptations assail us (not beyond our strength), looking to our souls' profit; let us therefore beseech the Lord to grant us patience in afflictions and to strengthen us that we may be enabled to fulfill His All-Holy will, which always results in the purification of our souls....

Having in mind that these temptations come to us by God's allowance, and that they are given to us for our souls' benefit, we should not sorrow above measure; we should even rejoice, considering that these things come to us by the love of our heavenly Father for the cure and complete healing of our sick souls. "Remove temptations, and no one will be saved."

And the Apostle James exhorts us to rejoice in temptations, saying to us: *My brethren, count it all joy when ye fall into diverse temptations* (James 1:2).

Being himself in pain and tried "like gold in the furnace" of sickness, he could console and strengthen others, both by his living voice and by correspondence. In one letter to his spiritual child in Athens, he writes:

...I would very much like to learn about the sickness of this girl, whom, as you remind me, we visited.... I hold her blessed for this suffering; it suffices only to practice patience, and, if possible, to glorify God for the good things He has prepared for her. One saint says: "When you are sick, say, 'Blessed is he who is counted worthy to be tried by God for the health of his soul.'" Again another saint says: "God does not rejoice so much in any other virtue, as when someone is sick and thanks Him...." And St. Peter

Damascene says: "We must thank God because He gave sickness as a crown of patience."

Trust in the providence of God became a living experience for Fr. Gerasim. In his letter of October 1, 1953, from the Monastery of St. Paul, see how he speaks of the beneficent and all-powerful Providence of God:

> ... Glory to our all-good heavenly Father Who uses various means and manifold contrivances to save us ungrateful ones and lead us into His heavenly Kingdom. This disease of my heart, being organic and therefore incurable, can be counted as one of these means. Furthermore, since His goodness and compassion is infinite, together with the temptations He gives us also the strength to easily confront and bear them....

As a "two-edged sword" in his refined conscience was the memory of his "terrible deeds" and the "old reckonings" which time had discharged.

> Great is my consolation, feeling that all these sufferings come from the love of the All-Merciful God, Who looks to the profit of our souls, and even of those who, as I, have grieved Him and angered Him above measure by their lives. May His All-Holy Name be blessed and glorified, in that He uses all kinds of medicines for the salvation of men. *My Father worketh hitherto, and I work* (John 5:17), He says to us in His Holy Gospel. What other work do they do if not to save the souls of men?... Keep always in mind the holy words of the Gospel: *Not a hair of your head falls without the will of your heavenly Father...* (*cf.* Matt. 10:29-30).

> Glory to our heavenly Father, that by the granting of these evils (as we foolishly call them) He has only one aim: that by the patience we show He may bring us, as far as possible, closer to Himself.... A certain saint says about this: "He who is wise and knows the truth confesses God not by the memory of past deeds, but by patiently enduring all that comes to him." Again, another saint says: "We must know this also, that there are three ways of piety towards God by which a man can be saved. The first is to

not sin, the second is for the sinner to bear patiently the afflictions that come to him, and the third is for one to mourn over one's lack of patience...."

St. Athanasius the Great asked St. Niphon: "Does sickness, then, benefit a man, Father?" St. Niphon replied and said to him: "Just as gold when cast into the fire expels rust and comes out pure, so also a man, if he thanks God in sickness, expels his sins."

3. *IT IS GOOD FOR ME THAT THOU HAST HUMBLED ME*

As he described in his letters, his health was attacked by the symptoms of many illnesses, and day by day his condition worsened in the cave of St. Athanasius. During an acute crisis of his illness he entered the infirmary of the Lavra. From there he sent notification to Fr. Andrew of St. Paul's, beseeching him: "Come and take me, my brother."

Abbot Seraphim, then the Abbot of St. Paul's Monastery, did everything he could to care for and give repose to the sick man. They all considered him as a brother of the Monastery. The serious condition of his health, however, constrained him to go to Athens to be treated there and recover his health. The year was 1950. His soul's pain was greater than his body's, because he was abandoning his beloved silence, the peace and serenity of the Athonite life.

He stayed in the home of his sister, in the district of Cypriadou. *Much peace have they that love Thy law* (Ps. 118:165). The peace *that passeth all understanding* (Phil. 4:7), a fruit of the Holy Spirit and of silence, shone forth from his face to all. Gentle, sweet, approachable, gracious, he naturally exercised, without intending it, a pastoral work. A multitude of faithful Christians came to receive his blessing and to harvest from him *a good word* (Ps. 44:1). Twenty-five years of ascetic life had made the white-haired elder-hermit a "mystical vineyard."

More than any other subject, his speech turned around the central axis of Christian spiritual life, of both monks and laymen: prayer.

"Pray," he repeated to many souls who came to see him. "Pray unceasingly with the great prayer: 'Lord Jesus Christ, Son of God, have mercy on me!' But when you say this prayer, take care that it pass through your heart like a knife."

Following the course of the Holy Ascetic Fathers, having as a heritage the spiritual tradition of his Elder Callinicus, Fr. Gerasim lived and taught unceasing prayer with the safeguards of the Philokalia. His saying, "take care that it pass through your heart like a knife," was, in the language of the Philokalia, "have the mind in the heart." Prayer must be joined with attention and sobriety, and the attention must be on prayer. This meeting of the mind and the heart creates feeling, compunction, contrition, pain, fear, love of God, tears, and the uniting of all the powers of the soul to the central aim of union with her Lord and God.

> The virtues, since they resemble the virtues of God, make a man fit to receive the Divine, but the virtues do not unite (him to it). The power of prayer, however, acts in a divine manner and effects the lifting up of man and his union with the Divine, because prayer is the bond that links rational creatures with God; prayer surely acts thus when, helped by warm compunction which burns the passions, it rises above the activity of the passions and the various thoughts, for the union of God with a passionate mind is impossible. (St. Gregory Palamas)

Fr. Gerasim's stay in Athens at that time was according to God's economy, that he might transmit his patristic Orthodox experience to the people of God in a popular form.

But as long as he stayed far from the Garden of the Panagia, he felt like a fish out of the sea. His soul quivered with longing, yearning for the day of his return. *When shall I come and behold the face of God...* (Ps. 41:3)?

The opportunity came suddenly and unexpectedly. He was informed that the Theological School of the University of Athens had planned a pilgrimage to the Holy Mountain by ship on the eve of the feast of the Holy Apostles, 1953. He asked them to take him with them. His joy was indescribable.

It was an unforgettable journey. Fr. Gerasim became a pole of attraction to all the students, and he was greatly moved at seeing so many youths dedicated to Christ. In the ship he served the Vespers and Divine Liturgy of the Holy Apostles. "The students sang with such compunction," he wrote later in one of his letters, "that it seemed to us that the angels of Heaven were following the ship, singing and celebrating together with us."

Far off the conical mass of Athos began to appear on the horizon. Fr. Gerasim returned to his beloved spiritual fatherland with his inseparable companion, serious heart disease. Now neither the cave of St. Athanasius nor the desert of St. Basil was a suitable place for him to live. Where could he go? *Make known to me, O Lord, the way I should walk...* (Ps. 142:8) he prayed fervently. And the Lord showed him the way which led to his beloved Coenobium, the Monastery of St. Paul, that he might spend his last years there "in peace and repentance."

4. THE SNOW-COVERED MONASTERY OF ST. PAUL

For the reader who might not be acquainted with the Monastery of St. Paul, we will take the opportunity to introduce it briefly.

The Coenobium of St. Paul is located on the western foot of Athos, by the bed of a torrent which descends from the peak, in wild and majestic surroundings. Except for a few days in the summer, the summit of Athos has snow in its deepest crevasses all the year round. So we can justly call St. Paul's a "snow-covered" Monastery.

Tradition says that the Monastery was founded in the 10th century by St. Paul of Xeropotamou in the last years of his life, when he was seeking more silence amidst the cares of the great Xeropotamou Monastery. St. Paul was a prince, the son of Emperor Michael Rangave. How many kings and princes in the course of

Monastery of St. Paul.

history have abandoned the vanity of this world and, "exchanging the royal rank," embraced the simple, frugal life of monks!

It appears that in the beginning St. Paul founded a small Monastery, which existed until the 14th century. Two noblemen, Gerasim and Anthony, brothers according to the flesh, reestablished the Monastery, erecting beautiful buildings and endowing it with various metochia. Xeropotamou Monastery recognized the independence and self-governance of the Monastery of St. Paul, with the agreement that if it were ever abandoned it would return to the jurisdiction of the mother Monastery.

After various historical vicissitudes, including bankruptcies, a great benefactor and reformer of the Monastery appeared: Archimandrite Anthimus Comninus, an acquaintance of Patriarch Gregory V and of Prince Michael of Moldavia, who was Abbot from 1816 to 1820. He doubled the number of buildings, built the high north wall, the bell-tower, and the foundation of the new catholicon.

Noteworthy in its history is the year 1839, when St. Paul's Monastery was reestablished as a Coenobium, with Hieromonk Stephen of Dionysiou as Abbot.

The Monastery's first Catholicon was built in the 15th century by the Prince of Serbia, George I Brancovich, in honor of the Holy Great-Martyr George, whom the monks of St. Paul's especially honor up to today. Perhaps the chapel on the rock of the north side is the remnant of this ancient church.

The new Catholicon is dedicated to the Meeting of the Lord. It has a marble iconostasis, pillars, and shrines made of the marble of Athos, Tinos, and Penteles. Abbot Sophronius Kalligas, who came from Cephalonia, labored with great zeal and love for its completion.

Among the treasures of the Monastery are distinguished two large pieces of the Venerable Cross, the holy relics of St. Gregory the Theologian, and two coffers containing the Venerable Gifts of the Magi, which were given by the queen of Serbia, Kyra Maro.

This devout queen expressed the desire to bring the Venerable Gifts of the Magi to the Monastery in person. She disembarked with great ceremony at the harbor of the Monastery and set out on foot for the Monastery, which is about a half hour away from the sea. But the Holy Mountain had long since been barred to women. When, therefore, she had gone some distance, almost half-way, a majestic Woman stopped her and did not let her go further.

"Who are you," she said to her, "who dare to enter my Garden?"

"I am the queen of Serbia, and I am bringing the Venerable Gifts of the Magi."

"Here I am Queen; therefore go back."

And the Woman, who had shone like a star with divine beauty and glory, disappeared. It was the Panagia! Kyra Maro fell to her knees, worshipped, asked forgiveness, gave the Venerable Gifts to the fathers, and returned. At the site of this miracle was built a shrine which is there to this day.

The barring of the Holy Mountain to women is a centuries-old tradition, and is one of the basic prerequisites of the monks' hesychastic, holy, and otherworldly life. Although some modern people heap this rule with accusations about a "medieval spirit," etc., it remains a protecting shell, an umbrella which safeguards the essence of monastic life. It preserves the dew of the Holy Spirit, that His fruits might be borne far from the hot desert wind of the various temptations of fallen human nature. This is especially necessary in our day, when contemporary man, driven by dire psychological necessity, seeks to find silence, to find his lost self, away from disturbance and confusion. The exclusion of women from the Holy Mountain cannot be characterized as a depreciation of women. The fathers of the Holy Mountain honor the Panagia, the New Eve and the Mother of God, and in Her person, full of divine grace, they honor every woman with the honor and worth the Creator gave her. But the monastic life is called and is angelic. And since the senses, before they are purified, tyrannize over and subjugate the "sovereign mind," and since "from sight comes lust," this rule is of great help in the incorrupt monastic life. It is a precaution that the fathers of the desert take in the struggle of purity. This rule is also established in other monastic arenas outside the Holy Mountain; and in women's monasteries, where it applies to men, it exists for the same spiritual reasons.

IV

"The Righteous Live Forever"

1. A HOLY END

Within the blessed enclosure of St. Paul's Monastery, Fr. Gerasim found every possible consolation and repose. The brethren of the Monastery esteemed and revered him, and eagerly cared for all his needs.

From almost the first moment of his coming to the Holy Mountain, St. Paul's was his own Monastery, his home. There was a special sympathy between him and the fathers there, who traditionally were mostly from Cephalonia. So strong were his relations with this Monastery that he was thought by many to be one of its monks. And now the Lord granted him to be counted among its brethren and to spend the last five years of his life inside its warm and loving enclosure.

Despite his trip to Athens for medical treatment, his illness took its course. But "glory to God for everything!" As he travelled towards the sunset of his earthly life, he spoke and wrote this saying of St. John Chrysostom with ever more zeal. He increased his patience, multiplied his praise and thanksgiving to his Benefactor.

"I can find no words," he wrote in one letter, "to thank our Lord for delivering me from the vanity of this world, even though up to today I have not been able to requite this great gift of the All-Holy

God. Therefore I beg you also to pray that our Lord may grant me before my departure, and even at the end of my life, to be well-pleasing to Him."

Casting an eye to the past, with the clear eyes of his soul he gazed at the vanity of the world. He experienced that "vain are all the things of man which after death are no more." He heard the truthful voice of the Eternal One: *For what is a man profited, if he shall gain the whole world, and lose his own soul* (Matt. 16:26)?

And with these conclusions he weighed the worth of monasticism, which is a longing and desire of the heart which "maddens" the souls of God's creations.*

> "What else is this longing of yours," he writes to a youth, "and this concern which occupies you, how to save your soul? This gift, my brother, is sent to us who are weighed down by sins and ingratitude only from on high, and by such summons our heavenly Father draws us to His own will. Sometimes he draws us by inspiring our souls with the fear of hell; sometimes He pulls us after Him, even involuntarily, by the sweetness of His love—love which He implants in the souls of His creatures, and as if mad they run behind their Creator like thirsting deer, sometimes forgetting even their own selves, while the whole world with all its enjoyments seems to them like an insupportable burden; and then they depart from the world, in order to be perfectly undistracted, and thus be able to love their sweetest God and worship Him day and night...."

Fr. Gerasim's five years of coenobitic life in the Monastery of St. Paul were the best preparation for the great journey. All who visited there were attracted by his peaceful figure and wise words. The present Abbot of St. Paul's, Archimandrite Parthenius, who was there during his lifetime, told us: "I remember him in the old-age infirmary. I was young then. He advised me kindly: 'Learn to pray, my child, pray a great deal.' And he gave me a beautiful book about prayer by St. John of Kronstadt. He was a man with a will like steel."

---

*The Greek adjective *allofronos*, "mad", means literally "of another mind"—*trans. note*.

Despite his medicines and the care of the fathers, his sick and exhausted heart confined him to bed for the last time. Yet the vigor of his soul remained invincible. His sacramental life became more intense. "He communed every Saturday of the divine Body and Blood of the Master, and asked that Holy Unction be served often," attested the Abbot of that time, Archimandrite Seraphim.

With these spiritual provisions he prepared for the journey to heaven, until the day of his departure arrived: January 30, 1957, the feast of the Three Hierarchs. The evening before he asked to receive the Immaculate Mysteries. Later he bade farewell to the brethren, who were around him, made the sign of the Cross, and in the third hour after midnight delivered his holy soul into the hands of God. *The souls of the righteous are in the hand of God* and *their reward is in the Lord,* and *their hope is full of immortality* (Wisdom of Solomon, Ch. 3). With his soul joining in the all-night doxologies of the fathers to the three "great lights" of the Church, he was offered up as fragrant incense to the throne of God, to rejoice eternally with the choirs of saints.

Everyone who knew Elder Gerasim well discerned something of his gifts and rare personality, and had something to say about his spiritual stature.

We would like to close this brief biography with the impressions of certain men of letters, who with a few final strong brushstrokes will give yet more life to the elder's portrait.

The well-known author Zacharias Papadoniou visited the Holy Mountain in 1928 with a large dose of prejudice, curiosity, and unbelief. He made the acquaintance of Fr. Gerasim, and on his return wrote a special article in *Free Rostrum* (Oct. 28, 1928), entitled "The Frantic Leap: Science Wears a Rassa," referring to the ascetics who live in great silence, their only possession their satchels. We cite here an excerpt of this article:

> ...One might think that illiteracy and ignorance are the first requirements for making this frantic leap. But no! On Athos there are scientists who have humbled themselves until they have be-

come purer than the hermit, and more flaming than he in their faith.

I met in Karyes the chemist, Mr. Menagias, a graduate of the Zurich Polytechnic, who after working in his scientific field in Egypt and Athens, while still young withdrew to the Holy Mountain and is already an ascetic in a distant skete, seven hours from Karyes. Fr. Gerasim, as he is now called, is not yet forty years old. He lives in rare asceticism, forgetting every subject and denying what chemistry taught him. If one exchanges two words with him, one is convinced that this man, with his modest manner, large eyes, face deepened by religiosity, indeed made a 'frantic leap.'

When we had climbed the hills of Karyes one afternoon and he was talking to me about his asceticism, I asked how he had settled his accounts with chemistry.

"Chemistry is a science which examines the laws of nature," he answered. "But what does it know beyond them? If it thinks that the ways phenomena appear to us is everything, so much the worse for it."

"And the world?"

"The world! I saw it two years ago, when I went to visit my family. It hasn't changed its mind. It's a good fortune to live far away from its greed."

...Fr. Gerasim, sitting on a high place, looked towards the desert of Athos, regarding wild Katounakia and his Skete with love and longing. But he entertained his brother there for a few days, the well-known electrical engineer, formerly the director of the electrical department of the Ministry of Communications. The two scientists often went for walks in the country. They represented two opposite worlds. But I think that each one respected the other's convictions.

In one chapter of his book *Holy Mountain*, the skeptic Papadoniou remembers Fr. Gerasim and his unshakable faith in Divine Providence. He writes:

> The pharmicist Balsamakis suddenly sold the clinic he had kept in Cephallinia, and went to become an ascetic in Katounakia on Athos. He had brought medicines with him in order to place

his science at the disposal of the monks. "Throw them away," said the elder of the kalyve. "What use are medicines? It is lack of faith in the Divinity." And he threw them away.

Of the same opinion with the elder and the pharmicist is their co-ascetic, Fr. Gerasim, a chemistry graduate of Zurich. "I don't believe in medicines," he told me. "I only believe in God. Medicines are made by chemistry. It is a science that examines some of the laws of nature; but it doesn't know what happens behind those laws.... My brother did well, and he doesn't use medicines anymore. If we were to bring our science here, he would be a pharmacist and I a chemist; namely, phenomena would still be misleading us. But we came here to draw near to their cause!"

On the other hand, the Greek-American university professor C. Cavarnos writes about Fr. Gerasim, whom he knew on Mount Athos, in his book *Anchored in God* (Athens, 1959, p. 116). On this page he lets the elder himself recount his return to the Church:

> In my youth I was indifferent to religion. In my final student years, however, I began to be interested in telepathy, mediums, and other psychic phenomena, and gradually I was convinced of the existence of the soul and the spiritual world. Their exact nature didn't interest me very much. For me, the important thing was that these things actually existed. Later, I grew so interested in religion that I came to the Holy Mountain, even though my brother and my mother tried to dissuade me.
>
> When I was in Switzerland I loved a young German girl. I loved her so intensely that I wanted to see her constantly, and I thought about her continually, even in my dreams. But as my interest in religion grew, my love shifted to God. I came to love God more than I had loved her. And my desire was to live the quiet "contemplative" life of a monk, devoted to unceasing worship of Him.

Archimandrite Sophronius Zakharov, the spiritual father and Abbot of the Monastery of the Honorable Forerunner in Essex, England, had created a strong spiritual bond with Fr. Gerasim which he preserved until the end. In his letter of July 4, 1955, Fr. Sophronius writes to Fr. Gerasim:

> ... You have given me much evidence of your unshakable kindness to me, who am unworthy of your attention. God deigned to join my spiritual being with your blessing and protection. And I, according to my strength (or rather weakness), strive to not appear ungrateful and a cause of shame for you when you will appear before the Lord.
>
> Every communication with you is for me joy and relief and consolation—which life does not let me receive.
>
> I wanted to spend much time with you in order to submit everything I do and preach to your enlightened judgment, according to the example of the Holy Apostle Paul: *and I communicated unto them that gospel which I preach ... lest by any means I should run, or had run, in vain* (Gal. 2:2). And this, namely the preaching, I again do from necessity. My desire is to live in silence with you and under your supervision just like before, when we three (you, my ever beloved in Christ Fr. Andrew, and I the wretched one) traveled the holy peninsula of Athos to find a corner for silence. But God did not grant this.

In the same letter he writes down the impressions of a Swiss intellectual named Bruschweiler, who, having visited Fr. Gerasim in the Monastery of St. Paul, wrote about him to Fr. Sophronius:

> ...I was very happy to be able to speak for many hours with that holy man, and every time I left him I felt in my heart a peace which flooded my whole being. He spoke to me about prayer and how it must be preserved in love. Truly I thank God, who allowed me to meet such a man. He showed me friendship, and in particular showed me the holy relics of the monastery to venerate. I even received a small piece of cotton which he touched to each of the relics, begging me to bring it to you. I will do so on my next trip.
>
> Fr. Gerasim has now grown very weak because of his heart ailment, and he doesn't leave his cell anymore. In this he is happy, and holds on to the prayer, which continues inside him without stopping.

Archimandrite Elias Mastrogiannopoulos, in his book *Holy Figures of Modern Greece,* writes with realism and clarity:

...His story [Fr. Gerasim's] is not very usual, and shows exactly the hidden paths by which Divine Grace leads those whom It wants to draw to Itself....

With all his brilliance, Fr. Gerasim was continually shown to be a lamp which shone upon both friends and enemies, foreigners and our own people, monks and laymen....

He was simple and moderate in everything.... His good heart ever radiated a fresh and heavenly courtesy to those near him.... He was always sweet and gentle. His love was so deep and great that it reminded one of a man of the apostolic era....

Our revered and ever-memorable Elder, Archimandrite Cherubim, in his book *From the Garden of the Panagia: Nostalgic Remembrances* (pp. 201-202) describes his meeting with Fr. Gerasim:

I was approaching my destination after an exhausting journey, when a great downpour began. I was forced to knock on the door of the nearest kalyve for shelter. With surprise I found myself before the renowned monk, Fr. Gerasim Menagias.... I saw him for the first time. His words, love, and conduct impressed me.... In his face I saw a scientist, an ascetic, a disciple of Elder Callinicus the Hesychast, a man of mental prayer, whom the entire Holy Mountain honored and revered....

2. "THE BODY OF GOD BOTH NOURISHES AND SANCTIFIES ME"

As a conclusion to the present volume we thought it profitable to quote a few pages* of Fr. Gerasim's writings on Holy Communion.

Knowing that the hour of His sacrifice had arrived, our Savior Jesus Christ wanted to leave us before His Passion a greater proof of His love. Therefore He established the great mystery of the Divine Eucharist.

---

*From manuscript book no. 184 of the Monastery of St. Paul, p. 25.

The revelation of this love, which was made during the last moments before His death, makes a deep impression in the hearts of men, and is reckoned exceedingly precious. For the same reason, men also usually bequeath gifts to the persons dearest to them in their wills, in memory of the love they had for them.

"But Thou, O my Jesus, when Thou didst leave this world, what didst Thou leave us in remembrance of Thy love? Thou didst give us Thy whole self. Thou didst leave us Thy body, Thy blood, Thy soul, Thy Divinity—in a word, Thy whole self, holding nothing back."

And as a guarantee in case we should doubt His love, we find in this mystery an obvious proof of it, as if when He established it the Redeemer was saying: "Souls of Christians, attend to this mystery, because by it I give you My whole self. Having such a proof in your hands, therefore, you are allowed no doubt that I love you greatly."

One saint named this mystery "love above all other love," because this gift has within it all the other gifts of the Lord—namely, the gifts of creation, deliverance, and eternal glory. For Holy Communion is not only a proof of Christ's love, it is also a guarantee of the enjoyment of the Kingdom of Heaven, which, as our Church emphasizes, He desires to give us.

The Prophet Isaiah wanted to make known to the whole world the thoughts full of love which God showed in order to draw the love of men to Himself.... "How," says the holy Augustine, "does it not appear as madness for one to say, 'Eat my flesh, drink my Blood?'"

When Christ first spoke to His disciples about this mystery, certain of them could not believe it, and withdrew from Him, saying, "How can this man give us his flesh to eat?"

In this which the men could neither think about nor believe, the exceptional love of Christ was realized. "Take, eat," He said to His disciples, and through them to us all.

He exhorted us to do this, even promising us entrance to His Kingdom: *He who eats My flesh and drinks My blood has life eternal.*

Finally, he even used the threat of hell against one who does not wish to partake of this mystery.

All these exhortations, promises, and threats come only from the fervent desire He has to give Himself to us through Holy Communion.

But why does Christ so greatly desire us to receive Him by Holy Communion?

Because love desires and has as its goal our union with His Divinity.

By Holy Communion Christ is united with the soul, and the soul herself is united with Christ. This union is completely real. Christ gives nothing with so much love as He gives this Mystery, giving Himself as food in order to unite Himself with the hearts of the faithful. With this fervent love has Christ desired to be united with us, that we might make up one being with Him.

"O divine Bridegroom of our souls, through the mystery of love Thou hast willed that Thy heart and our own become one single heart, inseparably united!"

As Christ seeks the union of us with Himself, so also we for this love must frequently partake of Divine Communion, according, however, to the judgment of our spiritual father, to whom we must confess. In any case, absolutely no obstacle can exist to continual Holy Communion, which again the spiritual father will regulate.

Nothing in this world is so beneficial as Holy Communion. The eternal Father established Christ as the keeper of this matter, and gave all the divine treasures to His disposal. Consequently, when Christ comes to the soul through Holy Communion, He brings with Him infinite treasures of Grace, and after Holy Communion everyone can say that "all good things came to me together with this mystery."

St. Dionysius teaches that the sacrament of the Divine Eucharist is the most effective means of the soul's sanctification.

Through Holy Communion we are freed from our forgivable sins and preserved from deadly ones.

This sacrament kindles in our souls divine love. God is love. He is fire which drives from our hearts every earthly inclination; and this fire of divine love which our Christ brought upon the earth seeks nothing else than to see our hearts flaming with divine love.

Holy Communion draws us so much to love, that when we retire after partaking of it we become terrible to the demons.

Some say that they receive Communion infrequently because they feel but little love for God within themselves. "Why, therefore, since you are cold, do you distance yourselves from this divine fire? On the contrary, since you are cold you should approach this sacrament very often, if indeed you desire to love Christ."

When one is sick, one needs doctors so much the more. So also here: for our soul's healing we must approach its doctor very often.

It is said somewhere that there are two kinds of men who should receive Communion frequently: the perfect, that they may preserve perfection; and the imperfect, that they may reach perfection.

Monk Gerasim Menagias

APPENDICES

APPENDIX 1

AN EVENT THAT OCCURRED DURING THE SEBASTOPOL CAMPAIGN

A Letter of Fr. Sabbas to Fr. Denasius, a monk of the Russikon:

In 1853, during the reign of the pious Emperor Nicholas—may the Lord grant him rest in the Heavenly Kingdom with all the Saints, where the light of the Countenance of our Lord Jesus Christ shines, where is the dwelling of all them that rejoice—at that time I was living in stillness with my blessed Elder, Hieroschemamonk Hilarion, on a hillock at the outskirts of the Monastery of Dionysiou, and celebrated the Divine Services in the holy church of the Holy Apostle James, the Brother of the Lord. The terrible war between the Russians and the Turks with their heretic allies was then taking place at Sebastopol. And when we with sorrow learned about this, we grieved in our hearts, since my blessed Elder loved the Russians. And many times I heard him thank God that his own people had not fallen into the hands of the Turks or of heretics, but into the hands of Orthodox Christians.

As soon as we heard about this terrible war, my Elder told me: "Behold, my child, since our brethren, the Russian Christians, now find themselves betwixt the sword and blood, we must fervently and with tears entreat God that they may conquer their enemies and humble them, that thereby His All-holy Name and the Russian people, His inheritance, may be glorified. Sabbas, my child, in addition to the Liturgy which you serve daily and at which you supplicate God for the Russians, I order you to read also the entire Psalter of the Prophet-King David every day, and to make prostrations to aid our brethren."

I answered: "For your sake I will do everything I can."

When we began the Liturgy and I had said the exclamation: "Blessed is the Kingdom of the Father, and of the Son, and of the Holy Spirit..." he answered: "Amen." And I began the Litany of Peace: "In peace let us pray to the Lord..." The Elder would reply in Georgian: "Upalo, Shegvitskale" ("Lord, have mercy") quickly. I would continue: "For the peace from above..." and the Elder would say "Upalo, Shegvitskale," but more slowly and with great sorrow. Further: "For pious Orthodox Christians"—then the Elder with great contrition and tears, raising his hands to heaven, would sing slowly: "Upalo, Shegvitskale," beating his breast with his right hand, falling down to the earth, striking his head three times against the ground and sprinkling it with tears. Again: "For our most pious and God-loving Emperor Nicholas, his Consort, children, court, and army...." The Elder would answer with contrition, having his hands upraised and gazing upwards: "Upalo, Shegvitskale." "That every enemy and foe be brought into subjection beneath his feet...." The Elder replied: "Upalo, Shegvitskale," smiting his breast, falling with his face to the gound, and striking his face on the floor three times with great lamentation. Further, "For the Holy Synod and for the God-preserved Russian Dominion...," and the Elder would reply with contrition and many tears: "Upalo, Shegvitskale."

As I write this, my heart becomes contrite and I weep and cannot continue to write. The same would take place at the Litany of Fervent Supplication.

In such a manner did we celebrate Liturgy every day. After a certain time elapsed, the Elder said to me: "Let's go to the monastery [Dionysiou] to ask the Abbot what they know about the war, if the Russians or the enemy have been victorious."

When we arrived at the Monastery, the Abbot with the Monastery Council showed us a paper which the Patriarch had sent from Constantinople via a hierarch who had handed it out to the celebrating hieromonk in every monastery. The Patriarch wrote that during the Great Entrance of the Divine Liturgy they must ask God to grant strength to the Turkish army to subdue the Russians under the feet of the Turks. A special prayer had been provided which was to be read aloud.

When the Abbot, Elder Eulogius, read us the Patriarchal Epistle, the Elder said to us: "Do you understand what our Head, our father, has written?" My Elder was horrified and said, "He is not a Christian," and asked sorrowfully, "Did you read this in the Monastery during the Liturgy as he specified?" But they answered, "No, it cannot be done." But the Patriarch had threatened in his decree that any monastery that did not comply with this directive would be subjected to very severe punishment.

The next day we left for our cell. A week passed. A monk from Grigoriou Monastery came to my Elder for revelation of thoughts, and my Elder asked him: "Did you read that prayer that the Patriarch sent to the monasteries?" He answered, "Yes, we read it last Sunday during the Liturgy." The Elder said: "You did ill by reading it; you have deprived yourself of the grace of baptism, you have deprived your monastery of God's grace. Judgment will come upon you!"

This monk returned to the monastery and told the elders and Abbot: "We have deprived our monastery of God's grace, of the grace of holy baptism—so said Fr. Hilarion."

Right on that very day, a flood of water washed away the mill, and the fathers began to murmur against the Abbot: "You have destroyed the monastery!" With great sorrow, the Abbot hastened to make three prostrations before the icon of the Savior, and prayed: "O my Lord Jesus Christ, I will go to the Confessor Hilation to confess what I have done, and whatever penance he gives me, I will fulfill, that I might not die from grief."

Taking with him a hierodeacon and a monk, he went to the Cell of St. James, where we were then living. When they arrived, my Elder was outside his cell. Seeing my Elder, the Abbot with his companions fell to the ground, making full prostrations and saying: "Bless, Holy Confessor!" Then they came up to kiss his hand. But my Elder cried: "Away, go away, go far from me; I don't receive heretics!" The Abbot pleaded: "I have sinned, I have come to ask you to assign me a rule of penance." The Elder said, "How could you have dared to place Mohammed above Christ? The God and Father of our Lord Jesus Christ said to His Son: *Sit Thou at My Right Hand, until I make Thine enemies the footstool of Thy feet* (Ps. 109:1), and you have asked Him to place His Son beneath the feet of his enemies! Go away from me, I will not receive you." With tears the Abbot begged the Elder to receive him in repentance and give him a penance. But my Elder said: "I am not your confessor. Go, find a confessor to give you a penance." And leaving them outside the cell weeping, the Elder went inside alone and locked the door behind him.

What was there left for us to do? We went to my cell and there celebrated the All-night Vigil, beseeching God to incline the Elder to mercy and to give the Abbot a rule of penance. In the morning the Elder came to church to the Liturgy, without speaking a word to those who had come, and after the dismissal at Liturgy he quickly left for his cell alone. Those who had come with the Abbot began to worry that he might have a heart attack; they asked to me to go over to the Elder and contend with him; perhaps he would listen to me.

I went and fell at Fr. Hilarion's feet and asked him: "Be merciful to them, give them a penance—the Abbot might have a heart attack and die." Then the Elder asked me: "What epitimia should be given to them? God on high is wroth against them. What epitimia should be laid on them in order to make God merciful to them?"

Then I told my father: "Elder, since I read through the entire Psalter of the Royal Prophet David every day as you instructed me, there is there one Psalm appropriate to this incident, Psalm 82: *O God, who shall be likened unto Thee? Neither be silent nor be still, O God....* Order them to read this entire Psalm tomorrow during Liturgy while the Cherubic Hymn is being sung, during the Great Entrance. Let the hieromonk who earlier read the Patriarch's prayer stand beneath the great polyeleos, and when all the fathers have come together during the Great Entrance, then the priest will leave the altar carrying the Diskos and Chalice in his hands. Let a monk walk in front carrying a scroll with this psalm inscribed on it, and let the hieromonk waiting beneath the polyeleos read the entire Psalm aloud to all the brethren. During the reading, from verse two until verse nine, all must repeat frequently, 'Lord, have mercy.' During the reading of the remaining verses, let them say 'Amen!' to each one. Then God's grace will return again to their monastery."

The Elder accepted my advice and asked me to summon them. When they had joyfully entered the cell and made prostrations, the Elder said to them: "Fulfill this canon of penance, and God's mercy will return to you." Then they began to be troubled, fearing that the Exarch sent by the Patriarch and staying in Karyes to monitor the execution of the Patriarch's Ukase might find out, or perhaps the Turks themselves might learn of the event and bring great misfortune upon the monastery. They did not know what to do.

The Elder said: "You have nothing to fear. I am taking my hieromonk and going to the monastery; and if the Exarch or the Turks find out, then tell them: a certain monk Hilarion the Georgian thus instructed us, and that is what we have done. And so you will be without grief."

Then the Abbot said: "Father Confessor, we worry and sorrow for you as well, because when the Turks find out about this, they will come here, seize you, tie you in a sack, and drown both of you in the sea." My elder answered: "We are ready, both I and my hieromonk. Let them drown us."

Then all of us headed together in a launch to Grigoriou Monastery. When the brothers of the monastery caught sight of us, they rejoiced exceedingly.

In the morning they arranged that the hieromonk who had read the Patriarch's prayer should serve Liturgy. They lit the great polyeleos during the Cherubic Hymn. When all the fathers had gathered, the celebrant came out of the altar preceded by the candle and the censer, bearing in his hands and on his head the Chalice and Diskos. He exclaimed: "May the Lord God remember all of you in His Kingdom!" and stood beneath the great polyeleos. Then one monk, holding in his hands a scroll inscribed with the 82nd Psalm, stood before the priest and the latter began to read:

"In the Name of the Father, and of the Son, and of the Holy Spirit!

O God, who shall be likened unto Thee? Be Thou not silent, neither be still, O God.

For behold, Thine enemies have made a noise, and they that hate Thee have lifted up their heads.

Against Thy people have they taken wicked counsel, and have conspired against Thy saints.

They said: Come, let us utterly destroy them that they may be no more a nation, and let the name of Israel be remembered no more.

For they have conspired with oneness of mind together, against thee have they made a covenent; even the tents of the Idumeans and the Ismaelites.

Moab and the Hagarenes, Gebal and Ammon and Amalek, and foreigners with them that dwell at Tyre.

Yea, for even Assur is come with them; they are become a help for the sons of Lot.

Do unto them as Thou didst unto Madiam and Sisara, as unto Jabin at the brook of Kisson.

They were utterly destroyed in Endor, they became as dung for the earth.

Make their princes like Oreb and Zeb and Zebee and Salmana.

Yea, all their princes who said: Let us take to ourselves for an inheritance the sanctuary of God.

O my God, make them like a wheel, as stubble before the face of the wind,

As fire which shall burn the forest, as a flame which shall consume the mountains.

So shalt Thou pursue them with Thy tempest, and in Thy wrath shalt Thou trouble them.

Fill their faces with dishonor, and they shall seek Thy name, O Lord.

Let them be shamed and troubled unto ages of ages, and let them be confounded and destroyed.

And let them know that Thy name is Lord; Thou alone art Most High over all the earth.

Up to the tenth verse the fathers cried out: "Lord, have mercy," and then all repeated many times: "Amen." And all understood that once again God's grace was descending upon the monastery; and the elders embraced me out of sheer joy, giving thanks for what I had done for them, and all glorified and gave thanks to God.

Thus ends the letter of Fr. Sabbas.

(Taken from *The Life and Labors of Elder Hieroschemamonk Hilarion the Georgian* by Hieromonk Anthony of the Holy Mountain, Holy Trinity Monastery, Jordanville, NY, 1985, pp. 68-73.)

APPENDIX 2

THE BLIND CONFESSOR IGNATIUS: A CLAIRVOYANT ELDER

Among the many Russian hermits of Karoulia who had Fr. Ignatius as their confessor was Hieroschemamonk Theodosius, a former seminary instructor in Russia who had come to Mt. Athos at the end of the 19th century, in the 1880's. A certain young high school instructor teaching in Skopje, Serbia, the future Archbishop Seraphim of Chicago, having heard the previous year accounts of the ascetic life of the Russian hermits on Mt. Athos, conceived a desire to make a pilgrimage there and decide his future. Arriving in late June, 1926, he spent several days as a guest with Fr. Theodosius, attending the lengthy all-night services and preparing to receive the monastic tonsure. He asked Fr. Theodosius to tonsure him, and Fr. Theodosius agreed to do so on the condition that the young high school teacher remain forever in Karoulia.

"On the morning of the feast of Sts. Peter and Paul, I had confession with Fr. Theodosius. The next day after the feast, Fr. Theodosius told me: 'Let's do it this way: I'll send you to my confessor, Fr. Ignatius. He is 105 years old and is blind, but he is actually a real clairvoyant elder, the likes of which I have seen nowhere else. Tell him everything about yourself, but whatever he decides, that you must do. Are you willing to remain in Karoulia if he blesses this?'"

Elder Theodosius of Karoulia.

I liked Karoulia so much that I answered affirmatively.

Then Fr. Theodosius gave me one of the Karoulia desert-dwellers, Schemamonk Dorotheus, as a guide, and we began to climb together the steep mountain slope to Hieroschemamonk Ignatius. He lived about two miles away or less, above Karoulia, but on a more gently sloping part of the mountain. He had a cell-attendant, a Greek, a ninety-year-old elder. Learning from Fr. Dorotheus that I had been sent by Fr. Theodosius, he silently pointed out to me a separate cell where the elder lived. I entered. The entire front corner was covered with icons. Beneath the icons on a narrow wooden cot sat the noble blind elder, working his prayer-rope. I prostrated before him and said that Fr. Theodosius had sent me to him. I received a blessing. Fr. Ignatius put on an epitrachelion and gave the blessing for the beginning of the rite of confession. I read 'Holy God' to 'Our Father' and halted. For, to my shame, I did not then yet know the 50th Psalm.

The elder said, "Read 'Have mercy on me, O God...'" I answered that I didn't know it by heart.

"What do you mean, you don't know it? You're a monk and you don't know it?!"

I said, "I'm not a monk, but I came as a pilgrim from Serbia."

And the elder said, "And I tell you you're a monk..."

Then with his finger he pointed at a piece of cardboard hanging on the wall on which was written the full order of the rite of confession. I read it.

After this, the elder told me to stand on my knees before the icons near him. He covered me with his epitrachelion and said: "First confess all your sins and then tell me what you want from me."

I confessed almost my entire life, and then related to the elder that I was employed as an instructor of the Law of God in a Serbian high school in the city of Skopje in Yugoslavia, that I wanted to become a monk, and that I wished Fr. Theodosius to tonsure me. But the latter had set as a condition for tonsure that I remain forever with him in Karoulia, and he had sent me to Fr. Ignatius so that he could decide my fate. "Whatever you say, I will do," I added.

I spoke, of course, a little more in detail.

The elder patiently heard me out and said: "Let's pray to God." For a little while we prayed silently, during which time the elder held his hands on my head. Then he absolved me of my sins, almost striking my head as he did so, blessing me with his right hand in the form of a cross, and saying: "Go back where you came from;

A view over the roof of Elder Theodosius' cell in Karoulia.

you're needed there. Pray to the Great-Martyr Panteleimon. You'll find an elder in another country." With these parting words of the elder, I returned to Fr. Theodosius, accompanied by Fr. Dorotheus, who had been waiting for me with the Greek cell-attendant.

Fr. Theodosius attentively listened to me, and then explained to me the words of the elder. That he had twice insisted on calling me a monk indicated that he blessed my intention to receive the tonsure. His counsel to return to Yugoslavia and to pray to the Great-Martyr Panteleimon signified that Fr. Theodosius didn't need to tonsure me, but that I would be tonsured in St. Panteleimon's Monastery. The indication that I would find an elder in another land testified to the fact that I would not remain long in Yugoslavia, but would leave to labor in some other country.

In parting, Fr. Theodosius gave me as a gift his paramon with cross, which he had worn for more than twenty-five years, for all the time he had been a mantia monk. This paramon wore out long ago, but I have worn the cross for forty-five years already. Everything happened as the elder had foretold to me. I was tonsured in St. Panteleimon's Monastery. I spent only two more years in Skopje, and then went to Carpatho-Russia, to Vladimirova, to Archimandrite Vitaly, later Archbishop, in whom I found an elder.

I corresponded with Fr. Theodosius, though, it is true, infrequently, three to four times a year. This correspondence was interrupted by his death in 1938. Earlier I remembered more than a few accounts about the clairvoyance of Fr. Theodosius, which I heard on Mt. Athos, but now, unfortunately, I have forgotten them. The only thing that remains in my memory is that which personally concerned me. This I have recorded. Grant rest, O Lord, to the soul of Thy righteous servant, the ever-memorable Hieroschemamonk Theodosius, one of the last clairvoyant elders of our sorrowful times.*

Archbishop Seraphim
Vladimirova, near Chicago
June, 1970

---

*The St. Herman of Alaska Brotherhood is planning to publish a book on Fr. Theodosius of Karoulia.—*trans. note.*

Index

A

Abimelech, Elder, of Little St. Anne's Skete, 653, 657
Abraham the Confessor, Fr., of Kavsokalyvia, 397
abstinence, 179-181, 189-190, 402, 517-518
Acacius of Kavsokalyvia, St. 13, 63
Adam before the Fall, state of, 356
Adamis, Constantine, 638
"Against the Armenians" by Elder Daniel, 301
"Against the Chiliasts" by Elder Daniel, 300
"Against the Demotic Language" by Elder Daniel, 300
"Against the Evangelicals" by Elder Daniel, 301
"Against the Kalapothakistites" by Elder Daniel, 301, 302
"Against the Spiritualists" by Elder Daniel, 305
Agapius, Fr., of Cyprus, 16
Agapius, Hieromonk, of Constamonitou, 608, 634
Agapius Landos, Monk, 394
Agras, Tellos, 647
Alexander I, Tsar of Russia, 379
Alexander III, Tsar of Russia, 450, 451
Alexander of Rodostolos, Bishop, 257
Alypius, Abbot of the Monastery of the Annunciation on Skiathos, 22
Alypius, Fr., of Xenophontos Monastery, 262-265
Anastasia the Roman, St. 104, 129-133
Anastasius, Fr., brother of Elder Sabbas the Confessor, 397, 398
Anastasius, "Uncle," 227, 228, 255
Anchored in God by Dr. C. Cavarnos, 42 n., 689
Andrew, Abbot of St. Paul's Monastery, 536, 568, 669-670, 678
Andrew, Elder, of Karakallou, 540
Andrew, Monk, of Grigoriou, 161, 167
Andrew the Faster, Elder, 69
Andrew of Constantinople, St., Fool-for-Christ, 448
Andronicus II Paleologus, 593
Anecdotes of Archimandrite Joel Yiannakopoulos, by E. Theodoropoulos, 53
Angelis Kiousa, 510-512
Anna Philanthropini, Queen of Serbia, 593
Anthimus, Abbot of St. Sabbas' Monastery, 428
Anthimus Comninus, Archimandrite, 682
Anthimus, Elder, of Dionysiou, 350
Anthony, Elder, of Constamonitou, 590
Anthony, Elder, of Optina, 33
Anthony, Elder, of St. Anne's Skete, 414-416
Anthony, Hieromonk, of St. Nicholas Skete, 30
Anthony the Great, St. 108, 328, 401 n., 465, 502, 503
Antipas, Fr., of Patmos, 259
Antiphonitria icon of the Mother of God, 237

Apollo, Abba, 229
Archimandrite Theodosius of Sophroniev Hermitage, 13
Arsenios, Monk, disciple of Elder Callinicus, 196, 215
Arsenius, Elder, of Fr. Charalampus' community, 454
Arsenius, Fr., co-ascetic of Joseph the Cave-dweller, 519, 520 *ill.*, 565
Arsenius, Monk, of St. Anne's Skete, 448
Arsenius of Paros, St. 23-25, 228, 255
Arsenius of the Peloponnesus, Elder, 19-20
Arsenius Theodoropolos, Archimandrite, 183
Artemius, Monk, of Grigoriou, 165
Ascetical Homilies of St. Isaac the Syrian, The, 38 n.-39 n., 467-468
Athanasius, Abbot of Grigoriou, 36, 91-168, 92 *ill.*, 168 *ill.*, 323
Athanasius, Abbot of the Great Lavra, 673
Athanasius Balsamakis, Fr., 663, 688-689
Athanasius, disciple of Niphon of Chios, 22
Athanasius, Fr., disciple of Elder Daniel of Katounakia, 251-253, 249
Athanasius, Fr., of the Great Lavra, 217, 606, 663
Athanasius, Hieromonk, of Iveron, 533, 566, 567
Athanasius, Monk, of Constamonitou, 273
Athanasius, Novice, of Dionysiou, 434-437
Athanasius of Paros, Hieromonk, 15-16, 21, 38 n.
Athanasius the Athonite, St. 562, 673
Athanasius the Great, St. 401 n., 678
Athenagoras, Patriarch of Constantinople, 568
Athonite Academy, 14, 16

Athonite Patericon, 367
Athonite Witness, "Remembrances of My Elder Joseph" by Archimandrite Ephraim, 42. n.
Athos, map of peninsula, 8-9
Athos, Mount, 8 *ill.*, 11-38, 45 *ill.*, 49, and *passim*, 174 *ill.*, 505 *ill.*
Athos, the Gate of Heaven by N. Louvaris, 537
Athos: The Holy Mountain by Philip Sherrard, 42 n.
Augustine, St. 108, 268
Aurelius Antoninus Caracalla, Emperor of Rome, 537
Avercius, Fr., of Dionysiou, 352
Avercius, Fr., of Karyes, 573-574
Avvakum of the Lavra, Elder, 35
Avvakum the Barefoot by Monk Theodoritos, 42 n.

B

Balambani Village (New Marmara), 112
Balfour, 669
Banquet of the Ten Virgins by St. Methodius of Olympus, 518, 519 n.
Barlaam, Elder, of Grigoriou, 139-140
Barnabas, Elder, of St. Basil's Skete, 662
Barnabas, Elder, of St. Sabbas' Monastery, 426
Barsanuphius the Great, St. 234
Bartholomew, Fr., co-ascetic of Elder Gerasim Menagias, 666, 668, 669
Bartholomew, Fr., of Karoulia, 356, 531
Basil, Fr., of Karakallou Monastery, 556
Basil the Great, St. 103, 138, 194, 207, 547, 562, 582, 660
Bebis, George S., "St. Nikodemus the Hagiorite," 39 n.
Bes, Abba, 627

INDEX   711

Bessarion, Abbot of Grigoriou, 154, 621
Bessarion, Elder, of Dionysiou, 349
Bethlehem, Church of the Nativity, 654, 655 *ill.*
Between Heaven and Earth by Monk Theocletus of Dionysiou, 327
Biographies of Athonite Ascetics of Piety of the 19th Century by Hieromonk Anthony of the Holy Mountain, 41 n.
Blessed Elder Philotheos Zervakos, ed. S. Kementzentzidis, 40 n.
Blessed Paisius Velichkovsky by Schemamonk Metrophanes, 38 n-39 n, 42 n, 662 n.
Book of Barsanuphius and John by John the Prophet, 626
Bruschweiler, 690
By the Waves of the North by A. Moraitides, 226, 287, 474

C

Callinicus the Faster, Elder, of Dionysiou, 351
Callinicus the Hesychast, Elder, 26, 32, 36, 169-219, 170 *ill.*, 255, 303, 323, 653, 657-660, 666, 679
Callistratus, of St. Sabbas' Monastery, 265-269, 427
Callistus Cataphygiotes, St. 193
Cavarnos, Dr. Constantine, 37, 689
cell of St. Gerasimus, 176 *ill.*, 177, 178, 187
Charalampus, Elder, of St. Anne's Skete, 69
Charalampus, of Kavsokalyvia, 535
Cherubim, Elder, of St. Basil's Skete, 663
Cherubim Karambelas, Archimandrite, 11, 12, 23, 25, 31, 34-37, 40 n., 41 n., 43-45, 44 *ill.*, 51, 65 *ill.*, 365, 369, 589
Christian, The, 217

Christodoulos, Fr., disciple of Elder Callinicus, 32, 194 *ill.*, 195, 215, 498-499
Christology by St. Nectarius Kephalas, 291
Christopher, Fr., of Arta, 16
Christopher Papoulakos and Cosmas Flamiatos by C. Sardelis, 40 n.
Christopher Papoulakos, Fr. 22
Christopher the Martyr, St., 335
Chrysanthus, Elder, 43
Chrysanthus, Elder, of St. Anne's Skete, 520, 523-524
Chrysostomos Kartsonas, Fr., of St. Anne's Skete, 69
Chrysostomos, Metropolitan of Pelagonia, 568
Chrysostomos Papadopoulos, Archbishop of Athens, 153, 300-301
Chrysostomos Papasarantopoulos, Archimandrite, 55
Codratus, Abbot of Karakallou, 26, 250, 278-279, 398, 533-584, 534 *ill.*, 551 *ill.*, 580 *ill.*
Collected Works of St. John Chrysostom, 292
Concerning Continual Communion of the Divine Mysteries, by St. Macarius of Corinth, 20
Constantine, Elder, of Dionysiou, 352
Constantine, Fr., disc. of Elder Daniel of Katounakia, 250
Constantine I, King of Greece, 217
Constantine, Emperor, St., 591
Constantius, Emperor, 591
Constantopoulos, Constantine, 635
Contacts, "Les Sectes Dans Le Monde Orthodox" by O. Clement, 211
Cosmas of Aitolia, St., 14
Cyriacus, Fr., of Karakallou Monastery, 555
Cyrikus, St., 104
Cyril of Phileotes, St., 268
Cyril Papadopoulos, Fr., 24

D

Damascene, Archbishop of America, 60
Damascene, Fr., co-ascetic of Elder Gerasim Menagias, 667-668
Damascene, Fr., disc. of Elder Daniel of Katounakia, 250, 278-279, 569
Damian the Unmercenary, St., 104
Daniel, Abbot of Grigoriou, Elder of Elder Callinicus 32, 175, 177-185
Daniel, Elder, of Katounakia, 25-26, 36, 178, 221-320, 222 *ill.*, 274 *ill.*, 323, 569-570
Daniel, Elder, of Thessaly, 24
Daniel, Fr., disc. of Elder Daniel of Katounakia, 250
Daniel, Fr., of Koutloumousiou Skete, 140
Daniel, Hieromonk, disc. of Elder Callinicus, 191, 192, 194
Darwin, 648-649
Darwin and the Truth pub. by "Zoe," 649
"Defense of Monasticism, A" by Elder Daniel of Katounakia, 301
Demetriades, Epiphanius, of Logoitatou, 22
Demetriades, Maria, mother of Elder Daniel of Katounakia, 262-227
Demetriades, Stamatius, father of Elder Daniel of Katounakia, 226-227
Demetrius the Myrrh-gusher, St., 521, 531, 599
Denasius, Monk, of St. Panteleimon's Monastery, 34, 697
Develikia Metochion, 339
Diadochus Photikes, St., 342
Dionysius Farazoulis, Fr., 652
Dionysius, founder of Dionysiou Monastery, St., 335
Dionysius, Hieromonk, of Fourna Agrafon, 538
Dionysius Kartsonas, Fr., of St. Anne's Skete, 69
Dionysius, Metropolitan of Ierissos, 153
Dionysius, Metropolitan of Trikki and Stagon, 217
Dionysius the Areopagite, St., 156
Dionysius the Orator, St., 394
Dionysius the Scholar, Elder, of Konistria 22, 285
Dometius, St., 335
Dorotheus, Schemamonk, of Karoulia, 705, 707

E

Elder Hilarion the Georgian by Hieromonk Antony of the Holy Mountain, 41 n.
Elder Michael the Blind by Monk Moses of the Holy Mountain, 42n.
Elder Silouan of Mt. Athos by Archimandrite Sophronius, 513
Eleutherius, Elder, of St. Anne's Skete, 69
Elias, Abbot of the Monastery of St. George on Paros, 24
Emmanuel Papadovasilakis, disciple of Fr. Hilarion the younger, 454
Ephraim, Hieromonk, of St. Basil's Skete, 663, 665
Ephraim the Syrian, St., 138, 554, 556
Epiphanios, St., 490
Esphagmeni icon of the Mother of God, 237, 238 *ill.*
Eudocimus, Elder, of Philotheou Monastery, 536, 583
Eudocimus of Vatopedi, St., 256
Eugene Voulgaris, Fr., 15
Eustratius, Fr., disciple of Elder Ignatius, 518
Eustratius the Hagiographer, Fr., 511
Euthemius, Elder, of Constamonitou, 590
Evagrius, 626

INDEX 713

Evangelical School of Smyrna, 227, 303
Evergetinos, 20, 165
"Explanation of the Great and Angelic Schema" by Elder Daniel, 301

F

Fifth Mystical Catechism by St. Cyril of Jerusalem, 447
Flavian, Abbot, 22
Foulaki, Vasiliki, wife of A. Moraitides, 26, 286, 289
Free Rostrum, 687
From the Garden of the Panagia: Nostalgic Reminiscences, by Archimandrite Cherubim Karambelas, 691
From the Monkey? by Apostolos Frankos, 649

G

Gabriel, Archimandrite, of Dionysiou, 223, 321, 342, 351, 352 *ill.*, 356, 452, 498, 499-501, 526, 640
Gabriel Kartsonas, Fr., of St. Anne's Skete, 69
Galaction, Fr., of Karakallou, 540
Garifallos, Christina, 281
Gelasius, Elder, of Dionysiou, 353
Gennadius, Elder, of Dionysiou, 352
Gennadius, Fr., of Constamonitou, 628
Gennadius the Martyr, St., 335
George I Brancovich, Prince of Serbia, 682
George II, King of Greece, 86, 153
George, Metropolitan of Nevrokopios, 303
George of Hilandar, Elder, 35
George Papageorgiadis, Archimandrite, 276
Georgia, country of 377-379
Germanus, Hieromonk, of St. Sabbas' Monastery, 427

Gerasim, Abbot of St. Panteleimon's Monastery, 230
Gerasim, Fr., disc. of Elder Daniel of Katounakia, 250
Gerasim, Hieromonk, of St. Basil's Skete, 663, 665
Gerasim Menagias, Elder, 12, 32, 178, 194, 196, 217, 644-694
Gerasim of Cephalonia, St., 647, 657
Gerasim of the Jordan, St., 268, 639
Gerasim the Hymnographer, Fr. 209, 394, 532
German occupation of Athos, 86, 671-673
Germanus, Elder, of Constamonitou, 634
Gerontius, Fr., disc. of Elder Daniel of Katounakia, 223, 250
Gerontius of St. Anne's Skete, St., 65, 67 *ill.*
Gideon, Fr., co-ascetic of Fr. Neophytus Karamanlis, 28
Gideon, Monk-Martyr, St., 571-572
Glimanus, Hieromonk, of Velanidia Monastery, 54
Glykophilousa icon of the Mother of God, 623, 625 *ill.*
Golgotha, 423
Great and Wonderful Pilgrimage to Palestine and Sinai, A, by Archimandrite Philotheus Zervakos, 426
Great Lavra, the, 43, 74-75, 85, 251, 328, 474, 537, 568, 658, 673
Gregory, Elder of Archimandrite Cherubim, 43, 63, 64 *ill.*, 65, 72-88 *passim*, 208
Gregory, Fr., of Grigoriou Monastery, 404-405
Gregory Hadjistamatis, disc. of Niphon of Chios, 22
Gregory, Metropolitan of Chalkis, 289
Gregory Palamas, St., 109, 187, 405, 521, 524-525, 662, 679

Gregory of Nyssa, St., 166, 192, 342
Gregory the Byzantine, Metropolitan of Chios, 484-486
Gregory the Confessor, Fr., of Little St. Anne's Skete, 394-395
Gregory the Sinaite, St., 184
Gregory the Theologian, St., 94, 104, 287-288
Gregory V, Patriarch of Constantinople, 682

H

Holy Monastery of Dionysiou on Mt. Athos, The, by Archimandrite Gabriel of Dionysiou, 329, 333, 348
Hadji George, 28-30, 462, 466, 469, 470-472, 475, 477-487, 478 *ill.,* 517
Haeckel, 648-649
Handbook of Spiritual Counsel, A, by St. Nicodemus the Hagiorite, 20, 39 n.
Helen, Empress, St., 428
Hellenic Chronicle, The, "The Holy Mountain Today," 42 n.
Herald of the Serbian Orthodox Church, The, 41 n.
Hermitess Photini of the Jordan Desert, The, by Archimandrite Joachim Spetsieris, 429
Hesychius of Grigoriou, Fr., 130
Hesychius the Presbyter, St., 187, 193, 665
Hieronymus, Elder, Confessor of St. Parasceva's Monastery, 404
Hierotheus, Fr., disciple of Hadji George, 484, 485
Hierotheus, Metropolitan, 574
Hilarion, Abbot of Constamonitou, 592
Hilarion, Elder, of Dionysiou, 352
Hilarion, Fr., disciple of Elder Sabbas, 375-377, 397, 398, 433-434, 443, 451, 453, 454

Hilarion, Monk, of the Kalyve of the Nativity of Christ, 513-516
Hilarion the Georgian, Elder, 30-32, 374, 376-391, 398-399, 400-401, 443, 446-447, 697-701
"Historical Study of the Dispute in the Athonite Monastery of St. Panteleimon" by Elder Daniel, 300
History of the Monks of Syria, The, by Theodoret, Bishop of Cyrrhus, 381
Hitler, 671
Hodigitria icon of the Mother of God, of Constamonitou, 603-604
Holy Communion, 691-694
Holy Figures of Modern Greece, by Archimandrite Elias Mastrogiannopoulos, 691
Holy Mountain of Athos, The, by Archimandrite Chrysostom Moustaka, 540
Holy Sepulchre, the, 423, 644 *ill.,* 656, 656 *ill.*
Holy Twelve, the, 35, 41 n.

I

Iakovos, Abbot of Dionysiou, 337
idiorrhythmia, 12, 239, 543
Ignatius Brianchaninov, Bishop, 366-367
Ignatius, Elder, of Dionysiou, 349
Ignatius, Fr. disciple of Elder Ignatius, 491-493
Ignatius, Monk, 623
Ignatius the Confessor, Elder, 26, 36, 178, 365, 457-532, 458 *ill.,* 704-708
In Defense of the Holy Hesychasts, by St. Gregory Palamas, 525
Ioannicius, Fr., of Paraclete Monastery, 12, 590
Ioannicius the Great, St., 268
Ioannikios, Monk, of Grigoriou, 150

Ioasaph, Martyr, St., 335
Ioasaph, Monk, of Ravdachou Cell, 621-622
Irenaius, Metropolitan of Cassandra, 344, 570
Isaac of Dionysiou, Elder, 321-363, 322 *ill.*
Isidora, Fool-for-Christ, St., 448
Isidore, Hieromonk, of Ikaria, 229

J

Jacob, Elder, of Dionysiou, 352
James, Elder of Elder Athanasius, 106-107, 111
James, Fr., disciple of Elder Codratus, 536, 556, 567
James the Brother of the Lord, St., 380, 383, 387, 393, 485
Jerusalem, 420-423, 421 *ill.*
Joachim, Elder, of St. Anne's Skete, 12, 36, 43, 44, 51-90, 52 *ill.*, 58 *ill.*, 323
Joachim II, Patriarch of Constantinople, 236
Joachim III, Patriarch of Constantinople, 236, 255, 397, 483
Joachim Spetsieris, Archimandrite, 40 n., 418-419, 432, 443, 446, 453
Joel Yiannakopoulos, Archimandrite, 55
John Chrysostom, St., 121, 188, 485, 500, 526, 554, 615, 685
John Damascene, St., 424, 602
John, Fr., disciple of Elder Daniel of Katounakia, 249
John of Kronstadt, St., 450, 527, 686
John of the Ladder, St., 63, 103, 123, 138, 190-191, 249, 332, 344, 552
John the Baptist, St., 334, 348, 350, 354, 355, 359
John the Hesychast, St., 425
John V Paleologus, Emperor, 593
John XI Bekkos, Patriarch of Constantinople, 592

Jonas, Elder, of St. Basil's Skete, 662
Jordan River, 427-429, 430 *ill.*
Joseph of Chios, Fr., 21
Joseph the Cave-Dweller, 35, 502-503, 519, 565, 598, 663, 664 *ill.*, 666
Joseph the Martyr, St., 335
Julian the Apostate, Emperor, 591
Justinian, Emperor, 108, 425, 428

K

Kalamaria Metochion, 339, 344, 357, 359
Kalyve of St. George, 471 *ill.*
Kalyve of Sts. Menas and Demetrius, 479, 479 *ill.*
Kalyve of the "Danieloi," 250-254, 254 *ill.*, 320 *ill.*
Kalyve of the Dormition in Katounakia, 459-460, 460 *ill.*, 472-475, 495, 498
Kalyve of the Nativity of the Theotokos, 70 *ill.*, 71
Kalyve of the Resurrection, 372 *ill.*, 394, 495
Karoulia, 175, 223, 704-706
Karyes, 34, 43, 105, 106, 110 *ill.*, 197, 353, 356, 360
Kathisma of the Holy Apostles, 345-346, 360
Katounakia, 173-175, 223, 246 *ill.*, 247, 287, 459, 460 *ill.*
Kavsokalyvia, 43, 61, 62 *ill.*, 63, 175
Know Thyself by St. Nectarius Kephalas, 291
Kollyvades movement, 14-16, 19-27, 31, 77-78
Kontoglou, Photius, 23, 535
Korakis, Costas, 638
Kyra Maro, Queen of Serbia, 682-683

L

Ladder of Divine Ascent, 198 *ill.*

Ladder of Divine Ascent, The, 165, 199, 516, 518, 550, 560, 575, 597, 613, 616, 631, 635, 659
Lausaicon of the Holy Mountain by Archimandrite Gabriel of Dionysiou, 210, 374, 379, 407, 500 n.
Lazarus, Elder, of Dionysiou, 43, 329, 345-346, 350-351, 360
Lemonie, French Under-Secretary, 217
Leontius, blind Elder, 212
Leontius, Elder, of Dionysiou, 352
Leontius, Monk, of Dionysiou, 345
Leontius the Confessor, Fr., 69
Leontius the Myrrh-Gusher, St., 335
Life and Labors of Elder Hieroschemamonk Hilarion, The, by Hieromonk Anthony of the Holy Mountain, 703
Life of St. Cosmas of Aitolia by S. Cristodoulides, 38 n.
Life of St. Nectarios by Archimandrite Joachim Spesieris, 40 n.
Little Russian Philokalia, Vol. IV, 38 n.
Little St. Anne's Skete, 175, 394, 395 *ill.*
Lives of the Desert Fathers, 627
Long Rules, The by St. Basil the Great, 547
Longinus, Abba, 466

M

Macarius, Bishop of Ierissos, 591-592
Macarius, Elder, of the Kalyve of the Nativity of Christ, 513, 514
Macarius, Fr., disciple of Hadji George, 484, 485
Macarius, Martyr, 335
Macarius, Hieromonk, of Karakallou Monastery, 581
Macarius of Corinth, St., 14-22, 18 *ill.*, 26
Makrakis, Apostolos, 261-262
Marianon Metochion, 340

Mark, Abbot of Dionysiou, 349
Mark, Metropolitan of Achilsk, 594
Mark, Monk, of Constamonitou, 587, 641
Marmara, Costis, 304-307
Martinian, Elder, of St. Basil's Skete, 662
Mavros, John, "On the Writings of St. Nectarios," 40 n.
Mavros, John, "St. Nicodemus of the Holy Mountain," 39 n.
Mavros, John, 26
Maximus, Fr., confessor of Iveron Monastery, 536, 578
Maximus, Fr., disciple of Elder Gerasim Menagias, 32
Maximus, Hieromonk, of Karakallou Monastery, 581
Maximus Kavsokalyves, St., 61
Maximus the Confessor, St., 207
Melania, St., 317
Melas, Paul, 652
Meletius, Fr., disciple of Elder Daniel of Katounakia, 250
Meletius, Metropolian of Smyrna, 240
Memoirs, Vol. I, by Fr. J. Spetsieris, 41 n. 374, 419 n., 427, 430, 455
Menagias, Panagis, 646-647
mental prayer, 19-20, 184-185, 192-193, 207-213 and *passim*
Metagitsiou Metochion, 340
Methodius of Olympus, St., 518, 518-519 n.
Michael Paleologus, Emperor, 592
Michael, Prince of Moldavia, 682
Michael the Archangel, St., 639
Michael the Blind of St. Anne's Skete, Elder, 35
Mihas, Panagiotis (later Archimandrite Bessarion), 147
Mitrophan of Hilandar, Fr. 41 n.
Mitrophan, St., disciple of St. Dionysius the Orator, 394

INDEX 717

Modestus, Elder, of Dionysiou, 345, 360
Modestus, Elder, of Constamonitou, 590
Modestus, Monk, of Constamonitou, 272-273
Monastery of Constamonitou, 35, 273 *ill.*, 591-595
Monastery of Dionysiou, 35, 43, 329-363 *passim*, 329 *ill.*, 381, 383, 389, 392 *ill.*, 393, 394, 499, 698-699
Monastery of Grigoriou, 96-168 passim, 99 *ill.*, 100 *ill.*, 109 *ill.*, 699
Monastery of Iveron, 172-173, 568, 378, 378 *ill.*, 379
Monastery of Karakallou, 535, 536, 537-542, 539 *ill.*, 543, 562, 564 *ill.*, 585 *ill.*
Monastery of Longovarda, 23-25
Monastery of Nea Moni, 21, 27
Monastery of Philotheou, 35, 537, 568
Monastery of St. Anastasia, 236
Monastery of St. Gerasim of the Jordan, 428
Monastery of St. Panteleimon, 25, 34, 228, 230-232, 231 *ill.*, 236, 380, 388-389, 708, 709
Monastery of St. Paul, 677, 678, 680-683, 681 *ill.*, 685
Monastery of St. Sabbas, 423-427, 424 *ill.*, 656
Monastery of the Annunciation on Skiathos, 22
Monastery of the Holy Forerunner in Palestine, 428
Monastery of the Paraclete, 43
Monastery of Vatopedi, 19, 35, 237-240, 238 *ill.*, 247, 256
Monastery of Xeropotamou, 35, 179, 682
Monastery of Zographou, 496, 637
Monks' Handbook, The by Elder Daniel, 301

Monoxilitis, metochion of Dionysiou, 339, 342, 357, 434-436
Moraitides, Alexander, 22, 26, 217, 223, 225-226, 247, 249, 279, 285-289, 290 *ill.*, 298, 299, 308, 647
Moses, Elder, of Optina, 33
Most Holy Mother of God, 2 *ill.*, 84, 85, 96, 104, 132, 156-157, 173, 237-239, 510, 622-625, 653, 683
Mystagogia by St. Maximus the Confessor, 610

N

name-worshippers, heresy of, 210-211
Nectarius Kephalas, St., 26-27, 289-296, 290 *ill.*, 668-669
Neophytus, Fr., disciple of Elder Ignatius, 487-491, 508-510, 515-516
Neophytus, Fr., of Kavsokalyvia, 14-15
Neophytus, Monk, disc. of Elder Callinicus, 187, 191, 192, 194
Neophytus of Katounakia, Elder, 30, 462-477, 487
Neophytus of Kavsokalyvia, Elder of Hadji George, 28, 30, 468, 470-472, 477
Neophytus VII, Patriarch of Constantinople, 593
New Evergetinos, The, by Archimandrite Gabriel of Dionysiou, 374, 436
New Martyrs of the Turkish Yoke, The, tr. by L. Papadopoulos and G. Lizardos, 38 n.
New Spiritual Meadow, A, by St. Nicephorus of Chios, 22
Nicephorus of Chios, St., 21, 27
Nicander the Confessor, Fr., 69
Nicetas Stethatos, St., 162
Nicholas, Archpriest, 217
Nicholas, Fr., of Grigoriou, 361

Nicholas I, Tsar of Russia, 387-388, 697
Nicholas II, Tsar of Russia, 451
Nicholas the Wonderworker, St., 126-129, 159
Nicodemus of Cyzicus, Patriarch of Jerusalem, 420, 422, 430
Nicodemus of Mt. Athos, St., 15-21. 17 *ill.*, 26, 94, 335, 650
Nicodemus the Cypriote, Elder, 71
Nikodim of Karoulia, Elder, 365-370, 370 *ill.*
Nilus, Metropolitan of Kasus and Karpathus, 250
Nilus the Desert-Dweller, St., 181, 192, 340, 463, 559
Nilus the Hermit (Kalogronomos), 21
Nina, enlightener of Georgia, St., 378
Niphon, Elder, of Constamonitou, 590, 618, 629, 629 *ill.*
Niphon, Fr., of Vatopedi, confessor, 239
Niphon, Fr., disciple of Elder Daniel of Katounakia, 223, 250
Niphon of Chios, Hieromonk, 22
Niphon of Kavsokalyvia, St., 63, 470
Niphon, Patriarch of Constantinople, St., 331 *ill.*, 332-335, 341, 350

O

obedience, 72-76, 337, 385-386, 468-476, 659, and *passim*
"On Fasting Before Holy Communion" by Elder Daniel, 301
"On Fleeing the World" by Elder Daniel, 303
"On Mental Prayer" by Elder Daniel, 301
On Schism by St. Nectarius Kephalas, 296
"On Suspicion" by Elder Daniel, 301
"On the Bonds Not Even Loosed at the Death of the Body" by Elder Daniel, 301
"On the Desert-Dwellers of the Roslavl Forests" by Fr. Clement Sederholm, 41 n.
"On the Salvation of Heretics and Heterodox" by Elder Daniel, 301
"On Untimely Sorrow" by Elder Daniel, 301
"On What a Spiritual Father Should Be" by Elder Daniel, 301
"On Whether the Stars are Inhabited" by Elder Daniel, 303
Onouphrius, Fr., disciple of Elder Sabbas, 375, 397-398, 401, 402, 443, 451, 453, 454
Onouphrius and Peter of Mount Athos, Sts. 394, 395 ill.
Optina Elder Moses by Juvenal Polovtsev, Archimandrite, 41 n.

P

Pachomius, Abbot of the the Monastery of the Holy Fathers on Chios, 27, 484, 484 n.
Pachomius, Fr., of Constamonitou, 590, 609, 612, 620-621, 638
Pachomius, Hierodeacon, of Grigoriou, 152
Paisius, Elder, 43
Paisius, Fr., of Constamonitou, 632
Paisius, Fr., of Karakallou, 540
Paisius, Monk, disciple of Elder Joachim, 63
Paisius Velichkovsky, St., 12-15, 19-20, 33, 38 n., 662, 662 n.
Palaiokapas, Constantine, 538
Panagoulakis, Elias, 53-55
Pandects of Antioch by St. Nectarius Kephalas, 291
Panselinos, Manuel, 23
Panteleimon, Bishop, Exarch of the Holy Sepulchre, 56-57
Panteleimon, Elder, of New Skete, 495

INDEX 719

Panteleimon, Fr., professor at St. Sergius Academy in Russia, 217
Panteleimon Giamon, Fr., 277
Panteleimon, Hieromonk, of Simonopetra, 141
Panteleimon, Monk, writer, 34
Panteleimon, St., 104
Papa-Nicholas Planas, 23
Papa-Nicholas Planas: The Simple Shepherd of the Simple Sheep by Nun Martha, 40 n.
Papa-Diamante of Morea, 22
Papadiamantes, Alexander, 22, 647
Papadoniou, Zacharias, 644, 687-689
Papoulides, C., "Dukhovnoe Polozhenie na Svyatoy Gore vo Vtoroy Polovine 18 ovo Veka" 40 n.
Papoulides, C., "Le Starets Paissij Velitchkovsky," 39 n.
Papoulides, C., "Alcance ecomenico do la renovacion monastica del siglo XVIII en la iglesio ortodoxa" 39 n.
Paramithia icon of the Mother of God, 237
Parthenius, Abbot of St. Paul's Monastery, 686
Parthenius, founder of the Monastery of St. Mark, 484, 484 n.
Parthenius, Fr., Russian ascetic, 217
Parthenius, Metropolitan of Thessalonica, 333
Pateric Romanesc by Protosinghelos Ioanichie Balan, 42 n.
patience, 674-678
Patriarchate of Jerusalem, 59
Paul of the Great Lavra, Physician, 455
Paul of Xeropotamou, St., 680, 682
Paul the Apostle, St., 207
Paul the Martyr, St., 335
Peter and Paul, Sts. 538, 538 *ill.*
Peter, Fr., disciple of Elder Sabbas, 397, 398

Peter, Fr., of Karakallou Monastery, 561
Peter the Athonite, St., 624
Philaret, Elder, Abbot of Constamonitou, 12, 587-642, 588 *ill.*
Philaret, Fr., of Constamonitou, 590
Philip, Fr., of Karakallou Monastery, 580-581
Philip, Fr., of the Great Lavra, 673
Philokalia, 13, 19, 32-33, 142, 188, 227, 248, 662
Philokalia of St. Theophan the Recluse, 367
Philotheus, St., 335
Philotheus Vysniotes, Abbot of Longovarda, 23-24
Philotheus Zervakos, Archimandrite, 24-26, 40 n., 276, 426
Photini, Hermitess of the trans-Jordan, 429-430
Photius, Patriarch of Alexandria, 454
Pilgrim's Journal by John Domnenos, 65
Portaitissa icon of Mother of God, 173, 174 *ill.*
Portaitissa Icon of the Mother of God, of Constamonitou, 608, 609 *ill.*
Priest's Handbook by St. Nectarius Kephalas, 291
Proclus, Patriarch of Constantinople, St., 600
Prophet Isaiah, 354
Purant, Professor J, 649
Pythagoras, 108

Q–R

Quickhearer icon of the Mother of God, 540
Radits, Commander-in-Chief of Serbia (later Monk Romanus), 593-594
Rareş, John Peter, Prince of Moldavia, 538, 539 *ill.*

Recollections of Mt. Athos by Archimandrite Cherubim Karambelas, 11, 38 n., 44 n.
Remoundos, John, 386-387
Rengos, Nicholas, 241, 275-276, 298-300, 317, 319, 320
Romanus IV Diogenes, Emperor of Byzantium, 538
Rostislav Gan, Fr., 368
Roxandra, Princess of Walachia, 538
Russian Ascetics of the 18th and 19th Centuries by Br. Nikodim, 367
Russo-Japanese War, 387-388, 697-703

S

Sabbas, Abbot of St. Panteleimon's Monastery, 236
Sabbas, Elder, of St. Panteleimon's Monastery, 232-233
Sabbas, Fr., disciple of Elder Sabbas the Confessor, 397, 398, 451
Sabbas the Confessor, Elder, 26, 31, 41 n., 371-455, 488, 495, 697-703
Sabbas the New of Kalymnos, St., 27, 35, 65
Sabbas the Sanctified, St., 124, 423-424
Seraphim, Abbot of St. Paul's Monastery, 678, 687
Seraphim, Fr., disciple of Elder Nikodim, 369, 370
Seraphim, Fr., of Kavsokalyvia, 563
Seraphim, Hieromonk, writer, 34
Seraphim Kartsonas, Fr., of St. Anne's Skete, 69
Seraphim of Chicago, Archbishop, 704-708
Seraphim of Sarov, St.., 519
Sermons on the Sunday Gospel Readings by Nicephorus Theotokis, 38 n.
Sikia Metochion, 339
Silouan of Mt. Athos, St., 35, 513

simplicity, 518
Sinners' Salvation, by Monk Agapius Landos, 394
Skete of St. Anne, 43, 65, 66 *ill.*, 175, 248
Skete of St. Basil, 13, 32, 44, 175, 660-665, 661 *ill.*
Skete of St. Elias, 34
Skete of St. John the Forerunner, 43
Sophronius Kalligas, Abbot of St. Paul's Monastery, 682
Sophronius, Monk, of Grigoriou, 144-145
Sophronius Zakharov, Archimandrite, 689-690
Soul-Saving Converser, 367
Spiritual Homilies by St. Macarius the Great, 442 n.
Spiritual Meadow, The, by John Moschus, 431
spiritualism, 304-307, 650-652
St. Anne's Skete: The Holy Altar of Athos by Hieromonk Anthimus, 71 n.
St. Arsenios of Paros by Dr. C. Cavarnos, 40 n.
St. Macarius of Corinth by Dr. C. Cavarnos, 39 n.
St. Nikephoros of Chios by Dr. C. Cavarnos 39 n.
St. Savvas the New, by Dr. C. Cavarnos, 41 n.
St. Xenia's Skete, 369
Stephen, Abbot of St. Paul's Monastery, 682
Stephen, Fr., disciple of Elder Daniel of Katounakia, 250
Stephen, Monk, disciple of Elder Joachim, 63, 75-76
Stephen the Proto-Martyr, St., 594, 599-602, 601 *ill.*, 606, 608, 617
Stergioglidis, Theodore, 301
suspicion, 315-316
Sylvester of Cappadocia, Fr., 19

INDEX

Symeon, Abbot of Constamonitou, 593
Symeon, Abbot of Grigoriou, 102
Symeon, Elder, of New Skete, 402, 409-410
Symeon, Fool-for-Christ, St., 448
Symeon, Fr., of Kerasia, 147-148
Symeon of Thessalonica, St., 508
Symeon the New Theologian, St., 143, 157, 185, 207, 208, 359, 462, 552, 578
Syncletica, St., 558
Thalassios, St., 190
Theocletus of Dionysiou, Monk, 91, 162, 673-674
Theodore of Edessa, St., 277
Theodore the Studite, St., 103
Theodoret, Bishop of Cyrrhus, 381 n.
Theodosia, Abbess of Kechrovounio, 26, 279-285, 280 *ill.*, 317
Theodosiades, Demetrius, 104
Theodosius, Elder, of St. Paul's Monastery, 650, 657, 667, 670, 671, 672, 675
Theodosius of Karoulia, Elder, 35, 217, 365, 368, 369, 370, 704-708, 705 *ill.*
Theodosius the Confessor, Fr., of St. Anne's Skete, 68
Theophan, Monk, of St. Anne's Skete, 315
Theophanes the Cretan, 23
Theophanes Troungas, 418-419
Theophylactus, Elder, of St. Basil's Skete, 662-663

Theophylactus of Kavsokalyvia, Fool-for-Christ, 448
Theotokarion by St. Nectarius Kephalas, 291
Theotokis, Nicephorus, 38 n., 468
Thomas, Elder, of Little St. Anne's Skete, 495
Thomas Mastoras, 616-617
Three Alexanders, The by I. Gizeli
Tikhon, Hermit, 444, 445 *ill.*
Tikhon of Zadonsk, St., writings of, 367
Timothy, Abbot of Paraclete Monastery, 45
To Kinima ton Kollyvadon by C. Papoulidis 40 n.
Tryphon, Elder, of Constamonitou, 590
Victorin, Elder, of St. Anne's Skete, 68
Vigla, 175, 328
Vimatarissa icon of the Mother of God, 237
virginity, 288, 518-521
Vladimir, Hierodeacon, of Jordanville, 366
"Voice from the Holy Mountain About the Impending Ecumenical Council" by Elder Daniel of Katounakia, 300, 303
Voultista, Metochion of, 114, 151, 160, 161
Zacharias, Archbishop of Ochrid, 333
Zacharias, Fr., of Grigoriou, 620

ST. HERMAN OF ALASKA BROTHERHOOD

For over three decades, the St. Herman Brotherhood has been publishing works of traditional spirituality.

Write for our free 96-page catalogue, featuring sixty titles of published and forthcoming books and magazines.

St. Herman of Alaska Brotherhood
10 Beegum Gorge Road
P. O. Box 70
Platina, CA 96076